Almost Yankees

Almost Yankees

The Summer of '81 and the Greatest Baseball Team You've Never Heard Of

J. DAVID HERMAN

University of Nebraska Press

LINCOLN

Lyrics to "Hey Canaries," by Frank and Pauline Verdi and
"Hometown Heroes" and "Ring Your Bell" by the Columbus
Clippers are printed with permission.

Library of Congress Cataloging-in-Publication Data
Names: Herman, J. David, author.
Title: Almost Yankees: the summer of '81 and the greatest
baseball team you've never heard of / J. David Herman.
Description: Lincoln: University of Nebraska Press, [2019] |
Includes bibliographical references and index.
Identifiers: LCCN 2018038915
ISBN 9781496208897 (cloth: alk. paper)
ISBN 9781496215369 (epub)
ISBN 9781496215376 (mobi)
ISBN 9781496215383 (pdf)
Subjects: LCSH: Columbus Clippers (Baseball team)—
History—20th century. | New York Yankees (Baseball
team)—History—20th century. | Baseball teams—Ohio—
Columbus—History—20th century. | Baseball teams—New
York (State)—New York—History—20th century. | Baseball
players—Ohio—Columbus—Biography. | Baseball team
owners—Ohio—Columbus—Biography.
Classification: LCC GV875.C83 H47 2019 | DDC 796.35709771/57—
dc23 LC record available at https://lccn.loc.gov/2018038915

Set in Sabon Next LT Pro by Mikala R. Kolander.

For my dad, and for his dad, whom I
never had a chance to know

Columbus Clippers are the best team around
They'll outhustle any team that's in town
Whoever they are playin' had better watch out
Land ho Columbus! We're the best without a doubt
The Clippers, Columbus Clippers
The Clippers are
Our hometown heroes
The Clippers, Columbus Clippers
The Clippers are
Our hometown heroes

—From "Hometown Heroes," one of two Columbus Clippers
fight songs played at Franklin County Stadium in 1981
(Courtesy of the Columbus Clippers)

CONTENTS

ILLUSTRATIONS

PROLOGUE

MY DAD HAS BEEN gone for several years now, but I can still hear his voice, rising above a chorus of others, urging the ball to clear the right-field wall.

It's June 12, 1981. Major League Baseball stadiums across the country are dark and empty tonight. For the first time in the history of professional sports, a labor strike has halted an entire season in midstream, with no end in sight. The players' association, unwilling to cede ground to team owners in matters involving free agency and soaring salaries, walked away from negotiations early this morning. Fans face a summer with no baseball. At least no Major League Baseball.

At Chicago's Wrigley Field, midmorning arrived with flags flying atop the scoreboard as if nothing had changed, but the Cubs' game against the San Diego Padres was the first contest canceled. A busload of disappointed Padres fans angled to at least get a tour of the stadium. Organist John Henzl performed for a half hour before learning that no one was coming. Sunshine gave way to a threat of rain, and tarps now cover the infield dirt, batter's box, and pitcher's mound in the vacant stadium. Fans on Chicago's North Side, already long-suffering, are once again cursing their misfortune. After a horrid start even for them, the Cubs had perked up enough to win five of their last six. The strike snuffed out any rekindled optimism.

Players scattered. Groups of New York Yankees, denied access to the team bus in the wee hours this morning, hitched rides on the streets of Chicago's South Side. Hours later in Milwaukee, Brewers pitcher Mike Caldwell pulled a 16-gauge shotgun from his locker in the team's clubhouse and started cleaning it, intending to fill at least part of his summer going after pheasants instead of hitters. On the road for a series in California, Red Sox star Carl Yastrzemski made plans to go fishing and watch his son play in the Cape Cod League. Back in Boston, outside Fenway Park, John Picardi, a young souvenir salesman, stood in his empty shop, played solitaire, and wondered how he'd afford to pay for tuition in the fall.

The Baltimore Orioles are the farthest from home of any Major League team. Tonight they're opening their own wallets for lodging in Seattle. A handful of Kansas City Royals are spending the evening at Detroit's Joe Louis Arena, watching Larry Holmes knock out Leon Spinks. Down along the Gulf Coast, any Houston Astros fans tuning in to hear Gene Elston and Dewayne Staats on KENR radio can't find them. The announcers are busy preparing to fill the airwaves tomorrow night with a historic recreation of the team's first-ever game in 1962.

Major League Baseball is over. For the moment, at least.

The reserve clause that bound a player to a team for life has been dead five years now. With players able to sign with the highest bidder, salaries have exploded. Owners with the deepest pockets, who embraced this new era, have benefited, some playing the new game better than others. George Steinbrenner, the capricious king of the New York Yankees, parlayed the biggest free agent signings into World Series titles in '77 and '78, and a 103-win regular season in 1980 before a loss to Kansas City in the American League Championship Series increased his mania.

Most owners though, Steinbrenner included, have had enough. Tired of losing control over player movement and salaries, they're demanding that every time one of their star players signs with another team, they receive a high-value player in return. Their desire to thwart the free agent market isn't lost on the players. Ownership has underestimated their resolve and, this time, both sides are determined not to give in.

And so the season has stopped cold, with Philadelphia's Pete Rose just one hit from the all-time National League record, Fernandomania sweeping through Los Angeles, and Steinbrenner's increasingly harried Yankees among the teams sitting atop what will come to be known as the "first-half" standings. Before it's over, the strike will wipe out more than seven hundred contests and change the game forever.

YET IN MINOR LEAGUE cities such as Columbus, Ohio, there will be baseball through the rest of the spring and summer. The Columbus Clippers, the top Minor League affiliate of Steinbrenner's Yankees, stocked with an unusual blend of experience, talent, and potential for a Triple-A team, are in the midst of a blitzkrieg against the rest of the Triple-A International League. The IL is strong this season, with Cal Ripken Jr. (Rochester), Wade Boggs (Pawtucket), Brett Butler (Richmond), and Von Hayes (Charleston) among its rising stars. But for the next two months at least, the Clippers—King George's super-talented collection of spare parts—will be the greatest baseball team on the planet.

In my mind, they already were. And it hasn't been close.

I'm eleven years old, a newly minted fan living through a coming-of-age, live-and-breathe baseball summer. I've been devouring write-ups and box scores in the *Columbus Dispatch*, mourning contests wiped out by thunderstorms, and listening to every game I can on WBNS radio. Most nights the sounds of the broadcast fill my room, tucked away in the city's Old Beechwold neighborhood, overlooking the Olentangy River amid dense trees and fireflies. Well past bedtime, I quietly click my radio back on, under the covers, and sneak in another inning. Those daydreams about the eighth-grade girl who sits next to me in the trombone section of my youth jazz band? Not even she can compete. I love this baseball team as only a shy young kid in his first season as a rabid baseball fan can love them. Even before the strike, they loomed in my consciousness, far more important than their Major League counterparts.

I don't care about Reggie Jackson. I have Marshall Brant, the Clippers' veteran slugger, coming off a Most Valuable Player season. My obsession with Dave Righetti, the Yankees' star rookie pitcher, wasn't born out of his success in New York but in Columbus, where he started the season 5-0 with a 1.00 ERA before the big club called him up.

The Yankees are just names in the paper. The Clippers are real. Any chance to watch them in person provides another level of magic, an extended version of that moment during any trip to the ballpark when you emerge from the walkway and catch your first glimpse of the field. The green turf, the white baselines straight as lasers, the perfectly kept infield. The buzz of the crowd. The excitement in the air.

COLUMBUS LIKES TO THINK of itself as a Major League city, but at this point, in 1981, it hasn't had a Major League team in nearly a century. Ohio State University football has long been the only game that really matters. Coach Woody Hayes, deposed more than two years ago for striking an opposing player in the 1978 Gator Bowl, is still worshipped. I was only seven years old, but I remember what a massive event his firing was in Columbus, and how shaken people were. A Kroger marquee on the way to my school declared: "WOODY, OHIO STILL LOVES YOU."

These days, the city's subpro image is beginning to change. Columbus is on the rise, and the Clippers are part of that. Franklin County Stadium, their home park in the city's West Side—a part of town known locally as the Bottoms, where nearly everyone has their roots in Appalachia—is one of the best stadiums in Minor League Baseball.

The city lost its baseball team after the 1970 season when the Columbus Jets, a Pittsburgh Pirates farm team, moved to West Virginia. For six seasons, Jet Stadium sat unused and crumbling, a reminder of all the things Columbus was not. But six years later, Harold Cooper and his fellow county commissioners bought the decrepit venue with visions of luring baseball back to Columbus. Construction crews rebuilt the stadium and laid down AstroTurf. The Columbus Clippers were born, as an affiliate of the Pirates for their first two seasons before the Yankees took over as the big club in 1979. After high attendance but poor play as a Pirates affiliate, the Clippers have won everything in sight under the Yankees, including both the International League pennant and the season-ending Governors' Cup playoffs in '79 and '80. In 1981, they're seeking an unprecedented three-peat of both.

Tickets are only a few dollars. A family of four can see the game, park, and grab a bite for twenty bucks. A new electronic scoreboard renders pictures of players in lights against a black background like a giant Lite-Brite. A picnic area sits past the fence in left field. Mount Calvary Cemetery lies beyond the outfield fences and a row of spruce trees. Fans ring cowbells to spark rallies, and nearly every game features some kind of promotion: Farmers' Night, Dime-a-Dog Night, Bat Day . . . even Halter-Top Night.

On this evening, with Major League parks shuttered, the Clippers are hosting the only baseball in the entire country that really matters. The Tidewater (Virginia) Tides, the top affiliate of the New York Mets, are in town for two games—the completion of a contest suspended earlier in the season, and the regularly scheduled game. First place is on the line, with Columbus (34-20) up by a game over the Tides (31-19).

The Clippers opened the season 9-11, a bit of a faceplant considering expectations. Tidewater spent most of May in first place. But while the Tides were high, the Clippers were moving up. Columbus overtook Tidewater on June 1, and since then, no more than a game and a half has separated the two teams. How hot are the Clippers? Heading into tonight's games, they've won twenty-five of their last thirty-four, a blistering .735 clip. But they haven't been able to shake the pesky Tides in the standings.

A Mets-Yankees proxy war on the strike's first night means national attention for Tidewater at Columbus. News outlets from around the country are eager to show the impact of the strike and desperate to fill sports pages and airwaves with baseball. *New York Times* reporter Ira Berkow is in town, along with Moss Klein of the *Newark Star-Ledger*, Jack Lang of the *Daily News*, and Steve Jacobson from *Newsday*. A fledgling new cable network, ESPN, is on hand to broadcast the second game nationwide. New York radio powerhouse WABC isn't here yet but will soon reassign its venerable Yankees play-by-play crew—Phil Rizzuto and all—to broadcast games back to New York, in hopes of filling this summer's baseball void.

The added attention might bother some of the younger Clippers, but it doesn't faze Brant all that much. He's had a handful of Major League at bats with the Yankees, and he's been on TV before. He does worry, however, that he might swing at a bad pitch with Yankees coaches watching from their homes in New York. Under Steinbrenner, these things matter.

The man they call "the Boss" is a free agent junkie who almost always trades away his top Minor League talent, usually for overpriced Major League veterans. He *hates* losing to the Mets, even by proxy. And a single failure can sour Steinbrenner on a Minor League prospect forever. Righetti aside, playing your way onto the Yankees out of the farm system these days is damn near impossible. Even for Brant, the reigning Topps Minor League Player of the Year. Even for Steve Balboni, the Yankees best power prospect in a decade, who's hit a few home runs that haven't landed yet.

Some players are traded away and inadvertently receive a huge break—a real chance to make the Majors with another team. Major League rosters these days are littered with ex-Yankees prospects who made good elsewhere. But it can still hurt.

Just this morning, the Yankees shipped promising second baseman Pat Tabler—one of the Clippers' leading hitters—to the Cubs as part of a deal for veteran pitcher Rick Reuschel, a rotund right-hander who won twenty games for Chicago in 1977 but will only win four for the Yankees. The trade was a tough one to swallow for both Clippers fans and Tabler, who found out about the deal from a teammate as he pulled into his driveway with a bag of Wendy's food. Tabler walked inside his apartment, took the burger out of the bag and chucked it against the wall. But his chances of sticking in the bigs just got a whole lot better.

Other Clippers, whether they would admit it to themselves or not, have gone as high in pro baseball as they'll go. Outfielder Wayne Harer, a singles hitter who won an IL batting title for Pawtucket in '77 with a .350 average, wasn't even invited to spring training with the power-hungry Red Sox the following year. He has settled in as a

"4A" player, not quite good enough for the Majors. Dave Coleman got twelve at bats for the Red Sox in '77, appeared on a rookie base-ball card, and continued to hit for power in the Minors, but then struggled through injuries and hasn't tasted the Majors since. In the Yankees system, players like this stand ready to serve as trade filler, as a temporary replacement for an injured big leaguer, or as insurance to keep those Minor League wins coming as Steinbrenner demands. But their odds of sticking with the Yankees? They aren't much bet-ter than those of the folks buried over the fence at Mount Calvary.

The Clippers are treated well compared to other Minor Leaguers. Yankees farmhands get more coaching, better uniforms, and bet-ter facilities. But it's still the Minors, far removed from Yankee Stadium, Broadway, Studio 54 nightlife, and not having to worry so much about money.

On this night, however, the spotlight is theirs.

I'M AT FRANKLIN COUNTY Stadium with my dad, a somewhat weary Jim Herman, sitting down the third base line. We're con-tinuing a tradition. He brought me here in '79 and '80 for my first live baseball games, exhibitions the Clippers played against the Yankees. His dad had taken him to White Sox games as he grew up on the South Side of Chicago. As the family story goes, my grandfather didn't have much money as a young man. But he bet most of the money he did have on the soon-to-be-infamous 1919 World Series–throwing White Sox team that would be redubbed the "Black Sox." It took my grandfather a long time to get over that. Perhaps he never completely did. I never had a chance to ask him—he died when my dad was only twenty, after a hard life.

My dad was a brilliant guy who always worked hard, from hospital orderly walking through a pair of socks in one night, to combat aide man in Korea, to promising young hospital admin-istrator, to father of five. This spring is no exception. He's bounc-ing between Ohio and California, where he accepted a new job. He's been gone a lot, working and getting ready to move us to the West Coast. So spending time with him at the ballpark is a rare treat, and not just the baseball part.

In the first game, the visiting Tides are poised to ruin things for us. Tidewater—with a roster full of rising stars, such as infielders Wally Backman and Ron Gardenhire, catcher Bruce Bochy, and reliever Jesse Orosco—rolls across six runs in the top of the ninth to grab an 8–5 lead. Backman, Gardenhire, and Bochy will become big league managers; Backman and Orosco will play in the infamous 1986 World Series five years later; and Orosco eventually will appear in more games than any other Major League pitcher ever. But that is all in the future.

Three errors in the ninth appear to doom my Clippers. Among the miscues, usually uber-dependable shortstop Andre Robertson missed a throw at second and allowed the go-ahead run to score. Columbus is three outs away from slipping back into a first-place tie.

And I can feel it in my young stomach. Dad doesn't say much, but I can sense his disappointment as well. Were it not a doubleheader, cars would already be snaking through the gravel parking lot toward Mound Street.

Bottom of the ninth. Mike Boitano pitching for Tidewater. He walks second baseman Tucker Ashford, the Clippers' leading hitter, a former first-round pick with the Padres who was rushed to the Majors and is trying to find a home in his third organization. Coleman comes up but manages only a pop-out to short.

In the Clipper dugout, grizzled manager Frank Verdi, twenty-eight years removed from his own "Moonlight" Graham moment in the Majors, looks to his bench. A baseball lifer from Brooklyn, he knows the game, and he knows that in this organization he'd better win. Particularly this night, with so many eyeballs on the outcome. The way Steinbrenner hires and fires managers and coaches, Verdi may be only one King George tantrum away from the big leagues himself, or from getting fired or demoted. He sends up three consecutive pinch hitters.

The first is Brad Gulden, a catcher who just rejoined the Clippers following a trade ... for himself. Yep. In 1980 the Yankees sent Gulden and cash to the Seattle Mariners for infielder Larry Milbourne and a player to be named later. Three weeks prior to this night, Gulden became the player to be named later. Two years earlier, he was one of two men to play catcher for the Yankees the night after Thurman Munson was killed.

His experience shows. Gulden walks.

Runners at first and second, one out. Lefty Dave Von Ohlen comes on to pitch for the Tides. Harer hits a ground ball and forces Gulden at second.

That brings up Balboni, who had been sitting out with Brant playing first and Rick Stenholm getting a rare start as a designated hitter. Van Ohlen works carefully—a lot of eyes in New York are watching him, too. Balboni is a Minor League Paul Bunyan, a colossus whose moon-shot home runs brought him national attention last season at Double-A Nashville. *Sports Illustrated* showed up after the six-foot-three, 250-pound, already balding Balboni slugged twenty-one homers in his first thirty-nine games with the Sounds on his way to Southern League MVP honors. He's a soft-spoken, heavily accented New Englander. "I think I've hit a few that I haven't seen anybody hit as faaah," he's noted.

His first season in Triple-A hasn't gone well. Balboni homered on opening night, then didn't hit another homer until thirty-three games in. His numbers through those first thirty-two contests: a .195 batting average, the one home run, and a measly eight RBIs. "Bye-Bye Balboni," a nickname he has never liked, was being used to describe his many strikeouts instead of home runs. But after that slow "staaht," he's beginning to come around, with five homers in the last twenty-two contests—including a blast against Richmond that left the stadium and cleared the cemetery wall, more than five hundred feet from home plate.

Balboni, too, is cautious. The Yankees are concerned about all those strikeouts. This time he refuses to chase Van Ohlen's pitches off the plate, and he earns a base on balls.

Trailing by three, the Clippers (albeit with a lot of help from the Tidewater bullpen) have loaded the bases with two outs. In the Tides' dugout, Boitano seethes as he watches the bullpen flounder. Verdi makes another move, sending pitcher John Pacella into the game as a pinch runner for the lumbering Balboni. Pacella, another Brooklynite, has dubbed himself the "Fordham Flash." Unless he's playing poker; then he'd like to be known as "Stacks."

Up to the plate steps Robertson, all 150 pounds of him. He's a twenty-three-year-old, Afro-wearing, right-handed-hitting Texan known far more for his dazzling plays at shortstop than his bat. He was the first black Little League player in the city of Orange, his hometown by the Gulf Coast. He became the first black scholarship player at the University of Texas. He'd heard slurs from the stands. Stuff he didn't even know existed. But the easy-going Robertson had a way of making it no big deal, like there was never any doubt in anyone's mind that he should be there. After he was drafted by the Texas Rangers, Robertson became the Yankees' shortstop of the future when they acquired him in a deal that included 1976 playoff hero Chris Chambliss, much as they did to acquire second baseman Willie Randolph from the Pirates a few years before. Now Robertson is tagged as "can't miss" in an organization where pretty much every Minor Leaguer is doing just the opposite. If not for Bucky Dent (Bucky Fucking Dent, for Boston fans), Robertson might already be playing at Yankee Stadium. Like Righetti and Balboni, he is a top prospect, a player the Yankees hope will become the core for the next edition of the dynasty.

The fans are on their feet, realizing this is more than just another game. With the count one and one, Von Ohlen serves up a fastball, high and away. Robertson reaches out and sends a fly ball down the right-field line, where the fence is only 330 feet away.

Robertson is not known for power. In more than 1,500 Minor League at bats entering the 1981 season, he had only twelve home runs.

But the crowd gasps as the ball carries. Tidewater right fielder Gary Rajsich drifts back, back. The ball clears the wall . . . just as it hooks foul. "After you hit one like that," Robertson would say, "people are thinking 'Man, that could have been it.'"

Now the home team is down to its last strike. The crowd stays on its feet.

It is 9:13 p.m. Von Ohlen should probably throw a curve. But he comes back with the same pitch, a fastball high and away. What are the chances that Robertson can hit the ball that far again? Only fair? One in a hundred? Worse? He was late on the first pitch.

He swings at the offering, late again, but perhaps a millisecond quicker, and lifts another fly ball to right, a near mirror image of the first swing. In the press box, Clippers radio play-by-play man Rick Rizzs—one of the people who got me hooked on baseball—has the call.

"Heeere's the 1-2 on the way, swung on, fly ball to right field!" Rizzs cries. "Going back is Rajsich . . ."

It seems everyone in Franklin County Stadium has their mouth open and their hands up, waving the ball out of the park like 8,625 Carlton Fisks.

"Near the wall, going, GOING . . ."

The ball drops white before the backdrop of the trees, curving toward the right-field foul line as it falls, but not so much this time. It carries. And carries. And carries.

And disappears over the wall. Just fair.

"GOOD-BYE, BASEBALL!" Rizzs roars into his mic. "It's a grand slam home run! And the Clippers have won the ballgame, 9 to 8!"

Euphoria! Dad and I wrap our arms around each other, jump up and down, and offer high fives to strangers nearby. The Lite-Brite flashes "WOW! HOME RUN! WE WIN!" The victory bell rings, and the Clippers' fight polka spins to life over the public-address system. Ashford scoots home, followed by Harer and then Pacella. Robertson is still running, floating, rounding third. Jubilant teammates mob him at home plate.

From a private box above the celebration, another George S.—not Steinbrenner—quietly savors the scene. George Sisler Jr., son of Major League Hall of Famer "Gorgeous George" Sisler and the Clippers' general manager, was never one to get overly excited.

"George, it doesn't get any better than this," offers team attorney Frank Ray, sitting nearby.

"It'll get better," Sisler replies calmly. "We'll win the championship."

For Ray, it may not get better, at least in terms of baseball. More than three decades later, still the only attorney the team has ever had, he'll recall that moment with more fondness than any championship run.

"That home run," he will say, "is the beauty of the game. That kind of moment, it encapsulates why this game is so special."

For the rest of 1981, WBNS radio will play Rizzs's emphatic call at the start of every baseball broadcast. For the team, Robertson's walk-off will be the springboard to a wild rest of the season, rich with baseball and life stories, on the way to one of the strangest endings to a baseball playoff series you'll encounter at any level.

For me, it's a perfect baseball moment. It seals me as a fan forever. It provides a template for daydreams that will transcend boyhood and cross my mind for the rest of my life. It will stand forever as one of my favorite memories of my dad, with whom my relationship is a blessing but very far from perfect. A crisp snapshot from a time when things were indeed simpler, before much heartbreak, or what seemed like more than a fair share of fear and despair, or the hostile takeover of soul-crushing addictions.

From there I'll enjoy a lot of amazing moments as a sports fan, with and without my dad. I'll have kids of my own, and we, too, will share wild moments of sports-fan elation. But as sports memories go, that moment in Columbus will be tough to top. The drama, the perceived highest of stakes, my age at the time, the father-son moment . . . it's total joy, wrapped in a warm Midwest vibe, at the far edge of young childhood.

IT'S AUGUST 19, 1981, the day before we leave Ohio for our new home in California, and I'm saying good-bye to my best friend, Darren. He's a "Stand by Me" sort of buddy I've known since first grade, someone with whom I've shared conversations about *Star Wars* and growing up and preliminary observations about girls on countless warm summer days like this one. This afternoon, we've been to see *Raiders of the Lost Ark*, a final day together in the last summer we'll remember together.

My mom arrives to pick me up at his house. With tears in my eyes, I stare out the back of our nine-passenger Country Squire station wagon as Darren runs behind us, trying to keep up as we pull away. He gets smaller and smaller, we turn a corner and he's gone.

The next day, scared and nervous about leaving Ohio, I climb into that station wagon with Dad, Mom, my younger sister, Julie, our dog, two cats and a litter box in the back alongside our luggage. Our new home is 2,500 miles away.

We roll out of Columbus and head west on Interstate 70, cornfields and stands of trees unfolding before us. Somewhere near the Indiana border, the Columbus radio stations fade to static. Among the many items in the side mirror, closer than they appear but still turning small and distant, are the Clippers. There's no internet, and Minor League scores aren't easy to come by. I'm just a kid, not savvy enough to think of calling up old friends, or the local paper, to find someone to tell me how my beloved team is doing.

The season goes on and plays out without me. The strike eventually ends, Major League Baseball returns, and the Yankees make the playoffs and once again fall short, leading George Steinbrenner to pursue even more free agents.

For a long time, I have no idea what happened to the 1981 Columbus Clippers, what happened the rest of that summer.

Almost Yankees

1

"I Wouldn't Ship Anything to New York Just Yet"

A DAY AFTER JOHN Hinckley Jr. nearly killed President Reagan, the San Diego Padres' team bus pulled out of Phoenix, and John Pacella felt good about himself and his future.

It was the last day of March 1981. Songs such as Kool & the Gang's "Celebration," Blondie's "Rapture," and the late John Lennon's "(Just Like) Starting Over" played on the radio. Unemployment remained high with the nation between economic recessions. Spring training was winding down and Pacella, a hard-throwing right-hander, had just tossed four solid innings in an exhibition game against the San Francisco Giants. He was poised to grab the number three spot in San Diego's starting rotation. In less than two weeks, he'd be taking the mound against those same Giants at Candlestick Park, in the opening series of the season.

Pacella had a full year of Major League service, albeit a ragged '80 campaign with the New York Mets. Traded in December, he signed a guaranteed two-year deal with the Padres. He possessed an upper-90s fastball, a hard slider, and a good changeup. He owned a condo on the beach in San Diego, just purchased. His new ride, a '75 BMW bought from teammate Rick Wise, was on its way to his new Southern California home.

He had one of the best mustaches in the game, an impressive handlebar.

Pretty good for a twenty-four-year-old kid who'd grown up in Brooklyn with no grass around, much less visions of a professional baseball career.

Pacella struggled that spring, but against San Francisco that day, he'd been sharp. He made a mistake against Joe Morgan, and the Giants' veteran second baseman tagged him for a two-run homer, but those were the only runs Pacella allowed in his four frames. He

FIG 1. Before he joined the Yankee organization, John Pacella pitched for the New York Mets. Courtesy of the New York Mets.

struck out three and walked one. With other Padre pitchers struggling through injuries and poor outings, it would be good enough.

On the bus leaving Phoenix that day, Pacella settled into a seat next to outfielder Jerry Mumphrey, who'd contributed two hits and San Diego's lone RBI in the just-completed exhibition. A bizarre scene unfolded. The bus screeched to a halt on the highway, flagged down from behind. The players looked back and saw flashing lights, police cars, and a black car, out of which stepped Padres general manager "Trader Jack" McKeon and the team's traveling secretary. McKeon boarded the bus.

"Mumphrey, Pacella!" he barked.

Pacella glanced at Mumphrey, whom he barely knew, and asked in his Brooklyn accent, "What did you do?"

"I don't know," Mumphrey replied. "What did *you* do?"

They shuffled to the front of the bus. McKeon delivered the news. The Padres had dealt them to the New York Yankees, and they needed to get their gear off the bus and head back to Yuma. Both were expected at the Yankees' spring training home in Fort Lauderdale the next day.

It was spin-cycle time in Pacella's head. Usually one to pick up on trade vibes, he hadn't this time. The New York freakin' Yankees. He was headed back to New York, to play for a team he'd worshipped growing up. Things were happening quickly. Arrangements needed to be made. He asked McKeon about getting his possessions sent ahead to New York.

"I wouldn't ship anything to New York just yet," McKeon said. "You may be going to Columbus."

"Columbus?" Pacella thought. "Columbus . . . Ohio?"

Not that Pacella was a stranger to the Triple-A International League. He'd pitched in Virginia for the Tidewater Tides during parts of the 1977, '78, and '79 seasons. He just hadn't figured on coming back to the International League, ever. The Minor League assignment left him shocked and confused, and many of his new teammates felt, or would be feeling, the same way.

The Columbus Clippers, the jewel of George Steinbrenner's New York Yankees farm system, weren't your typical Triple-A team.

TEN DAYS EARLIER IN Hollywood, Florida, Clippers general manager George Sisler Jr. drew deeply on a cigar and pondered his team's prospects for the '81 season.

"This club," Sisler told Columbus newspaper columnist Kaye Kessler, "is a cinch to be better than our 1980 team."

Pitching coach Sammy Ellis concurred.

"Talentwise, prospectwise, toolwise, there's no comparison," Ellis said.

The words were as strong as the aroma from Sisler's stogie. The 1980 team had won 83 games in a 140-game regular season. After a hard-fought win against Richmond in the Governors' Cup semifinals, the Clippers thumped second-place Toledo in the finals. Columbus boasted the best pitching in the league, by far, and the International League's MVP in Marshall Brant, their slugging first baseman.

Yet here were Sisler and Ellis, claiming the '80 team was nowhere near as good as the bunch likely to coalesce in Columbus this season. Many players destined for Columbus were working out with the Yankees in Fort Lauderdale but would soon be reassigned to Minor League camp at Hollywood's Dowdy Field.

How loaded were the '81 Clippers? Consider Pacella's situation. He found himself in a battle for the last spot in the New York Yankees' starting rotation with a group of pitchers—Dave Righetti, Andy McGaffigan, Gene Nelson, and Greg Cochran—that was arguably more talented than the Major League Padre rotation Pacella left behind in Arizona. Combine whoever *didn't* make the Yankee rotation with a solid cast of new and returning Triple-A pitchers and the Clippers looked formidable. You could count Yankee pitching legend Whitey Ford among the impressed.

"It's the best group of young arms I've seen in a Yankee camp," Ford told a Florida newspaper earlier that spring. "And if I didn't believe it, I wouldn't say it."

More from Ellis: "If I don't screw this staff up, we'll have a better pitching staff in Columbus than half the teams in the Major Leagues. These guys are so good they scare me to death."

A bit of hyperbole, perhaps, but at least some giddiness was merited.

The Clippers also upgraded defensively, and the new batting order looked scary good for Triple-A.

Brant, who smiled and hit home runs and never said no to autograph seekers, was back. He became my biggest hero on the team. He was pretty much *everyone's* hero. In 1980, his first season with the Clippers after five years in the Mets organization, Brant hit .289 with twenty-three homers and ninety-two RBIs. Stellar numbers, though still not good enough to earn him a meaningful look from the big club in spring training the following season. With the '81 Clippers, Brant didn't even have a full-time role locked up, at least not a well-defined role.

That's because another first baseman, Steve Balboni, was up

from Nashville, where *he* earned league MVP honors. Balboni was already something of a Minor League legend and had New York fans drooling, anticipating the day he'd take over at first base in Yankee Stadium. He and Brant might already have a shot with other Major League teams. Not with Steinbrenner's New York Yankees. Both would start the season at Triple-A, trading off between first base and designated hitter. And behind them in the organization, rising quickly, was an outfielder beginning to play more first base named Don Mattingly.

The Clippers also upgraded at third base, where newly acquired Tucker Ashford, an IL All-Star, would take over, and at second, where red-hot prospect Pat Tabler would roam. Rising star Andre Robertson, the smiling, soft-spoken young Texan, was up for good at shortstop. The outfield was strong and about to get stronger via trades and demotions of top-notch talent by the Yankees, whose outfield was beyond loaded with megastars like Reggie Jackson and free agent prize Dave Winfield.

On March 22, the Yankees cut nine players—including Brant—from their Major League roster and sent them to the Clippers' camp. Rick Rizzs, the Clippers' new play-by-play man, arrived in Florida and soon filed daily reports on the team for WBNS radio.

Columbus dropped its first exhibition game 13–6 against the Richmond Braves—an International League foe—at Dowdy. Most of the Clippers who played in that game were ticketed for Double-A Nashville. First baseman Jim McDonald singled and tripled. He was a former first-round draft pick who played well for the Clippers in 1980. Now, with Brant coming off an MVP season and Balboni present, McDonald would have to fight just for a spot in Double-A. Before long, he'd be suiting up for Veracruz in the Mexican League.

ABOUT SEVENTY MILES WEST of Columbus, star-turned-utility-player Dave Coleman, who helped the Clippers win it all the previous season, spent the first part of March at home in his native Dayton, unsure whether to journey to Florida or retire. He faced a twelfth season in the Minors, interrupted only by his few at bats

PHOTO COURTESY OF TOM WATSON

Columbus Clippers
Outfielder
DAVE COLEMAN—17

FIG 2. Dave Coleman's 1980 baseball card.
Courtesy of the Columbus Clippers.

for the Boston Red Sox four years earlier. Even in the rough economy, there were job opportunities offering a lot more money than
he'd earn for another season with the Yankees organization, particularly considering the team's latest, underwhelming offer. Maybe
driving a truck for a distributorship. Was suiting up for one more
baseball season worth another round of long bus rides, early morning plane trips, injuries that became an issue late in his career, and
what figured to be less playing time? He still believed he had the
talent to play in the Majors, but did—or would—anyone else?

Coleman played six different positions, and played them well, but to call him a phenom at any point in his career would be overstating things. He was terrific for Dayton's Stebbins High School, earning all-league honors as well as the MVP Award for the annual All-Ohio Baseball Series in Columbus, during his senior season in 1969. Getting drafted wasn't on his radar. He was taken in the eighteenth round, and only after his high school coach, Jim Murray, convinced some scouts to come give the young third baseman a look. When Coleman was selected with the 419th pick by the Boston Red Sox, it didn't even earn a mention in either of Dayton's two daily newspapers. He drew more attention from the local papers when he pitched a no-hitter for Dorothy Lane Market, his Little League team, at age seven.

In the Minors, he showed athleticism and some pop—twenty-four home runs for Pawtucket in '78 and twenty more for Toledo the following season. It wasn't enough. He was thirty now and would be the oldest player on the Columbus roster. Metaphors like "out of gas" and "hitting my head against a wall" were on his mind. But he also feared quitting too soon and facing that regret from behind the wheel of a delivery truck in a few years.

He decided to sign and report. One more season.

I Ran the Ballclub for about Five Minutes, Then I Got Shot in the Head

The man tasked with shuffling all this talent into another title winner was manager Frank Verdi, a vino-drinkin', horse-bettin', front office defyin', tough guy with a heart of gold out of Brooklyn's Boys High School. The '81 season was Verdi's first with the Clippers. His career in professional baseball had touched five different decades, all in the Minor Leagues, save for the briefest of moments.

Verdi, fifty-four when he took the Columbus job, was lucky to be alive. Among his most remarkable life stories, he once took a bullet to the head while coaching third base. It happened during the early morning hours of July 26, 1959, in Havana, Cuba.

Full appreciation of the story requires a bit of Cuban history. On July 26, 1953, a twenty-six-year-old baseball pitcher named Fidel

Castro led an armed attack against the Moncanda Barracks in Santiago de Cuba. He took the loss. But the attack came to be recognized as the start of the Cuban Revolution, and Castro dubbed his forces the 26th of July Movement.

Just shy of six years later, Verdi—then a thirty-three-year-old player in his fourteenth Minor League season—and his Rochester Red Wings traveled to Cuba for an International League series against the Havana Sugar Kings, a club flush with talent from the Cincinnati Reds organization. Castro had taken control of the Cuban government the previous winter, and wild celebrations—often involving guns—broke out frequently in and around the capital.

On the night of July 25, the Red Wings and Sugar Kings got a late start in their regularly scheduled game at Gran Stadium after completing a suspended contest. Rochester led the first game 3–2 in the bottom of the ninth when Havana's Rogelio Alvarez tied the game with a dramatic home run. As the clock struck midnight and July 26 arrived, the three thousand locals in the stands erupted with flag waving, singing, and plenty of gunfire into the air. Well, those bullets eventually came down, many of them on the field, sending players and umpires running for cover. Verdi and some of his teammates found some under a jeep near the Rochester bullpen, beyond the left-field fence. The game was suspended but eventually the gunfire subsided, at least enough that play could be resumed.

The Red Wings, increasingly anxious to finish the game and make their escape, grabbed a 4–3 lead on Billy Harrell's homer in the top of the tenth. In the bottom of the inning, Havana's Jesse Gonder doubled. Rochester manager Ellis "Cot" Deal argued that Gonder missed first base. The disagreement with first base umpire Frank Guzzetta ended after Deal delivered the international symbol for "choker" and was thrown out, further riling the crowd. Verdi, who was not playing after getting beaned two weeks earlier, took over for Deal as manager. After Gonder came around to score the tying run, Rochester and Havana headed into inning number eleven.

Verdi trotted out to coach third base in Deal's place. He clapped his hands and provided the usual banter. "C'mon, baby!" As Dick Rand started the inning by grounding out to Leo Cardenas at short, more shots rang out.

"I was standing there coaching," Verdi would recall, "and Pow! Down I went."

He was hit, knocked to the ground. He thought at first that he'd been clocked by a wildly thrown ball. A spent bullet had struck him in the head, earlobe, and shoulder. Players and umpires again ran for cover.

Verdi remained conscious but felt groggy. He tried to get back on his feet, but he couldn't.

"Frank, are you alright?" umpire Ed Vargo said, half yelling. "They almost got me too."

Vargo found the bullet that struck Verdi. "This is what hit you," he said. It appeared to be a .45 caliber.

Vargo felt two bullets whiz by, one past his chest and another past his leg. Cardenas was grazed in the back, enough for a hospital visit. Verdi was carried off the field by his teammates, and the game was called. It was the beginning of the end of American baseball in Cuba, at least for several decades.

Verdi's life may have been saved by a rubber-and-plastic liner, which he wore inside his cap with extra fervor after the recent beaning. It wrapped around the sides of his head but left the top exposed. His cap had a bullet hole in it, but the shell apparently deflected off the liner, and Verdi dodged serious injury. Maybe much worse.

"I ran the ballclub for about five minutes, then I got shot in the head," Verdi recounted. "If that bullet had been two inches to the left it would have gone right through my head and all the team would have had to chip in five bucks a piece for flowers."

Back in the states, the incident was national news. Verdi himself penned an account for United Press International. The Red Wings refused to play in Sunday's scheduled twin bill, over the protests of pretty much the whole island, including the Sugar Kings' management. "An atmosphere of peace, tranquility, and happiness reigned in the city when Rochester refused to play due to an incident of no importance the night before," a statement read.

After an anxious Sunday night in their hotel, the Red Wings flew home. Verdi and his manager sat next to each other on the plane, mulling over how getting thrown out of the game may have saved Deal's life.

As soon as he was able, Verdi called home to Bay Shore, Long Island, and checked in with wife, Pauline.

"I read in the paper you got shot in the head," she told him.

He assured her he was okay.

FRANK VERDI WAS A salty character, politically incorrect before the term was invented. He was known to summon rainouts with a mock Native American dance. "Kiss a fat lady's ass" was his go-to expression for frustration or displeasure. Players, umpires, front office types, or others who disappointed him were "cock-knockers." During one practice, he shook his head in disbelief at a young infielder's bad form. "You see him fielding that ground ball?" Verdi asked the team's GM. "It looks like he's fucking a beach ball."

And man, could he get angry. The '81 Verdi had mellowed somewhat, but crossing him was always ill-advised.

Once, during his tenure managing the Syracuse Chiefs, Verdi literally tore his office door off its hinges. A couple of years earlier, during a road trip with the Oneonta Yankees, he got so angry over an umpire's blown call that he went berserk, turned beet red, and refused to leave the field after he was ejected. The umpires summoned a sheriff and deputy sheriff handling security at the ballpark. "Get him off the field!" the sheriff ordered his deputy. "*You* get him off," the deputy responded. Verdi went eye-to-eye with defiant players, umpires, or anyone else who'd incurred his wrath. He'd flip his cap backward, put his hands in his back pockets, get right up in his target's face and let him have it, bobbing his own face from side to side around the visage of whomever was on the receiving end. Even much larger men were sometimes intimidated.

Sisler said he'd never seen anyone who hated to lose as much as Frank Verdi. Family members said each time Verdi lost a baseball game, a bit of his soul was lost too. He felt a deep responsibility to the people in whichever city he was managing to put a winning team on the field, and he knew his family's livelihood depended on his success. He loved the game and had no tolerance for those who disrespected it, or showed incompetence around it.

Verdi also had a gentle side. He could royally chew players out or put his arm around their shoulders, whichever he felt was needed. He took some of the younger guys around his '81 team, like pitcher Paul Boris and trainer Mark "Rookie" Letendre, into his care. When Jim Massie, a young reporter covering the Clippers for the *Columbus Dispatch*, lost his dad unexpectedly just before the season started, Verdi took him into his office and consoled him through those raw, early moments. A small group of players over the years, particularly pitcher Mike Bruhert, were treated like sons by Verdi.

The Verdis brought a family feel wherever Frank managed. His wife, Pauline, was an exceedingly patient baseball spouse who set up their lives wherever needed and expertly played the organ at games. Their four boys were ballpark mainstays during their childhoods, serving as bat boys, scoreboard operators, or in other roles. In Syracuse, when Verdi wasn't tearing his office door out of its sockets, he might have been drinking homemade wine with the grounds crew and playing bocce in right field. Visit the Verdi home at any point during his career and you'd likely see homemade pasta noodles draped over the back of the couch and be offered a glass of wine.

Usually the life of the party, Verdi told jokes and stories. He expertly belted out tunes by Louis Prima, Johnnie Ray, and other headliners of his day. When Frank Verdi walked into a room, Letendre recalled, there were no longer any strangers in it.

FOR SOMEONE WHO BARELY sniffed the Majors, Verdi had quite a list of Major League friends. In addition to close buddy Whitey Ford, Verdi hung out with Mickey Mantle, Yogi Berra, and Johnny Mize, among other Yankees legends. They liked Frank Verdi very much.

So it wasn't unusual when, during spring training in '81, Frank and Pauline received a dinner invitation from Whitey and his wife, Joanie. They were joined at the Fords' Fort Lauderdale condo by

Mickey, Yogi, Yankees coach Mike Ferraro, and their wives. Whitey's sons, Tommy and Eddie, were also there.

Chili was served that night, in the dining room. The stories started to fly, as they always did when the old friends got together. Mickey shared a funny one from his Minor League days and really got the group laughing—particularly Whitey.

The laughter turned to panic after Whitey sucked a chili bean down his windpipe, where it lodged. He headed to the kitchen to try spitting it out, began choking and wound up passed out on the floor, his face turning purple. No one was sure what to do at first. Joanie tried squeezing his chest. Eddie prepped for mouth-to-mouth. Mickey was panic-stricken.

Verdi kept his cool and knew he needed to do something. Were it not for him, Whitey Ford might have died that night at fifty-two. The pitching legend's old friend, who'd thrown more than a few punches over the years, delivered the hardest he had in him, right into Whitey's chest. Seconds passed. No change. Verdi pulled his right hand back and delivered another shot. This time, the chili bean popped out, and Whitey started breathing again.

He wouldn't remember Verdi's powerful punches. He'd been unconscious. The next day, though, Whitey's chest hurt so much, he thought he was dead.

A few years later, Verdi was looking for work after an 18-40 fans-with-bags-over-their-heads start with the Rochester Red Wings got him fired. This time, it was Whitey Ford who stepped up.

"He was without a job, and I kept hounding George Steinbrenner to hire him," Whitey would recall in his autobiography. "Every day I'd send a note to George, 'Don't forget Verdi. Don't forget Verdi.' George finally hired him as a scout. It was the least I could do for a guy who saved my life."

FOLLOWING VERDI'S ARRIVAL IN 1981, Clipper players and coaches who hadn't been exposed to him previously soon picked up on some odd baseball practices. For example, he often positioned his left fielders unusually close to the foul line. He sometimes did the same with his right fielders.

1981 Columbus Clippers
Manager
FRANK VERDI—26

PHOTO COURTESY OF WATSON PHOTOGRAPHY

Fɪɢ 3. Frank Verdi's 1981 baseball card. Courtesy of the Columbus Clippers.

Perhaps Verdi had been burned one too many times by balls dropping in just fair. His pitchers hated this particular move, because positioning outfielders that way left huge swaths of open space in left-center and right-center field. There were certainly times when balls dropped in there that otherwise would have been caught.

The first time Verdi positioned his outfielders that way with the Clippers, Ellis and bench coach Jerry McNertney gave each other a "What the hell is going on?" look in the dugout.

"What's this crazy old man doing?" Andy McGaffigan wondered aloud.

"I've never heard of anybody defending a foul ball," players would say.

Verdi, whom Ellis would describe as "stubborn as a box of rocks," didn't just stand his ground. He gloated whenever a fly ball was hauled in near the line.

"You see?" he'd say, turning to players and coaches in the dugout. "That worked!"

Another thing that worked for Verdi: having a few sips of wine—or something stronger—during games. No one remembers him impaired while he was managing. But sometimes, when the tension got to him, he slipped out of the dugout and into his office for a quick nip of brandy or other hard stuff he kept on hand. He consumed wine more openly in the dugout. With the Clippers in '82, Verdi called for a small cup from time to time. The trainer that season, Steve Donahue, was on point.

"Donahue!" Verdi barked. "Grapes!"

Larger amounts of wine loosened up Verdi for the long bus trips, during which he'd talk baseball, often spiritedly, late into the night. Anything to get through those long rides, which Verdi had already endured during much of his long baseball life. There were still many, many more of those journeys in front of him.

Meet My Son, Reggie Jackson

Several players in camp with the Clippers in 1981 had recognizable names later on, but either wouldn't make the team or would be demoted before very long.

William "Buck" Showalter was an accomplished Double-A player. And an experienced one—he'd been stuck there for three seasons. The previous year in Nashville, he'd accumulated 178 hits and a .324 average. A line drive switch hitter, he figured to fare well on Franklin County Stadium's artificial surface.

Showalter made the Clippers roster out of spring training, but he was back in Double-A before the end of April. Steinbrenner acquired another former Major Leaguer in Dave Stegman, and

Showalter found himself suiting up for Nashville . . . again. His playing career ended in '83. Shortly after, he embarked on a career as a highly successful manager, including a four-year stint with the Yankees.

Willie McGee was in camp with the Clippers and *he* didn't make the team. Only twenty-two at the time, he reached the Majors the following season with the St. Louis Cardinals. He was only a few years away from winning a National League batting title and MVP Award. The trade that sent McGee to the Cardinals for pitcher Bob Sykes was one of the worst in baseball history.

Then there was Reggie Jackson. Not the star outfielder.

This other Reggie, known to his friends as "Jack," was a lanky, right-handed pitcher and a good sport about sharing a name with a superstar in the same organization. He'd averaged nearly sixteen strikeouts a game during his senior season at Fisk, a small college in Tennessee, but he wasn't drafted. The Yankees gave him a look. Not much of one, though. After failing to stick with them, he'd bounce around in the Mets organization for a few years, topping out at Double-A.

"Jack" had met the more famous Reggie Jackson once, during batting practice before a Yankees–Red Sox game. Jack's father, Al Jackson, a former Columbus Jet, original New York Met and Major League pitching coach, introduced them when Jack was still in college, and Reggie was near his peak of Yankee fame.

"Reggie Jackson, meet my son, Reggie Jackson," Al Jackson said.

"You got a superstar's name," the left-handed slugger said. "You play ball? What hand are you?"

Jack told Reggie he was a right-handed pitcher.

"Get lost," Reggie said.

LIKE "JACK" JACKSON, VERDI, and the entire Clippers coaching staff and players, head trainer Mark Letendre dreamed of the Majors. He'd get there more quickly and stay longer than most of them.

Letendre was just twenty-two when he joined the Clippers in 1979, a year removed from the University of Maine. He'd already earned his nickname, "Rookie." In his early days at Maine, he was a nervous-as-hell, low-level trainer who handled pregame tape jobs and wraps for football players unlikely to see any action that day. In the locker room before a game, Letendre fumbled a ninety-six-inch roll of wrap. That's eight feet. The wrap fell to the ground and unrolled. And unrolled. Everyone stopped to watch. Still unrolling. Until it finished unrolling and came to a rest at the feet of the senior staff, all of whom watched it finally come to a stop, then looked up in unison at the embarrassed young trainer.

"Ah, what a fuckin' rookie," head trainer Wes Jordan said.

It stuck. Thankfully, just the "Rookie" part.

Jordan was more than a nickname generator to Letendre. A legend at Maine, Jordan conducted camps for aspiring young trainers. Letendre attended one of them at age sixteen and the experience changed his life forever. After Jordan died in 2002, Letendre joined sportscaster Gary Thorne in raising funds for an athletic training facility at the school, with Jordan's name attached to it.

With the Clippers, Rookie was part of the team as much as anyone. He joined players in their off-the-field carousing. Frank Verdi treated him like family and let him tag along to bocce tournaments. When Gene "Stick" Michael was the manager, he and Letendre competed in an occasional footrace in front of the players, who'd yell "C'mon Rookie!" or "C'mon, Stick!" The young trainer loved his job and even his commute to Franklin County Stadium, along the Olentangy Freeway from his home on Henderson Road. Just driving to work pumped him up.

Rookie was much more than a trainer. In his first job after college at Double-A West Haven, he sold candy bars and potato chips to players on the side. Kessler described Letendre as the Clippers' "psychologist, medic, chef, friend/confidant, traveling secretary, father confessor, housekeeper, sanitary engineer, and contractual attorney." And one more: "Budding genius." Letendre wouldn't stick around the Minors for long. He joined the Yankees as an assistant trainer in 1982, and he was the head trainer for the San Francisco Giants by 1986.

ON OPENING DAY OF the 1996 Major League season, the Montreal Expos visited the Cincinnati Reds for the traditional lid-lifter at Riverfront Stadium. John McSherry, one of several umpires who were battling severe weight problems, took his place behind home plate. Seven pitches into the game, with Montreal's Rondell White batting against Cincinnati's Pete Schourek, the fifty-one-year-old umpire knew something was wrong. "Hold on," he said to Eddie Taubensee, the Reds' catcher. "Time out for a second."

"Are you alright, John?" Taubensee asked.

McSherry motioned to the second-base umpire that he needed a replacement, walked toward the stands, wobbled, and collapsed on the field, still wearing his umpire's mask. The crowd gasped. Medical staff rushed to his side and attempted to revive him, but McSherry died on the field from a massive heart attack. He is believed to be the only person to die on the field during a Major League Baseball game.

McSherry's shocking death was part of the impetus for Major League Baseball's creation of the Umpire Medical Services program in 1999. The umpires, who number about seventy, became a team of sorts themselves, with regular health screenings and programs to help with nutrition, fitness, and wellness counseling. Mark Letendre was picked to head up the program, and he's held the position ever since.

Healthwise, Major League umpires have come a long way since. Letendre likes to think of the program as taking care of the men who take care of the integrity of the game. He also speaks frequently on the dangers of chewing tobacco and has received numerous awards over the years for his charitable work, as well as his career as a trainer.

Not bad for a Rookie.

FOR ALL THE TALENT that came through Dowdy Field in the spring of '81, Steve Balboni led the team in buzz generated. He impressed even Steinbrenner with a home run that cleared a forty-foot hedge beyond the center-field wall at the Yankees' Fort Lauderdale facility. "Only man ever to do it," the Boss noted.

The soft-speaking Balboni was twenty-four when he arrived in Yankee camp that spring with a national reputation as a can't-miss prospect. He slugged thirty-four home runs with the Double-A Nashville Sounds the previous season, on his way to Southern League MVP honors, and many were blasts majestic enough to stir imaginations. Balboni clubbed twenty-one homers in his first thirty-nine games with Nashville, and *Sports Illustrated* reporter Steve Wulf showed up and wrote a story headlined "Hello Balboni, bye-bye ball." Baseball fans around the country learned of Balboni's exploits at tiny Eckerd College in St. Petersburg, Florida, and his Minor League stops to that point.

The six-foot-three Balboni was listed at 225 pounds but was probably closer to 250. Bulk aside, he didn't look like a legendary home run hitter. He stood out not only for his stature but also for his receding hairline and moonish face. Yankees coach Stan Williams noted the dichotomy. "You look more like a goddamn truck driver," Williams kidded Balboni. "Where'd you park the semi?"

Balboni swung a long, heavy bat, thirty-six inches and thirty-six to thirty-eight ounces. He first encountered a bat that size by chance during his college days at Eckerd. He picked up one that was left behind in the locker room by the Pittsburgh Pirates' Willie Stargell after the iconic slugger and some of his teammates worked out at Eckerd in the spring of 1976, during a Major League lockout. Balboni had a bat that suited him.

All this added up to give Balboni a Bambino-esque quality that endeared him to fans, even during rough patches. Balboni's strikeout totals were high, even for a power hitter. The strikeout issue was one of the reasons Balboni hated the "Bye-Bye" nickname he was tagged with early in his career. The moniker fed an easy pivot between home runs and strikeouts, between feast and famine. Now that Balboni had reached Triple-A ball, which of the two would it be?

2

Locked Out

THE LOCKOUT THAT CONNECTED Steve Balboni with Willie Stargell's bat also marked a crucial moment in professional baseball's long, contentious labor history, as well as professional sports history.

Major League Baseball's owners were losing the labor fight in the spring of '76, and they knew it. The previous December, an arbitrator named Pete Seitz had issued a game-changing ruling, favoring players who were fighting for the right to sign with whichever team they wanted, for whatever pay they could negotiate. Under a "reserve clause" system that had existed for decades, owners had the option of perpetually renewing a player's existing contract, one year at a time, for as long as the owner desired. Players had little freedom or bargaining power. They were usually stuck with the first club they'd signed with for as long as that club wanted to hold onto them. It could last for a player's entire career.

The Seitz ruling blew that system apart, and in the weeks that followed, owners desperate to reestablish their upper hand tried locking players out of spring camps. The existing Basic Agreement between the two parties had expired on December 31. Owners said they wouldn't open spring training facilities until a new agreement was crafted, and the new agreement they had in mind would have hobbled the players' just-obtained rights and freedoms.

AN OUTFIELDER NAMED CURT Flood had been one of the players' key freedom fighters, a godfather of sorts to the free agent movement. Flood starred for the St. Louis Cardinals of the turbulent 1960s with unparalleled defense as well as top-tier batting. He helped the Cardinals to World Series titles in '64 and '67.

Following the '69 season, the Cardinals attempted to trade Flood to the Philadelphia Phillies in a deal also involving Tim McCarver, Dick Allen, Cookie Rojas, and three others. Flood refused to accept the deal. He didn't want to play for a last-place team in a crappy stadium, in a city known to be difficult for black players, such as himself, due to racist behavior by some of the locals. He believed baseball's reserve clause was unfair and took his case to the courts, seeking the ability to negotiate with other teams. The day before Christmas, he sent a letter to MLB commissioner Bowie Kuhn. "I do not feel that I am a piece of property to be bought and sold irrespective of my wishes," Flood wrote. "I believe that any system which produces that result violates my basic rights as a citizen and is inconsistent with the laws of the United States and of the several states."

Kuhn denied Flood's request. Flood and the players' association filed a $1 million lawsuit. He sat out the 1970 season, foregoing a $100,000 salary, and was bombarded with hate mail, including death threats. His personal and financial life fell apart.

The case made it all the way to the Supreme Court, which ruled 5–3 against Flood. Largely blackballed from baseball afterward, Flood played only briefly for the Washington Senators in 1971 before retiring, but his unprecedented challenge started something that the owners couldn't stop. It lit up the issue for other players, and for the public. It factored into the owners' decision, as part of a new Basic Agreement with players in 1970, to accept arbitration for settling grievances, which players and their association would use to wear down the old system. It all added up to the beginning of the end for the reserve clause.

ANDY MESSERSMITH WAS ANOTHER key figure in the players' fight. From the late '60s through the mid-'70s, Messersmith was one of the best pitchers in baseball. After he won twenty games for the Los Angeles Dodgers in '74, Messersmith tried to get a no-trade clause added to his contract. The Dodgers refused and instead renewed Messersmith's existing agreement for another season. Messersmith wouldn't sign the renewal, though, and he played the 1975 season without a signed deal. When the season ended, Messersmith—along with Montreal Expos pitcher Dave McNally, who'd retired midway through '75—argued that owners' absolute control over players shouldn't last beyond one-year extensions. Seitz issued his ruling on December 23. It sent shockwaves through the sport:

> The grievances of Messersmith and McNally are sustained. There is no contractual bond between these players and the Los Angeles and the Montreal clubs, respectively. Absent such a contract, their clubs had no right or power, under the Basic Agreement, the uniform player contract, or the Major League Rules to reserve their services for their exclusive use for any period beyond the "renewal year" in the contracts which these players had heretofore signed with their clubs.

In other words, players could now become free agents after playing out a year without a signed contract, as Messersmith had done. The reserve clause wielded by owners for so many years was effectively dead. Owners were horrified. They fired Seitz immediately following his decision.

Oakland A's pitching ace Jim "Catfish" Hunter became a free agent the previous year following a different Seitz ruling, but that involved an individual contract dispute, not the entire system. Regardless, the ensuing Catfish sweepstakes gave everyone a taste of how free agency would change things. Steinbrenner pounced, bringing Hunter to the Yankees for an unheard-of $3.5 million over five seasons. The pitcher's annual salary jumped from $100,000 to $700,000.

After the Messersmith-McNally ruling, players and owners traded barbs and counteroffers for a new agreement as the owners futilely appealed in federal courts. The first day of spring training for the '76 season came and went with no real spring training. Players showed up in Florida on their own, figuring they'd get in shape, wherever they could find facilities. Mets ace Tom Seaver loosely ran one such faux training camp at Eckerd College, with about forty players from various teams taking part. But Seaver rethought the idea and shuttered the camp on March 12. He figured that players getting in shape on their own time was playing into the owners' hands. Seaver, Stargell, and the other Major Leaguers left Eckerd, in some cases leaving gear—such as really huge baseball bats—behind. The beneficiaries included Steve Balboni.

The owners proposed a complicated new system requiring at least eight years of service before a player could become a free agent, a draft for free agents, and compensation for teams losing a free agent. Players countered with a lower bar for service required, and much less compensation.

On March 18, Kuhn ordered owners to open the camps. Spring training—and the 1976 season—would go on. Players and owners singed a new agreement that year, and for the most part it allowed players with at least six years of service to become free agents—still a major victory for the union.

The two sides didn't resolve the issue of how to compensate owners for free agents they'd lost. It stayed unresolved through a barely averted strike in 1980. It showed up again in a big way the following year.

Dr. George and Mr. Hyde

Clippers on the bubble for a roster spot in 1981 anxiously wondered what the Yankees would do with players like Rogers Lee "Bobby" Brown, a talented, athletic outfielder who had played well for the big club the previous season. The Yankees' already loaded outfield included superstar free agent signee Winfield. Now Mumphrey was in the mix too. Would Brown make the Yankee roster again? Would he be traded? If Brown ended up back in Columbus, someone else would have to go.

Brown dominated for the Clippers in '79, sharing IL MVP honors with Pawtucket's Dave Stapleton. Brown stole bases standing up. He hit .349. He robbed batter after batter, snaring balls in the outfield that few others could have reached. Teammates and fans said he looked like a man playing in a kids' game. Sisler called him "the greatest Minor League player I've ever seen." Still, Brown rode Steinbrenner's famed "Columbus shuttle" that season, getting called up to the Yankees four different times and

Fig 4. Bobby Brown's 1979 baseball card. Courtesy of TCMA Ltd.

sent down three. With the Yankees in 1980, Brown—one of Reggie Jackson's few friends on the team—hit a solid .260, with fourteen home runs and twenty-seven stolen bases. But in March of '81, after a slow start in spring training, "B.B." topped Steinbrenner's shit list, and the Boss was warming up the Columbus shuttle for him once again. Some speculated that Brown was angering Steinbrenner by seemingly not taking his struggles at the plate hard enough, instead maintaining his confident and happy-go-lucky disposition. It's also likely the Boss was still sore about Brown's 0-for-10 performance in the 1980 American League Championship Series.

Brown brimmed with self-assuredness, at least outwardly, and at least before Steinbrenner turned him into a psychology experiment. Pulling up to filling stadiums on the bus, he would quip, "All these people here to see B.B." That confidence dated back at least to Northhampton High School in Cheriton, Virginia, where, growing up in a poor family, he starred in all things athletic. One night, after a football game, he approached a beautiful young woman named Leontine. "You're my wife," he told her, "and you don't even know it yet." Before long she would.

Despite his spring training struggles, he felt—with good reason—that he had nothing left to prove in the Minor Leagues. An order from Steinbrenner to only hit from the left side of the plate further infuriated him. When the Yankees assigned him back to Columbus after a 3-for-27 spring training start and told him to check in at the Thunderbird Motel, where Minor Leaguers stayed each spring, Brown initially refused to do so. He felt degraded and frustrated. "I'm going home," Brown told Yankees GM Gene Michael, his manager with the Clippers in '79.

Michael was a Bobby-whisperer that season, providing some sorely needed nurturing. Now, two seasons later, he counseled Brown to sleep on it and check back in the following morning. Brown eventually relented and headed back to the Clippers, though he was increasingly bitter.

Within a week, the Yankees recalled him. But in mid-April, they sent him back to Columbus yet again.

STEINBRENNER PRESIDED OVER A circus on the field, in the clubhouse, and in the front office, with regular tours de force in control freakishness. He meddled in on-the-field issues, suggesting lineup changes, batting orders, and trades based not on acumen but authority, criticizing his own players and team to the press. He drove managers and coaches crazy and would fire them at the drop of a batting helmet. His attempts to inspire his players with rah-rah speeches fell flat, usually alienating them instead. He browbeat his staff. "I don't like to hurt people," he once said. "Sometimes I just . . . well, I guess I can't help it."

Youth wasn't enough to get young players off the hook for poor performances. Quite the opposite. "We've seen enough of Tucker Ashford," the Boss said following a spring training game. Ashford hadn't even had an at bat. Five years earlier, Steinbrenner nearly let a young-and-struggling future superstar named Ron Guidry get away. Late in his life, Steinbrenner noted that a younger version of himself might even have passed on a young Derek Jeter out of a lack of patience. The Boss eventually warmed to less-established players, but this was the early 1980s, and players like Ashford and pitcher Mike Griffin were in Steinbrenner's line of fire. Especially if they screwed the family dog against the Mets, with whom Steinbrenner believed he was in a pitched battle for the hearts and minds of New York fans.

Hard-throwing Griffin starred for the Clippers in '79 and '80, winning the James P. Dawson Award as the Yankees' top spring training rookie in the latter. He pitched in thirteen games for the Yankees that season, continuing to show promise at the tender age of twenty-three. The following spring, he struggled. The Mets—oh God, not the Mets—clobbered him in exhibition outings on March 19 and 23. Steinbrenner, who watched the second game already boiling over reports that Mets GM Frank Cashen had likened Yankee Stadium to "Fort Apache, the Bronx," sent Griffin down to the Minors before the game was even over and let loose on the young pitcher afterward.

"We had to find out about our young pitchers," Steinbrenner told reporters after the game. "Well, we found out about Mike Griffin today. You say you can't tell from one outing? The hell you can't. This spells it for Mike Griffin. He has fooled us long enough."

Not exactly a good moundside manner.

Griffin sucked it up, worked through some issues with his slider, pitched well for the Clippers once again, and escaped via a trade to the Cubs during the labor strike. He never established himself in the Majors, but he did go on to a lengthy career as a pitching coach. Reflecting three decades later on Steinbrenner's antagonism, Griffin admitted to being hurt back then, but he bore the Boss no ill will.

"I had a bad spring," Griffin recalled.

"You know what? He was right."

• • •

The list of quotes about—and sometimes lobbed directly at—George Steinbrenner from the 1980s has some colorful entries. To wit:

"Fuck you, you fat motherfucker!"—Graig Nettles

"You're a fucking chicken-shit liar."—Yogi Berra

"Come out of there, you fat fucking Fauntleroy!"—Bill Kane, the Yankees' traveling secretary

"Fuck him! He never played a game for this team."—Dave Righetti

"If you want to fire me, then get your fat ass out here to Chicago and just do it."—Gene Michael

"Steinbrenner sucks!"—The crowd at Yankee Stadium on multiple occasions

"He's an overbearing, arrogant, arbitrary, authoritarian son of a bitch. . . . But I just love him. We all do."—Pete Smythe, a longtime friend of Steinbrenner

In the clubhouse following a doubleheader in 1983, Goose Gossage, fuming over Steinbrenner's criticism of the team and the media's tendency to regurgitate all the negativity, spun one of the greatest/worst sports rants of all time.

"All you motherfuckers with a fuckin' pen," Gossage told reporters, "and a fuckin' tape recorder, you can fuckin' turn it on and take it upstairs, to the fat man. Okay? 'Cause I'm fuckin' sick of this fuckin' shit. The negative fuckin' bullshit, you got it?"

And that was after Goose had saved both games of the doubleheader. Imagine if he'd just had a bad game. Fortunately for all involved, the Boss took this tirade with good humor, noting that he'd recently lost eleven pounds, and that perhaps Gossage was referring to Yankees vice president Bill Bergesch.

Following the '83 season, Gossage and Nettles left the Bronx for considerably more relaxed San Diego, where they promptly helped the Padres make the World Series for the first time, though Gossage didn't always endear himself to the ownership in San Diego, either, noting at one point that Joan Kroc and her hamburgers were poisoning the world.

MOST OFTEN, THE BOSS was exceedingly hard on his players. He paid them a lot, he expected a lot, and he often doled out public criticism when they fell short of his expectations. His abuse of a lengthy list of Yankees managers—including an increasingly unraveled Billy Martin five different times—is well-documented. Front office staff, coaches, and even their loved ones could be targets. One ugly example came after game two of the 1980 American League Championship Series against the Kansas City Royals. With two outs in the top of the eighth and New York trailing by a run, Mike Ferraro, coaching third base for the Yankees, waved Willie Randolph home on a Bob Watson double. Randolph was thrown out at the plate, sending Steinbrenner into a rage on national television, and the Yankees went on to lose. The Boss wanted Ferraro canned that very second and took his frustrations out on the coach's wife.

"Your husband really fucked this game up for us today!" Steinbrenner bellowed at her, after the final out.

Manager Dick Howser, who may have stood up to Steinbrenner better than any other Yankee skipper, refused to go along with firing Ferraro and ended up getting fired himself. Howser wound up in Kansas City, where he managed the Royals—with a slugging first baseman named Steve Balboni—to their first World Series title in 1985.

While some of Steinbrenner's abusive behavior was inexcusable, it was also, at least in part, explainable.

Born in 1930 on the Fourth of July, in Rocky River, Ohio, George Steinbrenner grew up in the Cleveland suburb of Bay Village. His mother, Rita, imbued in him a sense of kindness he would demonstrate throughout his life, usually quietly, behind the scenes. His father, Henry, well . . . that was something else. Dad was a humorless taskmaster and control freak, for whom young George could do little to nothing right. A Great Lakes shipping magnate, the elder Steinbrenner rarely trusted anyone but himself with important tasks and spewed venom at rare delegees when they fell short of perfection. George would spend much of his life trying to get his father's attention and impress him, with very little success.

As a young boy, George launched an egg-selling business he called the George Company and made a small mint. That wasn't enough to get his father's attention. His exploits at Culver Military Academy and Williams College weren't enough. At the latter, he played halfback for the football team and starred in track as a hurdler. His father had been a star hurdler himself and wasn't impressed. George also sang in the glee club and played the piano. An English major, he loved covering sports in the school paper and might have done it for a living someday, but the family business sidelined those dreams.

His service of his country in the air force wasn't good enough to please his father, but it did introduce George to Columbus, Ohio, as he was stationed at nearby Lockbourne Air Force Base. He launched a coffee business on the base. Not enough. He ran the base sports program. Not enough. After the air force, it was on to Ohio State, where he earned a master's in physical education. Not enough. While he was at Ohio State, Steinbrenner palled around with the Buckeyes' star running back, Howard "Hopalong" Cassady, and other members of the team. He married a beautiful young woman named Joan, a member of a wealthy local family.

Not enough.

George grew increasingly interested and involved with sports, against the wishes of his father, who wanted him home and involved in the family shipping business, Kinsman Marine Transit. Before joining Kinsman full time in 1957, the younger Steinbrenner worked as a graduate assistant for legendary Ohio State coach Woody Hayes, then as an assistant football coach under Lou Saban at Northwestern. He also assisted Jack Mollenkopf at Purdue, crossing paths with legendary quarterback Len Dawson.

George returned to Kinsman but detoured into professional sports, purchasing the Cleveland Pipers of the new American Basketball League. He developed a reputation for angrily berating officials and once sold one of his players to the opposing team at halftime. The Pipers won the ABL title in 1962. Not enough.

At Kinsman, George first served as treasurer and built on the company's success. He worked his way up and became an industry heavyweight, helping his family rake in millions, and became an influential lobbyist.

Not enough.

Even when George pulled off purchasing the Yankees in 1973, Henry Steinbrenner could manage only backhanded praise. "It's the first smart thing he's ever done," the elder Steinbrenner noted.

GEORGE STEINBRENNER'S ISSUES WITH his father undoubtedly contributed to the behavior that made him one of sports' most infamous owners. He was diagnosed in the New York media, with the *New York Post* and *Wall Street Journal* among the outlets that spoke to psychologists and psychiatrists for print. Neither of these two men had examined Steinbrenner, but their assessments don't seem far off. "Executives who are harsh with their people often are expressing their own feelings of inadequacy and self-disappointment," one of them told the *Journal* for a Steinbrenner profile. Another speculated in the *Post* that "George Steinbrenner would give a World Series ring if his father would hug him to his breast and say, 'I love you.'"

World Series rings, George Steinbrenner had. After he purchased the Yankees, their fortunes quickly reversed. By 1976, they were back in the Series for the first time in fourteen years. In '77 and '78, they won it. The remarkable transformation was fueled by Steinbrenner's willingness to open his bulging wallet during the dawn of free agency. He restored the Yankees to dominance. He also left tire tracks across the backs of numerous people who'd helped him, many of them dedicated and talented.

THE BOSS HAD ANOTHER side, gentler and more compassionate. Steinbrenner had a Jekyll-and-Hyde dynamic going on, though perhaps it was Hyde and Jekyll in that order, as if Hyde George was the default, and kinder Jekyll George emerged after the serum was ingested.

Sometimes with headlines but most often without, he helped many, many people over the years. In Cleveland, he ran the March of Dimes and funded trips for Special Olympics athletes to international events. He stocked local high schools with scoreboards and rebuilt a Bay Village playhouse that had burned down. Throughout his life, he privately funded the college educations of hundreds. He once heard on the radio about a little girl who needed a life-saving operation her family couldn't afford. He contacted the family the same day and wrote a check for the whole thing.

His generosity with players went beyond just providing extra spending cash and letting them run up tabs at fancy restaurants.

George Frazier, an '81 Clipper, recalls approaching the Boss when Steinbrenner's father, Henry, was ill, and asking how things were going. George Steinbrenner appreciated Frazier reaching out and didn't forget. When Frazier's dad had a stroke during the 1983 Mayors' Game against the Mets, Steinbrenner took care of him. He let Frazier and his family take his private jet down to Springfield, Missouri, where it remained for two days, as long as the Fraziers needed it.

In the years that followed, Frazier hosted a Special Olympics fundraiser in Springfield that included an auction. Steinbrenner always sent a treasure trove of autographed baseballs. Even after Frazier was traded away by the Yankees, the baseballs kept coming, year after year, for as long as the event continued.

• • •

The catching position appeared to be the '81 Clippers' only weakness. Columbus lacked experience behind the plate. Pat Callahan had decent Minor League hitting stats but had never played at the Triple-A level. Juan Espino had, but he struggled with the Clippers as a backup in 1980. Incumbent Bruce Robinson sat out the '81 season following a car accident the previous year. Robinson's biggest contribution to the '81 team was a series of memorable practical jokes.

Callahan had hit more consistently in the Minors and offered more speed. Espino seemed more confident at the plate, got rid of the ball quicker, and arguably called a better game.

Espino would have the longer career of the two. A native of the

Dominican Republic, he signed at just sixteen years old, having grown up—as much as he had, anyway—in a small shack with a mud floor. He spoke little English, and there were no ESL programs around in those days to help him assimilate. He still managed to earn the respect of his teammates, many of whom remember him for always having a smile on his face, as well as for his game-calling skills.

Espino would first taste the Majors in 1982, as part of the Yankees' crazy revolving door of personnel. Steinbrenner's mania may have peaked, and in addition to going through three managers, three hitting coaches, and five pitching coaches that season, his Yankees had so many players come and go that not all of them were sure who their teammates were.

Asked about Espino that season, Yankees outfielder Dave Collins famously responded, "Which one's Espino? I haven't met him." The young catcher had already been sent back to Columbus after just two plate appearances.

THE '81 COLUMBUS TEAM continued tuning with spring exhibitions against Richmond and Rochester, another IL opponent. On April 3, Columbus clipped Richmond 6–5 at Dowdy Field, with Ashford delivering a two-run triple in the bottom of the eighth. Newcomer Paul Boris, a reliever who starred in Double-A the previous season, closed out the win with two scoreless innings.

Ashford, an IL All-Star with Charleston in 1980 who would win the league's MVP Award in '82, might have ridden the bench for the Clippers in '81. The Yankees thought they had a rising superstar in Joe Lefebvre (pronounced luh-FAY), an outfielder who also played third base. If Lefebvre failed to make the Yankees' roster, he was destined to start at third for the Clippers and hone his skills there. Except third base was Ashford's usual domain, and Tennessee-born Tucker—who had one green eye and one blue eye—spoke openly with the local media about the mistake he thought the Yankees were about to make, shoving aside an All-Star for someone less tested at the position.

Thankfully for Ashford, the Yankees shipped Lefebvre to the Padres in the Pacella deal.

Another notch down the pecking order, Danny Schmitz would still need to wait for his opportunity. He'd been poised to start at third before *he* was shoved aside by Ashford, before Ashford was nearly shoved aside by Lefebvre. The incumbent third baseman, Roy Staiger, retired before the season began.

Schmitz was used to fighting for a spot, having grown up in Michigan with five sisters, a brother, and a single bathroom for all of them to share. He'd already made it further in baseball than many thought he would, considering his frame—just five foot seven and 150 pounds—and deficiencies in power and speed. He was a gamer, though, and he could hit for average. In 1980 Yankees GM Gene Michael was ready to call Schmitz up all the way from Nashville. Steinbrenner vetoed the deal at the last minute.

Relegated to a utility infielder role at the outset of '81, Schmitz was losing patience. Were it not for the struggling economy and lack of jobs back home in Michigan, he might have given up on baseball by then. He'd get more playing time later that season, after the Yankees traded Tabler away. There were no hard feelings with Ashford, who kept things loose before games. "Between the two of us," Ashford would tell Schmitz, "we're going to get four or five hits tonight." Ashford was often right.

Schmitz was solid for the Clippers throughout '81, even leading the team in average for a time. He never would get the call to the Majors, though, despite a career Minor League batting average of .270.

PITCHER GREG COCHRAN'S FIRST few months of 1981 were certainly eventful. He married his wife, Stacey, on January 19. Less than two weeks later, the Cochrans packed their bags and made the drive from Tempe, Arizona, to spring training in Fort Lauderdale, with forty-five dollars to their names. They spent forty of that for a night at a Days Inn. The rest funded a meal at Burger King. Oh, and they were about to find out they were pregnant.

PHOTO COURTESY OF TOM WATSON

Columbus Clippers
RH Pitcher
GREG COCHRAN—27

FIG 5. Greg Cochran's 1980 baseball card. Courtesy of the Columbus Clippers.

Thankfully, a kindly couple from Pembroke Pines took them in and looked after them all spring, even after $600 a week started coming in from the Yankees.

On the field, it seemed everything was coming together for the blonde-haired, twenty-seven-year-old righty. Cochran already had a Major League curveball. He was one of the Clippers' top hurlers in 1980, and the Yankees needed a right-handed starter. Around the time he and Stacey left for Florida, a headline in the *Sporting News* read, "Cochran: Clear Path to Yank Job?" He seemed destined to finally make the Majors and fill the number five spot in New York's starting rotation.

In Fort Lauderdale, Whitey Ford watched Cochran throw batting-practice pitches to Winfield. "The breaking ball looks pretty good today, kid," the legendary hurler told him.

Cochran missed his first spring training start with the flu, then made his debut against Atlanta. The Braves, helped by two Bucky Dent errors, loaded the bases in the first. Cochran battled back and escaped the inning unscathed, shaking off catcher Rick Cerone's calls for a fastball and striking out Atlanta slugger Bob Horner on a 3-2 curve. Leaving the locker room after the game, Cochran ran into Steinbrenner.

"You looked pretty good today," said the Boss, offering praise he rarely gave rookies. "We'll see what you've got the rest of the spring."

Through all this, Cochran had a secret. He'd been pitching in pain since the playoffs the previous season. After he threw, his elbow would swell and lock up. He didn't yet realize that there was a bone chip about a half-inch long and a quarter-inch thick floating around in his elbow joint. It hurt. But this was his shot.

THE SCRAMBLE FOR THAT precious, final spot in the Yankees' starting rotation was probably the most interesting battle in New York's camp that spring.

Returning starters Tommy John, Rudy May, Ron Guidry, and Tom Underwood combined for sixty-seven wins the previous season. All were left-handed, and the Yankees wanted a righty for the fifth starting job. Per usual, Steinbrenner's gaze turned toward expensive Major League veterans on other teams. Montreal's Steve Rogers perhaps? Steinbrenner's coaches talked him into considering his own organization's abundant young pitching talent, but the Boss issued an ominous warning.

"Okay, you guys want youth?" Steinbrenner asked them rhetorically. "We'll bring two or three in."

"It'd better work, or it's going to be all your asses."

The coaching staff put an exhaustive, pitch-by-pitch grading system in place to determine who would emerge.

Rising star Dave Righetti was a contender, but he was a left-hander.

Pacella was a late entry after the trade from San Diego. Despite his credentials, which included one of the best fastballs in the organization, he was stuck back in the pack, at least for the moment.

Andy McGaffigan, destined for a long big league career, had as good a chance as any to earn the final slot. He had pitched at Double-A Nashville the year before but dominated and was named the league's top pitcher. He was off to a strong spring start. Then on March 14, in the first inning against Baltimore, his elbow tightened up. The strain landed him on the disabled list, and it wasn't an injury he'd be able to rush back from. Pitching coach Stan Williams already had his doubts about McGaffigan's drive. To Williams, the young pitcher seemed a little too content with the idea of spending another year in the Minors if the Yankees deemed it necessary.

Cochran strengthened his position as the favorite with strong outings in his first two spring starts. Then *his* elbow issues started to catch up with him, and he struggled. To hear the colorful Williams describe it, he "went out there and shit on the mound." Perhaps a bit harsh.

Cochran stayed mum about the pain he was pitching through. It was something everyone dealt with, he told himself. He'd work through it. He was too close to the Majors to not work through it.

Cochran nearly made the jump as a Pittsburgh Pirate. No foolin', on the evening of April 1, New York swung a deal to send Cochran, first baseman Jim Spencer, Minor Leaguer Fred Tolliver, and cash to the Pirates in exchange for first baseman Jason Thompson. Cochran said good-bye to his Yankee teammates, he and Stacey had their bags packed, and a Major League debut with the Pirates in the Steel City awaited. Commissioner Bowie Kuhn nixed the trade, though, ruling that the cash incentives were too high and that the deal wouldn't be in the best interests of the game, and sending Steinbrenner into a rage. Cochran headed back to the Yankees' camp, where he was still in the running, and received a $7,000-a-year raise from the Boss, who felt badly for him about the voided trade.

There was one more pitcher in the hunt, the youngest of the young. Wayland Eugene Nelson II, known as Gene, was just twenty years old and pitched all the way down in Single-A ball the previous season. He won twenty, though, and he already carried himself like a Major Leaguer. Steinbrenner loved the young pitcher's toughness. So did Williams, who joked that the Florida-born Nelson's daddy must have been an alligator.

Young Nelson had another factor on his side—Steinbrenner's loathing of the New York Mets and guiding principle of grabbing more headlines than the Yankees' cross-town rival. In the spring of '81, the Mets had their own boy wonder in twenty-two-year-old Tim Leary, who was already drawing comparisons to Tom Seaver. Leary's white-hot spring had New York's media and fans buzzing, and Steinbrenner grumbling. Nelson was even younger than Leary. Promoting him would certainly recapture some of those headlines.

The decision between Nelson and Cochran didn't come until 11:00 p.m. on April 5, ten hours before the Yankees' team plane left Florida to head north. Gene Nelson ended up taking that flight and before long was accepting handshakes from a parade of New York Yankees in their locker room. "Good luck, kid," Lou Piniella told him. "We need you."

Cochran, the last player cut, would start the season back in Columbus.

THE CLIPPERS BROKE CAMP on April 5, flew to Ohio, and held their first workout at Franklin County Stadium on April 8, with twenty-five players but just twenty-two roster spots to go around. Pitchers Roger Slagle and Tim Lewis (no relation to teammate Jim Lewis) were soon shipped to Nashville, and Coleman—his season already off to a rough start—was placed on the disabled list. The opening night roster was set. Among those who held on: Schmitz, Showalter, and Nate Chapman, a speedy outfielder. Showalter and Chapman would be back in Nashville before the month ended.

The Major League season began in Cincinnati that day, awash in bunting and miniature American flags, with feting for two former hostages released from Iran less than three months earlier.

With President Reagan still hospitalized after Hinckley's assassination attempt on March 30, a moment of silence replaced the ceremonial first pitch.

Baseball's labor fight produced the other backdrop. With no compromise reached, owners had implemented their own free agent compensation plan on February 19. Any team signing a free agent would lose a player from its roster, plus an amateur draft pick, which of course would make free agent signings a lot less attractive. Advantage: owners.

The players, not seeking new gains so much as trying to protect what they'd already won, voted six days later to strike, setting a date of May 29.

3

For Openers

THE CLIPPERS PRIED THE lid off the 1981 season in Charleston, West Virginia, looking about as strong as expected. Columbus swept three games from the Charlies before the well-meaning but perilous backdrop of Watt Powell Park, a 4,500-seat stadium shared with the local Little League, with an outfield pockmarked with puddles and a rugged infield that turned routine grounders into tricky hops. Marshall Brant once lost a ground ball there—in the lights. He later referred to Watt Powell as "Fantasy Island in reverse." Charleston was also attendance-challenged in those days, once drawing a "crowd" of only thirty-five, including both the wife *and* the girlfriend of the Clippers' starting pitcher that day.

Columbus Citizen-Journal beat writer Jack Torry wrote a whole feature story on the field's hazards and got himself thrown out of the press box by a Charleston GM who *may* not have been completely sober at the time. The ban was later nixed by league president Harold Cooper, and Torry no longer had to cover games from the bullpen.

Prior to the '81 season, the fences were moved in by the parent Cleveland Indians in hopes of generating some offense and excitement. The new dimensions: just 365 in right- and left-center, 320 down the lines, and 370 to center. For pitchers, the stuff of nightmares.

At least three of the five homers hit on opening night would have stayed in most other ballparks. Among those: A first-inning grand slam off the bat of Charleston's Karl Pagel, which sailed over the head of Showalter in left and barely cleared the short porch. Rick Stenholm put the Clippers ahead for good with a pinch-hit, three-run homer in the seventh. Final score: Clippers 10, Charlies 6.

If any Charleston fans in the rare sellout crowd went home happy, it was probably because the San Diego Chicken had performed.

In his Triple-A debut, Balboni blasted a two-run homer that cleared the scooted-in, center-field fence by thirty feet. What no one knew, or expected, was that it would be a very long time before he homered again.

Like Balboni, Pacella had an auspicious opening night. The hard-throwing righty came on in relief and shut out the Charlies for three and two-thirds innings. His control wasn't quite there. Three walks and a wild pitch. But that part would come around. He could pitch in this league. He had before. A promotion to the Yankees couldn't be too far away. Right?

PACELLA HADN'T LEARNED BASEBALL from his father, who was always supportive but just didn't follow or know the sport. It was one of the reasons young John started the game somewhat late, first discovering he had a special talent around age eleven. The family had moved from Brooklyn's Flatbush neighborhood out to Long Island, where a baseball-loving uncle named Anthony Buglino first got John throwing. Uncle Anthony was stunned by the boy's velocity. After the throwing session, he took John home and briefed Mama Pacella. "D'ya know what kind of ahhm dis kid has?"

John started Little League. Before long he was facing kids several years older and striking most of them out. He figures he threw in the low 90s when he pitched for Connetquot High School. The local kids just hadn't seen that kind of heat, and not surprisingly, Pacella dominated. "It was like I could wave to my girlfriend from the mound," Pacella recalled, "and then say, 'Excuse me while I finish this guy off.'"

Even then, Pacella struggled with his control. He might strike out seventeen batters in a game, but also walk eight. The blazing fastballs, combined with the wildness, left many hitters terrified. Knees knocked in the batter's box with good reason. As one opposing batter bailed out on a fastball at his head, his batting helmet began to fly off. The ball struck the helmet and broke it in two.

The local legend and mystique grew. Pacella's outings drew an increasing number of scouts, with as many as fifteen showing up.

The New York Mets grabbed Pacella in the fourth round of the 1974 amateur draft. His pro career didn't start well. In forty-three innings for rookie-level Marion, Pacella gave up forty-eight hits, walked thirty-two, and served up six wild pitches. He won just one out of eight decisions. The instruction he needed to fully harness his power, as well as learn some pitches other than fastballs, was elusive. But Pacella managed to dramatically reduce his walks the following season, along with his ERA. Clocked with a radar gun for the first time that winter, he hit 97 mph, which was impressive, even though Juan "Señor Smoke" Berenguer hit 102 during the same session. A few months later, Pacella got his first small taste of big league life.

JOHN PACELLA ONCE STRUCK out the great Hank Aaron. Honest. Any doubters can look it up, but they shouldn't bother asking Pacella for the video.

It happened during Major League Baseball's Hall of Fame Game, an annual exhibition held in Cooperstown from 1940 until 2008. On August 9, 1976, the contest matched the Milwaukee Brewers and the New York Mets. As was customary, big leaguers were used somewhat sparingly and Minor Leaguers got a chance to play. Pacella was called up by the Mets to pitch in the contest, playing alongside Seaver and other players he'd idolized growing up.

Pacella was a wild, twenty-year-old, A-ball pitcher. Hammerin' Hank, forty-two years old and nearly three years removed from breaking Babe Ruth's career home run record, was entering the final weeks of his playing career. In an exhibition game, with the skies turning nasty as Hurricane Belle approached, hitters were more aggressive than they usually would have been. So it wasn't quite a clutch strikeout during a pennant race, or Roy Hobbs facing the Whammer in *The Natural*, but it was still pretty cool.

Pacella got the start, and the Brewers tagged him for five earned runs in the first three innings. In the fourth, Milwaukee manager Alex Grammas called on Aaron to pinch-hit. The crowd of nearly ten thousand, plus more fans just outside the fences, roared as the legend was announced. To Pacella, the standing ovation seemed to go on for ten minutes.

"Hank Aaron," Pacella thought. "Hank Aaron? Please just don't let me hit this guy in the freakin' head. Don't hit 'im. Don't kill 'im."

Still, Pacella went right after Aaron. First pitch fastball, swung on and missed. Majestic but futile. Then another fastball, swung on and missed for strike two.

Pacella was a few months removed from the 97 reading on the radar gun. He's not sure how fast the last two pitches he threw to Aaron were that day. Just that they were the fastest he'd thrown in his life to that point.

Aaron took another fastball, inside. One ball, two strikes. In the stands, Pacella's mother focused her 8mm video camera on her son's big moment. Catcher Ron Hodges set the target. A fourth straight fastball.

Swung on and missed. Strike three. Yer out.

The best we can do is read about it, though. Mom had been filming family members in the stands and other scenes from around the stadium, and she ran out of film just before the final pitch was delivered.

• • •

It's April 10, 1981, and I'm listening to WBNS radio's opening night broadcast in my boyhood room.

As was the case for baseball in general, I hadn't tuned in at first. I might have missed the first game altogether, had Dad not wandered downstairs—after himself taking in a few innings by radio—and shared the score. The Clippers had just taken the lead in their first game of the season. I hadn't followed professional sports much, but my interest was piqued. I walked upstairs, clicked on my own radio and found an excitement and level of importance in the voice of Rizzs, the Clippers' young broadcaster. I was on my way to being hooked on the broadcasts. And the sport.

I was coming of age a bit ahead of schedule, shy, awkward, not very good at sports myself, wound tightly for such a young age, more of a studious, daydreamer type. I always meant well and wanted desperately to be liked, perhaps more so than an average boy of eleven. I had friends, but also detractors—bully types who seemed to zero in on me. I felt scared a lot. On top of the standard challenges of growing up, I was developing a persona of isolation, a feeling of "less than."

In baseball, though, I found refuge from my confusion.

Having a winning team to cheer for at a young age increases one's odds of lifelong baseball fandom. Studies have been done on it. I had that winning team in the Clippers, but I wouldn't see the season through with them. My mother and father sat my younger sister and me down in the living room in late spring and started pouring us our first-ever glasses of champagne. We were celebrating something. There hadn't been any clues to that point, but I somehow sniffed out what was going on.

"Dad," I asked, "Are we moving?"

Jim Herman smiled faintly in midpour, his thunder swiped. He had a new job, and we were indeed moving, to California, at the end of August. As if life weren't confusing enough for me already. Many of the points of reference I did have at the edge of adolescence suddenly had a shelf life, and it was a short one.

It was an exciting and terrifying prospect for all of us, including my dad. He was uprooting us at a tender time for both my younger sister and me, and he was questioning whether he was making the right call. He would for years.

• • •

On April 14, Space Shuttle *Columbia*—a new manned, reusable spacecraft on its first mission—returned to earth. My new favorite team did the same.

In their home opener against the Richmond Braves, the Clippers rallied from an 8–2 deficit and grabbed a 9–8 lead in the seventh inning. Then, as Steinbrenner himself watched, Richmond scored twice in the top of the ninth with help from a controversial call, on which Richmond's Ken Smith was ruled safe at second despite running out of the baseline. The Braves held on for the 10–9 win on a cold night at Franklin County Stadium. Steinbrenner publicly ripped umpire Pete Calieri for the "awful" call and said Calieri would never make it to the Majors. The Boss was right, at least about the second part. Calieri did manage to land an uncredited role in the movie *The Natural*, two years later, playing an umpire. Verdi felt like Calieri had been impersonating an umpire that night.

The Clippers bounced back for a 9–2 win the next night, boosted by Ashford's 4-for-4, three-double performance. The new Columbus third baseman had nine hits in his first sixteen at bats, and he'd hit safely in the first fifteen games of the season.

Game three of the series went to Richmond, 10–5, with poor Calieri in the middle of things again. The umpire and Verdi argued about balls and strikes throughout the game, and after Calieri called Brant out on strikes with two men on in the seventh, Verdi screamed at the umpire for several minutes. The following inning, Calieri asked Verdi to clarify a lineup change.

"Where's Tabler going?" Calieri asked.

"You'll figure it out," Verdi said, turning around and throwing an arm up in the air.

That did it. Good-bye. Calieri threw Verdi out of the game.

DESPITE THE SERIES LOSS to Richmond, things seemed to be in order. The Clippers were 4-2, in first place by half a game. Brown was on his way back to Columbus, having been demoted once again by Steinbrenner, and figured to bolster an offense already off to a strong start. Plus, the Toledo Mud Hens were coming to town. The Clippers had absolutely owned Max Klinger's favorite team over the previous two seasons, winning an astonishing thirty-three of forty-four games, including the 1980 Governors' Cup finals, four games to one.

On the night of April 17, in the teams' first meeting in '81, Columbus trailed 2–1 in the bottom of the seventh. Robertson reached first on an error. Chapman sacrificed him to second. Showalter singled up the middle, and Robertson zipped toward home with the tying run. Then Toledo catcher Steve Herz did something that

Fig 6. Shortstop Andre Robertson first joined the Clippers in 1980. *Columbus Citizen-Journal*, Scripps Howard Newspapers/Grandview Heights Public Library/Photohio.org.

altered the trajectory of the season. He blocked the plate without the ball, which was twenty feet up the net.

Robertson described the resulting collision as hitting a "brick wall." He injured his right leg and had to be helped off the field. Herz claimed he was only trying to step back to catch the relay, but he was called for obstruction. Verdi and the Clippers were irate.

The injury was more serious than first believed, not once but twice. Initially expected back soon, Robertson wound up on the disabled list with a deep, painful contusion. He'd miss eleven games and play through pain after his return. Years later, he'd be diagnosed with a partial ACL tear, dating back to the collision with Herz. That collision would affect Robertson for the rest of his career.

The young Texan had always been somewhat of a good luck charm for the Clippers. When he first joined the team in 1980, after an injury to shortstop Dennis Sherrill, Columbus won twenty-one of its next twenty-seven games. After Sherrill returned and Robertson was demoted to Nashville, the Clippers lost nine of their next eleven. At that point, Sisler got involved and insisted on getting Robertson back. When he did, Columbus won six of ten.

Now the shortstop was gone again, and another Robertson-less struggle would soon commence.

Verdi, Robertson, and the Clippers didn't forget Herz's play. Baseball has unwritten rules about protecting your team, and retribution.

A few weeks later, pitcher Bill Castro joined the Clippers. Castro had barely set his bags down when he was pulled into Verdi's office and greeted with, "This is who we're going to throw at," along with a brief explanation of the Herz play. Oh, and welcome to the team.

Castro was a relief pitcher. That night, he made his first start since 1975. He went six strong, giving the Columbus pitching staff a much-needed lift. His control was terrific. No walks.

Sure enough though, Castro put one in Herz's ribs the first time he faced him.

"I drilled him pretty good," Castro recalled. "The next day, I found a bottle of whiskey in my locker."

AFTER ROBERTSON WENT DOWN, the Clippers started doing something they hadn't done since the Yankees took the reins two years earlier. They started losing.

On an overcast Easter Sunday, Columbus bumbled its way to five errors in a 6–1 loss to Toledo. Schmitz, filling in for Robertson at short, and left fielder Showalter misplayed a routine pop-up into a double. Balboni, struggling to adjust to Franklin County Stadium as well as Triple-A ball in general, slipped and fell twice on the artificial turf, committed two errors, and went 0 for 4 at the plate. "Balboni couldn't have caught a cold today," a Mud Hen was overheard saying after the game. Two Clippers were thrown out at home in one inning. McNertney got himself thrown out of the game in the ninth, after asking Calieri, "Are ya blind, Pete?"

Verdi said it could have been worse, noting that he once committed four errors in *one inning* for the Rochester Red Wings. Everyone and every team has bad days, he noted.

The bad days started to pile up.

The Clippers traveled to Toledo and dropped the next two games against the Mud Hens, their former tormentees. The first game was played in sub-forty-degree weather, with wind chills of about twenty, and lasted for thirteen miserable innings. McGaffigan, a Florida native, donned two pairs of thermal underwear, three pairs of socks, a hooded vest, and two warm-up jackets. Teammates noted that outfielder Garry Smith, who grew up in Maine, didn't seem fazed and dubbed him "The Eskimo." The players got a fire going in a fifty-five-gallon drum in the dugout before stadium officials made them put it out.

Coleman shared a story about once playing a doubleheader in Quebec City in seventeen-degree weather.

The Clippers committed four more errors in a 10–8 loss the next night. They dropped two of three games against Wade Boggs and Pawtucket, then three of four against Tidewater. With another loss at Richmond, Columbus sank to seventh place in the International League standings. "What's Wrong?," asked a *Citizen-Journal* headline on the morning of May 5. The front office in New York also wondered. Perhaps the arrival of versatile veteran Dennis Werth, on his way to Columbus for a rehab assignment, would help.

Verdi tried batting the hulking Balboni in the lead-off spot one night, just to shake things up. But the team's problems weren't centered on offense. Ashford was batting .338. Brant and center fielder Wayne Harer got off to blazing starts. Brown, back down from the Yankees, provided another boost. The Clippers stumbled defensively without Robertson, though. And the pitching, expected during spring training to be a strong point, was instead a pain point.

GREG COCHRAN, STILL PITCHING in pain, struggled as much as any Clipper hurler during the team's early-season woes. He started the home opener against Richmond, but he didn't make it out of the third inning. Facing Toledo in his next start, he looked more like his old self, holding the Mud Hens to a single earned run in a complete-game victory. Then he gave up double-digit hits and lost a game on a bases-loaded wild pitch against Pawtucket. He couldn't locate his breaking pitches, and hitters were increasingly teeing off on his fastball. Stacey Cochran warned her new husband that he'd better be careful not to get hurt, with all the line drives coming his way.

In Richmond on May 4, the Braves chased Cochran after two-thirds of an inning. It was time for the pitcher to come clean about his elbow troubles.

The Yankees shipped Cochran to New York to get the elbow checked out. Bone chips, including that one biggie, were found, and two weeks later, surgery officially ended his season.

He came back in 1982, but with no zip on his fastball. He tried a knuckleball, got people out ugly for a while, but realized it was over.

He had been part of a College World Series team at Arizona State that sent a whopping thirteen players to the Majors and came so close to being the fourteenth.

"I wasn't bitter," Cochran said many years later as a grandparent with a successful career in retail real estate. "I had a good run. The hard part was that you had the talent to pitch in the big leagues and just didn't get the chance. But I've been very blessed."

AMONG THE OTHER EARLY challenges faced by the '81 pitching staff, McGaffigan was still sidelined by injury. Two other pitchers who figured to play a significant role—Chris Welsh and Tim Lollar—had been shipped to San Diego in the Pacella-Mumphrey deal.

Most of the Clipper pitchers who were left struggled mightily in the early going, with numerous rain outs and cold weather not helping. Three starters—including Pacella—had posted ERAS over 5.00. It appeared only Righetti, a promising young lefty, was immune. He began pulling away from that pack.

"Can You Pitch in the Big Leagues?"

Just twenty-two years old in 1981, Dave Righetti had already taken a wild baseball ride. The son of a hot-tempered shortstop who never quite made the Majors and hadn't gotten over it, Righetti had the game drilled into him early, learning alongside his older brother, Steve, in the backyard of their home in San Jose, California. Their father Leo's relentless pushing and harsh words often left five-year-old Dave in tears.

Righetti switched from outfielder to pitcher in high school, further honed his skills at San Jose City College and emerged as a flame-thrower. Both he and Steve were drafted by the Texas Rangers, but the little brother had surpassed his infielder big brother, the one who was supposed to make it but never would. Pitching for the Double-A Tulsa Drillers in 1978, nineteen-year-old Dave Righetti, a self-described "skinny kid from California," set a Texas League record by striking out twenty-one Midland Cubs on a ninety-five-degree Oklahoma afternoon. After the Yankees acquired the young lefty that November in a deal with the Rangers involving Sparky Lyle, Righetti was hailed by Yankees GM Al Rosen as "the next Ron Guidry." Cue the pressure.

The Yankees called Righetti up on August 2, 1979, the day beloved team captain Thurman Munson was killed in a plane crash. Righetti, still just twenty years old, arrived at the ballpark to find everyone distraught.

He started three games for the Yankees, as their turmoil-filled season wound down, and held up well. No wins against one loss, but a 3.63 ERA and thirteen strikeouts in seventeen and a third innings. Manager Billy Martin liked Righetti well enough that he told him he'd be part of New York's starting rotation the following season. But in October, the volatile Martin got into a barroom brawl in Minneapolis—with a marshmallow salesman—and got himself fired as Yankee manager for the second time. The following spring, Righetti was among the last players cut.

FIG 7. Dave Righetti's 1981 baseball card. Courtesy of the Columbus Clippers.

Righetti took a big step backward in 1980 with a Nuke LaLoosh–
style meltdown. Back in Columbus, he tried to live up to the hype
and failed, going only 6-10 and leading the league in walks. He
started games in dominant fashion but then completely unraveled. He threw instead of pitched, relying on his fastball at the
expense of other pitches he needed to succeed. And he rebelled.
His after-hours exploits included a drunken, late-night hijack-
ing of a grounds crew golf cart, which he and a teammate took
for a spin around Franklin County Stadium, complete with Evel

Knievel–inspired bunny hops off the pitcher's mound. The golf cart never recovered, and Righetti's career flirted with the same disaster. A serious talk with Sisler followed. It was a turning point for the young pitcher.

Righetti went to the Instructional League in Florida that winter and "turned that league on its ear," pitching coach Ellis recalled. "Rags" found a windup he could stick with, stopped relying so much on the heat, and started throwing his curveball. "I've grown up," he told reporters at the outset of the '81 season. "I've found out this job is like other jobs. There is too much money to be made in this game."

He was the last pitcher cut by the Yankees out of spring training but didn't sulk this time. The woes that plagued the rest of the Clipper pitching staff early in the season largely missed him, and he won his first three starts.

Across the country in Southern California, a young pitcher with a quirky delivery from Sonora, Mexico, was capturing the nation's imagination. Fernando Valenzuela tossed seventeen and two-thirds scoreless innings for the Los Angeles Dodgers after he was called up late in 1980 at the age of nineteen. On Opening Day of '81, with ace Jerry Reuss injured, Valenzuela got the start and shut out the Astros on five hits. By late April, the young lefty was 5-0 with five complete games and a microscopic ERA of 0.200. For good measure, he hit .438. Fernandomania was born.

Righetti watched with interest. Though still in the Minors, he set a goal of matching Valenzuela. "Hey," Righetti would tell himself, "I'm a good young lefty, too."

On the night of April 30, in Norfolk, Righetti held the Tidewater Tides to just one run in nine innings and struck out eleven. He was officially back on Steinbrenner's radar. On the morning of May 4, Ellis took a phone call from the Boss.

"I want to put the heat on Righetti," Steinbrenner told the Clippers' pitching coach. "Tell him if he can put together two consecutive solid starts, he's coming to New York."

After the team arrived at the Holiday Inn–West in Richmond,

Ellis asked Righetti to meet him at a downstairs tavern. Righetti got his bag up to his room, then joined the coach. Beers were poured.

"Can you pitch in the big leagues?" Ellis asked Righetti.

"Hell, yeah," the young pitcher replied.

"The big guy called me. He said if you can pitch two more good games in a row, you're going."

The pressure wasn't insignificant, especially for someone still only twenty-two and less than a year into having his head screwed on right. Ellis later noted that many young pitchers in that position would have "folded like a cheap suit."

But this time, Dave Righetti was ready. On Tuesday night, with his fastball overpowering, he took a no-hitter into the seventh inning before settling for a one-hit, nine-strikeout, complete game as the Clippers rolled past Richmond 10–0. A week later in Columbus, the Charleston Charlies became Righetti's next victim. Mixing his pitches more effectively this time, Righetti scattered six hits and struck out eleven in a 5–0 win. The rising star had allowed just one earned run in his last twenty-seven innings.

That was apparently enough for Steinbrenner, and a trade soon created a roster spot. Righetti made one more start for the Clippers on May 20 in Syracuse, but he was pulled from the game after throwing a scoreless first inning, called up to the Major Leagues in mid-outing. Every other member of the Clippers wished they could join him. For Righetti, there were big things ahead, including an unexpected showdown with the other good young lefty he'd aimed to match.

PACELLA AND RIGHETTI WERE friends who brought out the wacky in each other. Letendre recalls the two pitchers talking to each other in some sort of strange code. During rain delays, they did belly flops onto waterlogged tarps. There was plenty of going out, goofing around, drinking, and chatting up women. Both men were single, at least early in the season.

After arriving in Columbus, Pacella plunked down $700 at Rent-A-Wreck for a Cadillac Eldorado. The company lived up to its name. Whatever year Pacella's new ride was built, it was barely holding together. He and Righetti would tool around Columbus in it while, unbeknownst to them, the car didn't have any water in the radiator, among other problems.

A rainout in May turned into an eventful evening. Pacella and Righetti hopped into the Eldorado and headed for TGI Friday's at Kenny and Henderson, where the old car sputtered its last in the driveway. It was still pouring rain, it looked like fun inside the Friday's, and the two friends, after a brief consultation, decided their best move was to abandon the vehicle and go in. They just left it there. "Will the owner of the Eldorado please move your car ..." became a familiar refrain as the drinks flowed. The two pitchers laughed each time they heard it.

Eventually the car was towed, the license plates were run, and the owner identified. The next day, after a call was placed to Franklin County Stadium, a somewhat bewildered Verdi approached Pacella and Righetti in the locker room.

"Did you really have to leave the car in the fucking driveway?" Verdi asked.

But it was a good thing Pacella went into Friday's when he did that night, because his future wife was in there. Caryn was sitting at the bar with her sister when he first saw her. Before long, he and Righetti had the two women laughing pretty hard. The pitchers hadn't even played the baseball card. The women didn't realize they were talking to professional ballplayers.

Then Caryn's ex showed up, wanting to talk to her. "The asshole's here," she told her sister.

Pacella intervened and told the guy that he was done, and to take a hike. After looking at Pacella and Righetti, both six foot three, the average-sized ex weighed his options, and left.

John and Caryn. She was from nearby Westerville. When he struggled on the field that season and his confidence was just about gone, she encouraged him. They'd go out for drinks, play bocce. By the time he was traded to the Minnesota Twins the following season, she was ready to go with him.

In his first start of the '81 season, on April 23 in Toledo, Pacella gave up five runs and didn't even make it through the second inning. Four days later, against Pawtucket, Pacella's first three innings of work included four walks, two wild pitches, and a three-run blast by Sam Bowen. In his next start, he walked six, threw two more wild pitches, and hit another batter. Columbus lost 5–0 at Tidewater for its eighth defeat in ten games.

Caryn would help him through with one form of support. Ellis, Pacella's new pitching coach, would provide another.

DAVE RIGHETTI HAD FINALLY gotten the call. Across the country, another young man's Major League dreams suffered a severe setback.

The Yankees made room for Righetti by dealing veteran lefty Tom Underwood, along with first baseman Jim Spencer, to the Oakland A's. In return, the Yankees received first baseman Dave Revering, lefty Chuck Dougherty, and a young outfielder named Mike Patterson.

Born in Santa Monica and raised in Los Angeles, Patterson offered a nice blend of power and speed. Plus a nice signing voice and a gift for drawing cartoons. He'd bloomed late at LA's Dorsey High School. Really late. As a senior, Patterson didn't even start until the city playoffs, when he hit a triple at Dodger Stadium. At Dorsey he'd befriended and played alongside future big league star Chili Davis.

Not surprisingly, considering his limited playing time in high school, Patterson was passed over in the 1975 draft. He appeared to be destined for a career as a graphic artist. Still, after graduating early, he caught on in the Oakland organization and broke in with Single-A Boise in 1975, at the age of seventeen. Promoted from Double-A Waterbury—where he was known to sing the national anthem before games—to Triple-A Ogden in '79, he homered in his first at bat and tripled later in the same game. In Ogden he'd enjoy a relative explosion at the plate, hitting .324 in '79 and .304 in '80, after posting middling numbers at lower levels in the Minors.

He made Oakland's Opening Day roster and helped the A's set a Major League record with eleven straight wins to start the season. He enjoyed playing in his native California. His mom was about to make a trip up from LA to watch him play in the big leagues. Davis, his good friend and now off-season workout partner, was one of the hottest prospects for the nearby San Francisco Giants. Patterson's dreams were coming true.

Then, suddenly, he was dealt and sent back to the Minors. Hello, Columbus.

The trade shocked and shattered the young Californian. He'd spent his entire career in the A's organization and knew most of his teammates well. He'd been off to a hot start as a big leaguer, hitting .348 in limited playing time. He'd been having fun playing baseball. He'd never played for a title-winning team at any level, but the A's appeared to be on their way. Mike Patterson had appeared to be on his way.

Now he felt unwanted. He'd heard about playing in the Yankees' Minor League system and how talented players tended to get stuck there. "Well, at least it will never happen to me," he figured. It was about to.

LIKE RIGHETTI, BRANT WAS called up to the Yankees in the midst of the Clippers' rotten start to the season. Sort of.

He enjoyed an uncharacteristic hot start with Columbus, hitting .300 with three homers and eleven RBIs in just nine games. Shopping with his wife on an off day, he was paged to the front of the store. Sisler was on the phone. Yankee first baseman Bob Watson was hurt. Marshall Brant was headed to New York.

Brant had been there before, briefly. A handful of meaningless at bats at the tail end of 1980. But this is no September call-up, he thought. This is it. I'm hot, in a groove. I tried too hard to crank when they called me up at the end of last season. This time, I'll stick.

This time, Brant never even attached. After arriving at Yankee Stadium, he realized something was wrong. Some kind of mix-up. He wasn't even allowed to dress for the game and instead sat in Steinbrenner's private box, eating prime rib, watching Jim Spencer fill in at first base in his spot, against the Detroit Tigers. The next day, Brant was headed back to the Clippers.

Major League Rule 2(F)(I): "ANY PLAYER who has been unconditionally released after midnight August 31, of any champion-ship season cannot be re-signed by the releasing club until May 15 of the next following championship season." Brant had been released by the Yankees the previous November, in what amounted to a clerical error, before re-signing with Columbus. New York's April roster move was protested by the Blue Jays and White Sox, keeping Brant from his big opportunity. He'd been sidelined by an obscure rule and a goof-up.

Back in Ohio, at the Toledo airport, Brant literally crossed paths with Balboni. Despite his early-season struggles, Balboni had been summoned to New York to take Brant's spot.

The next night, Balboni started at first base for the Yankees. In his first at bat, he crushed a Howard Bailey pitch to the gap in left-center, all the way to the wall, and rumbled around the bases for a triple. In the seventh, he walked with the bases loaded to force in the go-ahead run. The home crowd went wild. Yankee fans knew of the big man's Minor League exploits but hadn't expected to see him in New York so soon.

Brant sat alone in his hotel room, on a rainy night in Toledo.

In the Yankees' big league camp the following spring, a traveling secretary made the rounds with a large box of American League pennant rings, handing them out to members of the '81 Yankees. He brushed past Brant and handed one to Balboni.

"Bonesy," Brant said, mostly joking, "that's my ring."

4

"A Ball Never Comes to Me"

MARSHALL BRANT, NOW IN his sixties, still dreams about his baseball career at night. Bad dreams, sad dreams. Two, maybe three times a week. There are a hundred variations. The theme is always the same.

He's getting another chance to avoid failure, to become a Major League Baseball player. To stick.

In the dreams, he's not ready. He's not young and in shape. He's "now." This is it, though. Gotta do it right. He steps into the batter's box. He can smell the pine tar.

He looks down and realizes he's standing at the plate, for this last gasp, wielding his son's Nerf bat instead of his usual Louisville Slugger M110.

Call time out. You're not ready.

No, stay in the box. This is your last chance. You've got to do this.

Wrong uniform. No pants. No shirt. No glove. A bat made of plastic. Tennis shoes instead of spikes. A scramble to suit up in time for a crucial at bat.

"A pitch is never thrown," Brant describes, awake and back in his present-day Santa Rosa living room. "A ball never comes to me." The dreams parallel his baseball career, partially self-sabotaged, partially snakebit.

Brant starred for the Clippers from 1980 to 1983. He was one of those people who others joke "should run for mayor." He appeared to have it all: a beautiful young wife and children, a promising career as a baseball slugger, and hero status in Columbus, perhaps as much for his exploits off the field as on it. He never refused an autograph and praised those who said "please" and "thank you." He was great with kids, visiting them in hospitals and instruct-

56

1981 Columbus Clippers
Infielder
MARSHALL BRANT—33

FIG 8. Marshall Brant's 1981 baseball card. Courtesy of the Columbus Clippers.

ing them at clinics. He was central casting–handsome and lived a clean, wholesome life of unpretentious faith.

It turns out that the biggest things he lacked were belief in himself, and—at least when it came to baseball—luck.

BORN AMID THE TOWERING redwoods in Garberville, California, Brant grew up further south in the tiny town of Penngrove, a pit stop on the old highway between Petaluma and Santa Rosa. In the '60s, Penngrove offered a few bars, a general store, a post office, churches, and not much else.

Young Marshall had plenty of chores to do. The Brants didn't live on a full-on farm, but they had gardens and raised chickens. He never got an allowance but picked up a little money with a thirty-two-customer paper route and a janitor's job at Penngrove Community Church. He bought sodas for just a nickel. Having a couple of dollars in his pocket made him feel rich.

He watched Saturday morning cartoons and the moon landing on TV. There wasn't much else to do for fun, other than play sports, which dominated his youth. Competing against older, bigger brothers toughened Marshall. He grew early. In Little League, he kept hitting home runs until they stopped pitching to him.

His father, Kenneth, rarely came to watch Marshall play. Kenneth, a World War II veteran, was usually gone by 5:00 a.m. each day, off to his job as a truck driver with PG&E. The interactions between father and son never seemed to involve anything fun. Kenneth provided for his family, but he didn't speak much, or show much emotion, unless he was angry.

Mom Nancy stayed at home. One day as she washed dishes, Marshall approached her with a question. "Are we poor?" he asked. They were, but Marshall didn't usually feel like they were, in part due to her efforts. She didn't want to answer.

In school, Marshall was a B student who played the piano and the trombone marginally well. He truly excelled on the baseball field and the basketball court. There he was the star, and his athletic exploits started to earn him some of the attention his father didn't—and perhaps couldn't—give.

Marshall loved following pro sports, too, and he was a huge fan of the NBA's San Francisco Warriors. He once waited three hours before a game for autographs, only to have Warriors star Rick Barry push past him and curse him out. Preteen Marshall was crushed. He wouldn't forget that, even when he became a star athlete himself.

He reached six foot five in high school and starred in both sports for Rancho Cotate in Rohnert Park. He knew he was a good athlete, but even then, he had a hard time believing he was that good, or that anyone else would think he was. He recalls hitting a high

"A BALL NEVER COMES TO ME"

school home run in a key moment, circling the bases and hearing the opposing coach yell to his pitcher, "How could you throw a pitch like that to a guy who's probably going to get drafted?" It was the first time it ever occurred to Marshall that he might be a baseball prospect. "Is that true?" he wondered.

He was already approval-seeking, hoping to prove his worth in the eyes of others. He wanted the fans he played in front of to like him, perhaps more than most athletes. He liked playing sports, but he really liked succeeding. He was motivated primarily by a growing fear of failure.

MARSHALL MOVED ON TO Sonoma State and starred in both sports there too. After his freshman year, the student body voted to kill the athletic program. He transferred to Santa Rosa Junior College, where he played baseball for Len Read. "You're going to love playing for Coach Read," an older teammate told Marshall after his arrival. "He's got five great-looking daughters."

Marshall spotted one of them, a pretty young woman named Diana, across the dining hall one day. He was shy, unsure of himself. It would be up to her to make the first move. And the next few moves. Later that week, playing forward for the SRJC basketball team, he scored thirty-three points in an overtime win. Diana approached him the next day in the dining hall.

"I've gotta tell you," she said. "You played the best game last night. That was exciting."

His jaw hit the tray. He managed to mumble a thank-you. Was this woman actually talking to him?

Diana started turning up outside his history class. He assumed she had a class nearby, but later found out that she didn't. He started showing up at her trampoline class (yes, trampoline). Coach Read was the instructor. He eyed Marshall with a father's suspicion.

Baseball season started, and Diana showed up at every game. She traded notes with Marshall when he was in the on-deck circle. Finally, in May, they went on a proper date . . . to an Oakland A's doubleheader. The date took place on Mother's Day, so Marshall had some work to do to win over Diana's mother, as well as her dad.

He'd been drafted in the fourth round by the New York Mets the previous January, before he'd played any games for Coach Read. When Diana told her father about Marshall being drafted, and "have you heard the news," and wasn't this exciting, and he's so great, Dad wasn't so sure. Coach Read was a kind man, but also a concerned father. He barely knew Marshall, and as far as the coach knew, the young slugger was a hotshot punk who wasn't good enough to date one of his daughters.

"Well," Diana's father said, "I guess we'll see if he's as good as he thinks he is."

After the baseball season began, Coach Read warmed to Marshall, realizing the young man was pretty much the polar opposite of hotshot punk. A bunch of home runs didn't hurt either.

Brant shipped out several months later to Marion, Virginia, for a rookie-level team in the Appalachian League. His professional career began on a high school field. He remembers large insects, humidity, crappy locker rooms, crappy uniforms, crappy venues.

Playing professional baseball hadn't been a lifelong dream. It was an opportunity, something he felt he'd backed into and wasn't certain he deserved.

He also backed into his wedding proposal to Diana. He never really asked, but every day walked eight blocks down a hill to Marion's Piggly Wiggly restaurant and pumped coins into a payphone just to hear her voice. One day, he simply told her that he never wanted to be away from her again.

She finished school. They married less than two years later. For their honeymoon, they drove from California to Florida for spring training, in a '73 VW Bug, with Cat Stevens and John Denver playing, and one of Marshall's bats propped between the seat and the gas pedal, so he could stretch his long right leg across to the passenger's side. Carlsbad Caverns, Fort Stockton, Lake Charles, St. Petersburg. The whole thing cost them fifty-three dollars in gas. There were many more road trips ahead of them, as well as time apart. Her positive attitude rarely wavered as they bounced from town to town, dealing with forward and backward steps in her young husband's baseball career. "Alright," she'd say hopefully. "Let's load up the car." As a coach's daughter who'd been around baseball her whole life, she understood better than most women would.

He had a strong first season as a pro in Marion, hitting .327 with thirteen homers—good enough to be named the league's Player of the Year. Then it was on to Lynchburg. Jackson. Norfolk. Marshall would scuffle, then succeed, then scuffle and succeed again. Yet in his head, he almost always scuffled. All the while he was pleased—and somewhat surprised—that someone thought well enough of his skills to pay him to play professional baseball.

AT TIMES, THE MAJOR Leagues felt tantalizingly close.

Brant won the Carolina League MVP Award with Lynchburg in '76. He had another big season at Double-A Jackson in '77. In spring training with the Mets the following year in St. Petersburg, he hit a pinch-hit, walk-off home run against the Blue Jays, a one-hopper into the bay. Making the big club seemed possible, but the Mets sent him to Triple-A. After learning the news, he sat in front of his locker, crestfallen. A clubbie walked by and snatched away his Mets cap.

He played in Norfolk for Triple-A Tidewater, managed by Frank Verdi. A different manager than he would be for the Clippers, Verdi drove Brant crazy and added to his self-doubt. He messed with Brant's swing. He rarely gave Brant the green light to hit on 3-0 counts, on which the slugger might have feasted. Brant's two years with the Tides weren't statistically horrible but were filled with frustration. He was still hitting for power. The big club was in last place and needed power hitters. Why wasn't he getting a chance?

The only explanation he ever got came from Mets GM Joe McDonald. At first base, the Mets were partial to Lee Mazzilli, a bearded bachelor and New York native who figured to put more butts in the seats than the squeaky clean, California-born Brant.

In 1980 the Mets sold Brant to the New York Yankees for a paltry $8,000. The deal would work out quite well for the Yankees.

• • •

The night after Andre Robertson's injury, 740 miles to the east, in Rhode Island, the International League's Rochester Red Wings and Pawtucket Red Sox began one of the most incredible baseball games ever played.

The contest at diminutive McCoy Stadium included two future Hall of Famers—Rochester's Cal Ripken Jr. and Pawtucket's Wade Boggs—along with twenty-three others who had either played in the Majors or would. It began benignly enough as an early-season pitchers' duel between Rochester's Larry Jones and Pawtucket's Danny Parks. Rochester broke through against Parks in the top of the seventh, grabbing a 1–0 lead. When the hometown Red Sox scored with two outs in the bottom of the ninth to force extra innings, no one could have imagined what would unfold overnight and into the next morning.

As temperatures dropped below forty degrees and the winds blew in, hitters from both teams went into an even deeper freeze. Scoreless inning after scoreless inning piled up. The umpires should have suspended the game—still tied at 1–1 as the teams hit twenty innings, after 12:50 a.m.—per International League rules, but crew chief Jack Lietz's rule book was missing that information. The teams played on. And on. The stadium ran out of food and coffee. Players started fires with broken bats in the dugouts and ripped up benches in the bullpens, hoping for some shred of warmth.

Pawtucket relief pitcher Luis Aponte pitched the seventh through the tenth innings, allowing no hits and striking out nine. After the nineteenth inning, Pawtucket manager Joe Morgan let Aponte go home. The pitcher's wife confronted him in the wee hours of Easter morning and asked him to explain where he'd been. Aponte told her that he'd just come from the ballpark. "Don't you lie to me," his wife responded.

Rochester took a 2–1 lead in the top of the twenty-first. When Boggs singled home a run to tie it back up in the bottom of the twenty-first, his exhausted teammates growled at him.

It took a while, but Pawtucket team officials were finally able to reach IL president Harold Cooper by phone.

"It's from Pawtucket," Cooper's wife told him in the 3:00 a.m. hour.

"Tell them I'll call back," Cooper responded.

"They're still playing."

"They're still *what?*"

By the time Cooper intervened and the contest was suspended, the teams had completed thirty-two innings, the longest game in the history of professional baseball. It was 4:07 a.m. Nineteen freeze-dried fans were left in the stands. And it wasn't over yet. The teams reconvened on June 23 to decide a winner, with a packed house and media from across the world in attendance. Pawtucket's Dave Koza singled home the winning run. Final score: Red Sox 3, Red Wings 2, thirty-three innings. Time of game, eight hours, twenty-five minutes, also a record.

Rochester's Dallas Williams went 0 for 13, a record for single-game futility that will almost certainly stand forever. Rochester pitchers combined to strike out thirty-four batters, including Russ Laribee *seven* times. Rochester's Dave Hupert caught thirty-one innings, at one point asking home-plate umpire Denny Craig to call sixteen straight balls, so he could go home and go to bed. Craig, who refused, handled the plate for the entire game. Craig called 882 pitches. He claimed he never went to the bathroom.

You can find the official scorecard and a ball signed by the players in the Baseball Hall of Fame.

"Verdi, You Go to Shortstop!"

About that early-season Columbus losing stretch: despite their struggles, the Clippers stayed loose. No one panicked, *Citizen-Journal* headline aside. These players were too experienced, too talented to doubt that things would turn around, and be fine, before long.

Quite the opposite of fearful and morose, the tone in the clubhouse was one of confidence and even playfulness. The young men played music and told jokes. Ribbing continued. Behavior like this in the middle of a losing streak could sour a grizzled, old-school manager like Verdi, who took winning—and losing—

quite seriously. One might expect Verdi would chew out his players a la another "Bull Durham" character, manager Skip Riggins.

After the Clippers fell at Richmond for their ninth loss in twelve games—unheard of during the Yankee era—Verdi surveyed the clubhouse from just behind the doorway. *Kiss a fat lady's ass. These cock-knockers sure seem to be enjoying themselves.*

Verdi walked in and made his way toward the radio. His players paused, unsure what form of rebuke was coming.

"Alright, alright, I see," Verdi said. The manager grabbed the volume knob on the radio.

He turned it up, most of the way.

"Let's have a goddamn disco in here!" Verdi yelled. He then broke into some goofy dance moves, which Paul Boris, years later, would liken to those of Elaine on *Seinfeld*.

Most of the players got a good laugh out of it. They stayed loose. A younger version of Verdi might not have recognized this model. His approach was a master stroke, though, just what his veteran team needed. Things would indeed turn around, and be fine.

BORN IN 1926, FRANK Verdi grew up in Brooklyn, the son of a hardworking butcher, playing stickball in the streets amid peddlers hawking produce from horse-drawn carts. His neighborhood, Bedford-Stuyvesant, in the borough's north-central region, was a rough one, and Verdi toughened early.

Young Verdi made deliveries for his father's shop by bicycle. His other job, on Friday nights, was racing between Jewish households lighting candles and turning off electric lights for occupants who weren't permitted to do so on the Sabbath.

Three generations of Verdis shared a small brownstone. There wasn't a lot of room, so getting outside to play sports was particularly enticing. Young Frank and his friends would each chip in a penny or two for a rubber Spaldeen ball to play with. In addition to costing an exorbitant ten cents each, Spaldeens would wear out. Playing a game required an actual baseball. The group of friends would walk about a mile to Ebbets Field, home of the Brooklyn Dodgers, in time for batting practice. They'd station themselves behind the right-field fence, near a gas station on Bedford Avenue, and wait for any balls hit out of the park.

They weren't the only kids in Brooklyn who had the idea. When a ball did clear the fence, a small war ensued to see who would come up with it. With one or two in hand, Verdi and Co. would walk another mile to the famed Parade Grounds Park, hoping to secure one of two grass fields. To Verdi, that was like playing at Yankee Stadium.

Young Verdi was quick, competitive, and sure of what he wanted to do in life. By his preteens, he was telling anyone who'd listen that he wanted to be a big league baseball player when he grew up. Other kids talked about becoming doctors, lawyers, scientists. They'd hear about Verdi's baseball dreams and laugh at him. Even some teachers would join them. Okay Frank, but one out of a million people can do that, so let's be realistic. What's it gonna be? His answer never varied. Baseball player.

The street-tough Verdi kept pushing toward those dreams, working his way through Brooklyn's Boys High School, hustling in local pool halls for extra money while living and breathing all sports. In basketball he played for Boys High in the city championship game in his senior season. But he especially excelled in baseball, usually playing shortstop. After graduating, with World War II raging, Verdi joined the navy and trained as an antiaircraft gunner at Camp Shelton in Virginia. He was also a backup shortstop for the base team.

Verdi was literally on a train, moments away from departing for California en route to the fighting in the South Pacific, when he heard his name called.

"Seaman Verdi!"

He wondered what the hell he had done.

"Yes sir?"

"Get the hell off that train!"

Admiral Chester Nimitz himself had called the base that morning. His team in Hawaii needed a shortstop. The starting shortstop for Verdi's team was headed to Hawaii. Verdi stayed behind, and maybe stayed alive, because he was needed at shortstop for Camp Shelton.

AT AGE NINETEEN, IN 1946, he realized his professional base-ball dream and signed with the New York Yankees, inking a $200-a-month contract atop a wooden butcher's block in his father's Long Island shop. The St. Louis Browns were also in the running to sign Verdi but finished a distant second. The scout who signed him, Paul Krichell, was a Yankee legend whose previous signees included Lou Gehrig, Leo Durocher, and Phil Rizzuto. Krichell even noted that the pen Verdi would use to sign was the same pen the scout had signed Gehrig with.

After the deal was inked, Krichell attempted to pay his respects by purchasing some cuts of meat. "I don't want any money," Verdi's father said. "Just please take care of my son."

Short on bulk at just over five foot nine, maybe 170 pounds, Frank Verdi wasn't short on determination. He spent eighteen years—his entire playing career but for one brief moment—toiling in the Minor Leagues. He took the field for fifteen different teams in nine different leagues in six different classifications, under seven different organizations. He made countless journeys, many of them on rickety buses, across twenty-seven states from Maine to New Mexico to Florida, two Canadian provinces, and two Caribbean islands.

Verdi's teams battled Mud Hens, Maples, Senators, Red Roses, Coal Barons, Roughnecks, and Sugar Kings. He played for title-winning teams at Single-A Binghamton, New York, in '49 and '52, competing for the Eastern League batting title for the latter.

On the field, Verdi held his own. He wasn't known for his power, though he did hit a home run off the legendary Satchel Paige once. But he could hit for average, steal bases, and bunt like he was putting on a clinic. He was a master of little ball, the selfless style of play—appreciated by managers and teammates—that didn't always show up in the box score, a player whose value could not be measured by basic baseball statistics. His style was epitomized by his mastery of the "hidden ball trick." He pulled the play off seven times in 1949 alone. And were there a "will to win" statistic, Verdi might have won the crown in multiple leagues. One newspaper columnist described him as a "hollering, hustling, fighting kind of ballplayer that fans naturally take to."

Early in his career, Verdi made friends with a young teammate named Ed Ford, the pitcher later known as Whitey. They roomed together during Ford's first season of pro ball in '47, at Butler, Pennsylvania, about thirty miles outside of Pittsburgh. The two friends and their Butler teammates would play before crowds of about two hundred. Dreaming of the Majors, they'd pull Pirates games in on the radio and listen to Rosey Rowswell's unique call of Ralph Kiner home runs: "Look out, Aunt Millie, here she comes!" followed by a sound effect of breaking glass.

It was Whitey who introduced Verdi to his future wife, Pauline Pasquale, when the two men were teammates at Binghamton in 1949. Whitey met Pauline's sister after a game, asked her out, and got a yes. They needed a chaperone in those days, and Pauline filled the role. Whitey came home from the date and shook Frank awake in his bed with news of Pauline. "Frank! Frank! Wake up! I think I found the perfect girl for you!"

The first time Frank met Pauline, the eighteen-year-old Binghamton native was shooting baskets, making shot after shot. She also played tennis and could throw a baseball eighty miles an hour, debunking the whole "throw like a girl" thing decades before doing so was in vogue. Athletic AND beautiful. Young Verdi was smitten. Pauline's mother wasn't so sure—she had her doubts about his career as a baseball player. But she agreed to meet with his parents, who thoroughly won her over.

The following year, Whitey Ford reached the Majors with the Yankees and began his journey to superstardom. He was just twenty-one years old when he won Game Four of the 1950 World Series, completing New York's sweep of the Philadelphia Phillies.

Verdi had no such luck, at least professionally. He married Pauline in February of 1951, but his baseball career appeared to stall out. Verdi returned to Binghamton for parts of the '50, '51, and '52 seasons.

In spring training of 1953, though, he earned a spot as one of four "extra" players with the Yankees—teams were then allowed expanded rosters until May 15. These surplus players generally did not accompany the team on road trips and sat on the bench during home games. Verdi was told he was in New York only to work out with the team in advance of a possible trade to Philadelphia. But nearly a month into the season, Verdi learned he'd be joining the Yankees in Boston.

Sunday, May 10. A spring afternoon at Fenway Park, with just shy of twenty-nine thousand fans in attendance. The Yankees entered the contest in first place, a half game up on Cleveland, after splitting their first two games in Boston.

With New York trailing 3–2 in the top of the sixth, Yankees manager Casey Stengel lifted shortstop Phil Rizzuto for a pinch hitter. Moments later, eyeing the bottom of the inning, Stengel yelled, "Verdi! You go to shortstop!"

The stunned Verdi, who hadn't even been sure Stengel knew he was with the team, took his position between Gil McDougald at third base and Billy Martin at second, behind pitcher Vic Raschi. There were no defensive opportunities for the Yankees' very nervous rookie. Boston's Jimmy Piersall grounded out to third. George Kell flew out to center. Raschi then finished the inning by striking out Dick Gernert.

In the top of the seventh, Mickey Mantle ignited a two-out rally with a single off Sid Hudson. After Gene Woodling singled to send Mantle to third, Boston's Ellis "Old Folks" Kinder came on in relief of Hudson. But it wasn't Kinder's day. "Old Folks" gave up an RBI single to McDougald and a two-run double to Martin. He issued walks to Charlie Silvera (intentional) and Raschi. Now up 5–3, New York had the bases loaded. Verdi was due up, poised for a dramatic Major League debut after seven seasons in the bush leagues, ready to stake his claim to a full-on roster spot.

Verdi stepped into the box to face Kinder, thinking about all the radios back home in Brooklyn, friends and family listening in as his dream came true. This was it.

"Time out!" he heard.

The Red Sox were making a move. Coach Bill McKechnie went out to the mound, grabbed the ball from Kinder and summoned Ken Holcombe to pitch. As Holcombe warmed up, Verdi was still thinking about all those radios in Brooklyn.

"A BALL NEVER COMES TO ME"

"Play ball!" umpire Larry Napp cried.

Verdi stepped back into the box.

"Time out!" he heard again, and wondered what the hell was going on now.

This time, the voice was Stengel's. Verdi turned around and saw teammate "Big Bill" Renna swinging three bats. Verdi was out of the game, lifted for a pinch hitter. Renna grounded into a force out at third, ending the inning. Verdi didn't know it at the time, but his Major League playing career had also ended. One defensive inning. Zero at bats. He didn't appear in any more games for the Yankees, and two days later, the Yankees sent him back to the Minors for good.

Verdi's playing career lasted until 1963, the last two of those seasons as a player-manager. He'd begun a long, winding career of winning pennants, clashing with front offices, and terrorizing umpires as a field boss. There were interruptions. Heartbreaks, disillusionment, time spent away from the game. Jobs as a steamfitter, a car salesman, a Pinkerton man at the racetrack. But when chances to return to the game presented themselves, Verdi couldn't say no. His love of the game, those Major League dreams . . . they just wouldn't die.

Now, in 1981, Verdi found himself at the helm for the Clippers, one step below a return to the Majors with the Yankees as a manager or coach, a man still pursuing a dream as much as any player on his roster.

• • •

They passed out Columbus Clippers baseball cards that spring at my grade school, Our Lady of Peace. As if my budding fandom needed another boost. They were the first baseball cards I owned, and I loved them.

The cards were produced through a joint effort by the team and the Columbus Police Department. There were no stats on the backs, just tips on baseball and crime prevention for kids. The set included Marshall Brant, Steve Balboni, Dave Righetti . . . pretty much everyone who was with the team at the start of the season. Verdi had a card, as did GM Sisler, with an image of him kneeling next to the previous season's Governors' Cup trophy. The set also had a card for a member of the police department, Sgt. Dick Hoover. A memorial of some sort. I'd shuffle past it in the stack with little consideration.

Years later, I checked into it. It turns out that Sgt. Hoover was a hero in his own right, in life as well as baseball.

It was Hoover who started the card program in 1980, with an $8,000 boost from local philanthropist Hester Dysart. Hoover was a beloved figure in the department who'd served in the navy during World War II and held numerous positions during his twenty-six-year police career, many involving community outreach. He loved the Clippers and could usually be spotted at Franklin County Stadium in the same reserved seat.

Just a month before the '81 cards came out, he retired at age fifty-five. Less than two weeks later, he was killed in a car accident in Florida. The group completing the card set rushed to include him.

Hoover had also been a left-handed pitcher, and a good one. A Columbus native, he was just seventeen years old when the New York Giants signed him in 1943. He never caught on in the Majors, but he pitched briefly for the Boston Braves in '52, his teammates including Eddie Matthews and Warren Spahn. Playing for the brand-new Columbus Jets in 1955, Hoover threw a seven-inning no-hitter against the Richmond Virginians. He retired and entered the Columbus Police Academy just after that season ended.

The news of Hoover's death stunned Verdi, a friend of Hoover's since they were teammates with the Jets. Hoover and his wife had been touring Florida, checking up on his old baseball teammates.

I still have those cards. Several sets of them, actually, which means I have about eight Dick Hoovers. It no longer seems right to call his card a "common," though.

• • •

The news of the day in 1981 continued to fascinate. On May 13, a Turkish assassin named Mehmet Ali Ağca raised a Browning HP 9mm handgun above a sea of worshippers in St. Peter's Square and fired four shots at John Paul II. "I have killed the pope," read a letter found on Ağca after his apprehension. I watched the news coverage on a TV rolled into my Catholic school classroom and, for some reason, took notes.

John Paul II was seriously wounded, but he survived and would become the second-longest reigning pope in history, as well as one of the most important historical figures of the last one hundred years, and a fast-tracked Catholic saint.

• • •

After his April 17 demotion from New York, Bobby Brown got off to a hot start with the Clippers—six hits in his first fifteen at bats with a home run. Then some personality struggles with Verdi, along with the blows Brown's renowned confidence had taken, began to show up in his on-the-field performance, and the hits stopped coming. There was another factor. Brown had been self-assured in his abilities as a switch hitter, but he was still only hitting from the left side of the plate, per the Boss's orders.

In Richmond on the night of May 4, Brown, hitless in his first two at bats against Braves lefty Ken Dayley and mired in a 2-for-19 slump, decided he'd had enough. He turned around and hit from the right side, defying the organization's wishes. He promptly lined a single up the middle.

"I have to go back and do what's best for Bobby Brown," he told reporters after the game. "I am twenty-six years old and I will be twenty-seven here in a few days, and I'm too old to go back to just hitting left-handed. I don't have the time to waste.

"They can suggest I do something, but that doesn't mean I have to do it. And if it hurts their feelings, well fine, go ahead and trade me. I'm not giving it up. It's something I've worked on too hard and too long to give up."

If Steinbrenner or anyone else in the organization was annoyed over Brown's insubordination, they probably didn't stay that way for very long. There was no arguing with the results. Brown picked up twenty-nine hits—including four home runs—in seventy-one at bats after returning to switch-hitterdom, a sizzling .408 clip. He warmed to Verdi, who—along with McNertney and hitting coach

Mickey Vernon—helped straighten him out. "You can be the same player you were in '79," Vernon would tell him.

As Brown heated up, so did the Clippers. When the Yankees recalled Brown on May 28, Columbus had won thirteen of its last eighteen games and climbed to within two and a half games of first-place Tidewater in the standings. Brown was hitting .364 with his swagger back when the Yankees called. It was the sixth time he'd ridden "the shuttle" up to New York.

The Clipper resurgence was further fueled by the return of Andre Robertson on May 3. He provided an immediate defensive boost, despite playing through pain. What surprised most if not all was his explosion at the plate.

• • •

Andre Robertson was deep in the hole at short, in shallow left field, really. The ball was skipping away from him on the fast, artificial turf at Franklin County Stadium. It was going to be a tough play.

It was 1979 and he was only nineteen years old, appearing in just his fourth game at the Triple-A level, with the Syracuse Chiefs. He'd made the jump all the way from Single-A just a few weeks earlier.

Now in game seven of the '79 Governors' Cup championship series, he was starting for the Chiefs against his future team, the Columbus Clippers, filling in for an injured Garth Iorg.

The decisive contest of the series had already been a terrific baseball game. Bobby Brown, playing center for the Clippers that night, nailed Dave McKay at the plate with a perfect throw in the fifth. Robertson tied the game at 2 with a dramatic RBI single in the seventh, and the Chiefs had taken a 3–2 lead in the eighth, when slugging first baseman Boomer Wells was hit by a pitch with the bases loaded. In the bottom of the ninth, a passed ball by Syracuse catcher Ernie Whitt set up the tying run for Columbus. Now the Clippers and Chiefs were locked in a duel between superstar relief pitchers: Rick Anderson for Columbus and Steve Grilli for Syracuse. The two teams entered the twelfth inning tied at 3, with the 1979 Governors' Cup awaiting the winner. Syracuse, now the top affiliate of the expansion Toronto Blue Jays, was trying for its ninth cup. No Columbus team had ever won one.

"A BALL NEVER COMES TO ME"

With one out and no one on, Columbus manager Gene Michael summoned Danny Schmitz to pinch-hit. Schmitz shattered his bat and sent a Grilli pitch deep, deep into that hole at short. Somehow, Robertson got to the ball and fielded it cleanly. He fired the ball toward first.

It sailed over the head of Wells, fifteen rows into the stands. Airmail. E-6. Schmitz took second on the play, and the Clippers had the series-winning run in scoring position. Roger Holt lined the next pitch into center field, knocking in Schmitz. Game, set, and cup to Columbus. As the Clippers and their fans celebrated, Robertson slowly walked off the field, his head down. "It won't be the last one you throw away," Syracuse manager Vern Beeson told him. "At least you didn't throw it in the dirt."

Multiple lives would turn on that error. It would lead to a trade, a World Series appearance, a tragic accident that would change two lives forever, and much more. Robertson hadn't realized he could throw the ball so hard. Neither had the opposing manager, Michael, who was impressed.

Michael, just completing his first year managing, was already a rising star in the Yankees' organization and a Steinbrenner favorite. Following the season, he made the jump to GM for the big club. New York swung a deal with Toronto that winter, and Andre Robertson headed to the Yankees organization.

FIVE DAYS AFTER HIS return in 1981, Robertson hit his first home run of the season in a win at Pawtucket. Later that week, he began feasting on his former team, the Chiefs, with home runs in consecutive games. On May 20 he delivered an inside-the-park homer. The next night, his clutch squeeze bunt in the bottom of the eighth lifted red-hot Columbus past the Chiefs 6–5, the Clippers' sixth straight win. On Memorial Day in Rochester, Robertson doubled, homered, and drove in three runs. On the night of May 30, he beat a relay to first base in the bottom of the eighth, denying Toledo a double play and allowing Columbus to score the go-ahead run. The Clippers went on to a 5–4 victory . . . and regained sole possession of first place.

5

Signs of Life

ON THE NIGHT OF May 15, in nearby Cleveland, Len Barker took the mound for the Indians and did something no Major Leaguer had done in the previous thirteen seasons. Barker pitched a perfect game. Twenty-seven men up, twenty-seven down, no base runners in Cleveland's 3–0 win against Toronto. Perfectos are one of baseball's rarest—and most exciting—feats. Oakland's Catfish Hunter had been the last man to do it, stifling the Minnesota Twins back in 1968.

As a brand-new fan, I'd never heard of perfect games until that night. Rizzs educated me as he called the Clippers game against visiting Syracuse on WBNS. He received a heads up that Barker was close, picked up a phone in the press box and reached a contact at Cleveland Stadium. With the phone to his ear as he called the Clippers game, Rizzs provided updates on Barker's bid with increasing urgency. This was important. It was historic. It was fun. When Ernie Whitt flew out to Rick Manning in center for the last out, WBNS listeners were able to share in the excitement. "Len Barker has done it!" Rizzs shared joyfully.

Later that night, Rizzs went nuts when Columbus held on to beat Syracuse 4–2, ending the game with a Jim Lewis strikeout of Chiefs bopper Greg Wells on a 3-2 slider, followed by Callahan throwing out Creighton Tevlin at third on a double-steal attempt. A game-ending, strike 'em out, throw 'em out double play. An exciting night of baseball for any fan, but especially for a new one.

Were it not for the efforts of one Columbus baseball godfather, in particular, that evening might never have happened.

Birth of the Clippers

"We just bought old Jets Stadium," Harold Cooper told Frank Ray. "I hope that was legal."

It was Ray's first day in his new job, providing legal representation for the Franklin County Commissioners, in August of 1976. Ray was just twenty-seven and a few years removed from law school. Cooper, one of three commissioners, led a budding effort to lure professional baseball back to Columbus, Ohio, after a six-year absence.

Those years marked a dark time in the city's baseball history, the first time Columbus hadn't had a professional team since 1894. That history was rich.

In the beginning there were amateur teams like the Columbus Buckeyes, who played their first game in April of 1866 on the lawn outside the local insane asylum, presumably because the wide-open green space suited. Columbus fielded Major League teams in the late nineteenth century—professional versions of the Buckeyes (1883–84) and the Columbus Solons (1889–91). Minor League entries around the turn of that century included Reds, Statesmen, and Senators, who would be followed by the Red Birds and the Columbus Jets. The nicknames of some Columbus players during the early part of the twentieth century reflect the era's colorfulness. Cannonball Morris. Dirty Jack Doyle. Icebox Chamberlain.

By the 1970s a lengthy list of Hall of Famers had played for, or run, Columbus teams. The legendary Mordecai "Three Finger" Brown came through Columbus, pitching for the Senators in 1917 and 1918. Joe Tinker, of Chicago Cubs "Tinker-to-Evers-to-Chance" fame, arrived in Columbus in 1917 as a player-manager and executive. Branch Rickey, who later helped break baseball's color barrier by signing Jackie Robinson, was the Columbus Jets' vice president in the '30s and early '40s. Willie Stargell played for the Columbus Jets in '62. As of this writing no less than fourteen future members of the Hall had spent time with Columbus teams, and others—including Derek Jeter—were sure to follow.

Babe Ruth never played for a Columbus team, but he played *in* Columbus in Yankees exhibitions and as a barnstormer with his Bustin' Babes team, as well as Lou Gehrig's Larrupin' Lous. When in Columbus, Ruth would disappear for chunks of time. His teammates probably figured he was out drinking and chasing women, for which he was well-known. While there was likely some of that, Ruth quietly spent some of his downtime in Columbus visiting with children at St. Vincent's Orphanage. He made the nuns who ran the orphanage promise never to tell anyone. But stories trickled out over the years, of the mighty Babe showing up with armfuls of clothes and toys from a Lazarus department store, arranging trolley rides to old Neil Park so the children could watch his games, and of the iconic slugger paying for all of their concessions. The Babe had been an orphan himself, and he never forgot that.

As the 1970s approached, an unusual legal arrangement with a local youth foundation blocked any funding for sorely needed improvements to Jets Stadium. The Jets, a farm team of the Pittsburgh Pirates, left town for Charleston, West Virginia, following the 1970 season. The stadium fell apart in earnest, with portions of the roof caving in. The Central Ohio Transit Authority, in need of a new bus barn, eyed the land and licked its chops. It appeared the stadium would be completely razed and that professional baseball in Columbus might be gone forever.

Then Cooper, who had played a key role in saving Columbus baseball once before, after the Red Birds moved to Omaha in 1954, went to work. In late 1975 he and his fellow commissioners spent $600,000 of Franklin County's general fund to purchase the decaying stadium. There were no hearings, no ballot measures. It was a different era, and they just did it. Statutes allowed for the purchase, but not for the county owning and running a team. The following summer, Cooper and his fellow commissioners looked to their young attorney for the next steps.

"We're going to bring professional baseball back to Columbus," Cooper told Ray. "This is your assignment. I don't care what you do with your time, as long as you bust your ass and figure out how to do this."

Ray, with no legal precedents or models to work from, devised a plan within a month. The stadium would be classified as a parks-and-rec facility. The commissioners would resolve that the parks board could operate a baseball team and a stadium. With two newly formed, nonprofit corporations running the show, the franchise and stadium would be fully owned by the public.

Such an arrangement had never happened before, and nothing quite like it has happened since, anywhere. Ray had his doubters, but his legal maneuvers turned out to be strokes of genius.

OF COURSE, AN ACTUAL team was also required. Not long before he enlisted Frank Ray, Cooper convinced his good friend John Galbreath, the owner of the Pirates, to ditch Charleston and reestablish a Triple-A affiliate back in Columbus. The Clippers were born, with George Sisler Jr., another old pal of Cooper's who served the previous ten years as International League president, hired as their first employee that winter.

Old Jets Stadium, needing a near total overhaul, was stripped down to its concrete underpinnings. Bill Trautwein, an Ohio State football hero turned architect, handled the redesign. Fifteen thousand seats with overflow capacity. Luxury boxes. A two-hundred-seat restaurant. The price tag would top $6 million, and the Minor Leagues had never seen anything like it. Neither had any county government. Cooper and his fellow commissioners were taking a sizable gamble, with the full faith and credit of Franklin County in play. If the plan backfired, the county would be in serious financial trouble. "I think we would have all changed our names and moved into witness protection programs," Ray would joke, years later.

The young attorney's father, an agronomist who taught at Ohio State, was brought in to consult about the playing surface. His conclusion: grass wouldn't work, at least not in time for the home opener. The team opted instead for a carpet of green AstroTurf, another first for the Minor Leagues.

Completing the stadium in time for the first home game turned into a mad scramble. Columbus suffered through the infamous Blizzard of '77, putting the project behind schedule. When the Clippers returned home on April 22, after dropping three of their first five games on the road, the home wasn't quite finished, and neither was the miserable weather. On any other day, the game

Fɪɢ 9. George Sisler Jr. (*left*) and Harold Cooper were two of the Columbus Clippers' founding fathers. *Columbus Citizen-Journal*, Scripps Howard Newspapers/Grandview Heights Public Library/Photohio.org.

would have been postponed. But the stands were overflowing with nineteen thousand chilled-but-hardy fans, and too much had been pointed toward this moment for too long. The game went on, and the Clippers' new park was baptized with snow and sleet. Ed Whitson got the cold start for Columbus. Wayne Harer, then a young Pawtucket outfielder, got the nod in left for the Red Sox, with slugging Sam Bowen off to a horrendous start that season.

The city's baseball-starved fans cheered every play, good and bad. Trailing 5–3 in the bottom of the eighth, Columbus had runners at first and second with two outs. Mike Edwards hit a liner to left that skipped on the slick turf, gobbled up Harer, and got past him for a hard-luck error. Two runs scored, Edwards wound up at second, and the game was tied. Yogi Berra's twenty-year-old son, Dale, knocked home Edwards on a base hit between short and third, giving the Clippers a 6–5 lead they wouldn't relinquish. Columbus was the victor in the slick-in-more-ways-than-one new stadium, with the paint still drying, literally and figuratively. Trautwein may not have remembered much of it. He was so nervous that some part of the not-quite-completed stadium would fall down that he spent the game imbibing, and before the end of it, he was quite drunk.

Professional baseball was back in Columbus. The Clippers struggled on the field in their first season, finishing seventh in the eight-team International League, but drew 457,251 fans, about 10,000 off the Minor League record. They averaged 7,144 per game, better than the Oakland A's that season. Cooper and the commissioners had quietly figured the country would have to subsidize repaying the bonds. Instead, the county benefitted to the tune of $500,000. It was only the beginning.

It added up to a triumph for many people, but perhaps for Harold Cooper most of all.

• • •

Born in 1923, Cooper grew up in the Bottoms neighborhood in Columbus, often sneaking into the then newly built previous incarnation of the stadium in hopes of watching the Red Birds. On occasion he got caught, and the local police weren't very forgiving. One officer was applying lashes with a billy-club strap when Red Birds team president George Trautman walked up and asked what was going on. Trautman solved the issue by giving young Cooper an unpaid job at the stadium. The young man was handed a rag soaked in vinegar, pointed toward a container filled with hot dogs, and ordered to clean the mold off them. Yum.

Cooper worked his way up to clubhouse manager and eventually became a baseball executive, with military service in between. He led a group of Columbus investors who purchased an Ottawa team to replace the departed Red Birds in 1955, giving birth to the Jets. A picture run by the *Columbus Citizen* during the transition shows Cooper, crouching before a pile of letters from a sign that had spelled "R-E-D-B-I-R-D-S" on the stadium, with a pack of matches in hand. He ran the Jets as general manager for thirteen seasons before leaving to run for county office. After leading the way in birthing the Clippers, he became president of the International League, serving from 1978 until 1990. Franklin County Stadium was redubbed Cooper Stadium in 1984, and it came to be known, affectionately, as "The Coop."

The Clippers' current home, gorgeous Huntington Park, opened in 2009. A full-length, bronze statue of Cooper, holding a baseball head high, was unveiled that year and still sits outside the center-field entrance at Neil and Nationwide.

After Cooper's death in October of 2010, his ashes were quietly spread around second base.

Hopefully that was legal.

WHEN COOPER BECAME THE neophyte Columbus Jets' general manager in 1955, the first player he signed was Frank Verdi. The Jets' first batboy was Verdi's son, Paul. Frank Verdi hit respectably and played his usually stellar defense at shortstop and third base over the next two seasons, further endearing himself to local fans with his fiery play. For June of '55, he was named the Jets' Most Valuable Player and rewarded with a one-hundred-dollar wristwatch. The following season he even received an award from the local American-Italian Golf Association.

Unfortunately for local fans, the Jets finished well back in the standings those first two years, in seventh place both times.

Each day, Cooper handed Verdi and the rest of his Jets teammates a breakfast meal ticket, to be redeemed at a local restaurant.

The variety was sometimes lacking. One day, Verdi found himself staring down at scrambled eggs for the seventeenth straight morning. He asked a waiter if he could please change things up, just a little. Over easy, fried, but please no more scrambled.

"Naw, scrambled eggs, that's it!" the waiter snapped.

Verdi, never known for walking on egg shells around anyone, took the meal and his breakfast ticket, threw them in the waiter's face, and walked out the door. He had just begun to walk down the street when a car pulled up with the window rolled down.

"Hey Frank," said a voice from inside the car. "C'mere."

It was Cooper. He let Verdi know that he appreciated their friendship and all, but well . . . he'd just sold him to Rochester.

"Hey, I didn't hit the guy with the eggs more than thirty seconds ago," a shocked Verdi said. "Whaddya got, a two-way wrist radio?"

• • •

Less than two months into the '81 season, the Clippers starting rotation was barely recognizable from what Verdi and Ellis had in mind on opening night. With Steinbrenner punching bag Mike Griffin traded to the Cubs, Righetti promoted, Cochran and McGaffigan injured, and Pacella and Brian Ryder struggling, righty Dave Wehrmeister emerged as the ace of the staff, at least for most of the season—an upswing in a twisty-turny career.

Wehrmeister, who hailed from the Chicago suburb of Berwyn, shredded the record book at Northeast Missouri State and left early to turn pro in '73, drafted by the San Diego Padres. He spun two one-hitters that season but lost a combined twenty-five games in his first two campaigns. Then, via promotion, he escaped a losing, bad-atmosphere, Double-A team in Alexandria, Louisiana, and found himself four thousand miles away, pitching for a fun, relaxed, Triple-A Hawaii Islanders team chasing its first Pacific Coast League pennant. He debuted with a two-hit shutout and played a key role down the stretch. On September 8 Wehrmeister took the mound before 7,700 screaming Hawaii fans and shut out the Salt Lake Gulls, earning the Islanders the PCL championship. The Gulls were sick of seeing him. In forty-one and a third innings against Salt Lake that season, Wehrmeister allowed just one earned run.

He was just twenty-two years old and far, far away from Alexandria. Wehrmeister was now one of the Padres' top prospects.

More of the not-so-good from early in Wehrmeister's career: he battled hepatitis, lost sensation in his pitching hand and had to have an artery-pinching rib removed, found out he'd been tipping his pitches and spent time in the Instructional League to correct the flaw. He made the Padres in '76, '77, and '78 but got shelled each season. Shipped back to Hawaii early in '78, he dropped his first eleven decisions, one short of an ignominious league record.

Dave Wehrmeister didn't quit. He ended that streak with back-to-back, four-hit victories. Then, helped by a new submarine-style delivery, he dominated the following season. A top prospect again, he was traded to the Yankees organization. He changed his delivery back to over the top, regained velocity on his fastball, and starred down the stretch as a reliever for the 1980 Clippers. Now he was a starter again, and he was throwing as well as ever. Tailing, sinking, fastball. Hard slider. Good curveball.

It almost wasn't to be, for the Clippers at least. The Kansas City Royals selected Wehrmeister in the Minor League draft following the 1980 season, paying the Yankees $25,000 to acquire him. But Kansas City passed, returned Wehrmeister to the Yankees, and lost out on half of that money, as well as a pitcher who'd be back in the Majors before season's end.

Crafting a preview to the '81 campaign, Torry asked Ellis if he thought Wehrmeister had Major League ability. Ellis responded bluntly.

"That's a stupid question," the pitching coach said.

UP IN THE MAJORS, Righetti was rolling.

Three days after his May 20 call-up, the young lefty got the start, pitched seven solid innings, and beat the Indians 3–2 at Yankee Stadium. Six days later, in Cleveland, he beat the Indians again, allowing only a single earned run in eight innings. In his next outing, he shut out the Orioles for eight innings, striking out eight in a no-decision. The buzz swelled. In his last start before the labor strike, Righetti ran his record to 3-0 with a win at Kansas City.

During the same time period, Fernando Valenzuela, whom Righetti had quietly tagged as a rival, returned to Planet Earth. On May 18, at Dodger Stadium, Valenzuela's eight-game winning streak to begin the season came to an end against Philadelphia. In his final six starts before the strike, the skyward-looking lefty was a mere 1-4 with an ERA of 6.16, ballooning his season ERA from 0.50 to 2.45. He'd recover enough to win National League Rookie of the Year honors, but he'd never match his torrid, Fernandomania-inducing start. Baseball hasn't seen anything quite like it since and likely never will.

Righetti and Valenzuela might have been teammates. In 1979 the Dodgers backed out of a winter meetings deal that would have brought Righetti to Los Angeles in exchange for veteran pitcher Don Sutton. It was one of several times that Steinbrenner, eyeing another free agent bonanza, tried to trade Righetti, over the strenuous objections of his managers and coaches. In 1980 the Boss was ready to ship Righetti to the Rangers for fading veteran Doc Medich before the coaching staff talked him out of it. A year later, Righetti, pitcher Brian Ryder, and $400,000 were headed to the Cubs in exchange for 1980 National League batting champion Bill Buckner, but Chicago owner Bill Wrigley pulled out of the deal at the last minute.

Steinbrenner sometimes put potential trades and other roster moves to a vote, with himself and his coaching staff weighing in. When his proposals lost 6–1, he'd say it didn't matter because he got eight votes, anyway. Sometimes he'd relent. His coaches tried repeatedly to convince him to try bringing in some youth instead of more high-priced free agents. The Boss rarely budged, and when he did, he'd let the group know that their careers were on the line.

PLAYERS WITH MAJOR LEAGUE credentials joined the Clippers throughout the '81 season. On May 1 former Detroit Tiger Dave Stegman arrived. When the sun had come up that morning, Stegman was a member of the Pacific Coast League's Hawaii Islanders, across the continent for a series in Vancouver, British Columbia. Then word came that he was the "player to be named later" in the Pacella deal, headed to the Yankees organization.

When he heard "Columbus," the first thing that came to mind was Columbus, Georgia, a place he'd visited while playing in the Double-A Southern League four seasons earlier. He learned he was staying in Triple-A ball, in Columbus, Ohio, and that he'd join the Clippers in Norfolk. Where was that, exactly?

He flew all day and arrived by cab, just in time to see the Clippers team bus in front of the hotel, about to pull away for the trip to the ballpark. He could have jumped aboard, but he didn't. Too tired. He opted to get some rest instead. His new teammates would give him a lot of grief about that, especially considering that they'd had their own crazy-long day of travel, and that the game that night went eleven innings. And they lost, 2–1. A defeat that could "take the starch out of you," Verdi told reporters after. It was the manager's first game against Tidewater since the Tides had canned him after the 1980 season.

The next night, Verdi penciled Stegman into the starting lineup, in left field. He usually played in right, but as Verdi had explained to him upon his arrival, there were six outfielders, and getting all of them playing time required some creativity. Stegman didn't have the black shoes he needed, just the white shoes used by the Islanders. Verdi needed a quick fix. "You got any shoe polish?" the manager asked a young clubbie just before game time. The young man did, and they managed to get the shoes sort of black looking. But even that only lasted a few innings in the wet outfield grass at Met Park. A somewhat embarrassed Stegman found himself with shoes that were splotchy black on top and white on the bottom.

It wasn't an issue he would have faced as a member of the Tigers, with whom he'd spent parts of the three previous seasons.

The California native had made his Major League debut with Detroit in '78, hitting a respectable .286 in limited action. With the Tigers in '79, Stegman hit three home runs in just thirty-three at bats, including a blast at Yankee Stadium against then twenty-year-old Dave Righetti. It came on a 3-2 fastball and sailed out to left. Stegman loved fastballs, by the way. He struggled with sliders and curves. The home run was the first Righetti gave up in the Majors, and the pitcher was still kind of mad about it when Stegman became his teammate in Columbus. Perhaps Righetti had only himself to blame.

"You were throwing me nothing but fastballs," Stegman explained.

"Yeah," Righetti said. "I was out partying the whole night before. I was hung over."

There were more at bats with the Tigers in the 1980 season, 130 of them, but Stegman struggled and hit only .177. His stock in Detroit had already fallen when the Tigers ditched manager Les Moss—who'd managed Stegman before and liked him—to make room for Reds castoff Sparky Anderson, who hadn't managed Stegman and didn't like him as much.

Now Stegman was the latest in a long line of Major League veterans stuck in Columbus, where he'd play for three seasons, briefly returning to the Majors after escaping to the Chicago White Sox organization. With Columbus in the spring of '82 was Buck Showalter who was also mad at him. Stegman's arrival the previous spring resulted in Showalter's demotion to Nashville, so Buck gave him a hard time.

The friendships came along, and thankfully Stegman found at least one person in Columbus who really liked him. He met his future wife, Tonda, in a honky-tonk lounge there. She knew very little about baseball and was ready to pass on her future husband's invite to the ballpark. A friend, who'd accompanied her to the lounge, talked her into it.

ON MAY 7, WITH the Clippers still fighting to top the .500 mark, Dennis Werth added still more big league experience to the lineup. Werth hit over .300 for the Yankees in limited duty during the 1980 season. He was hardworking and versatile, able to play catcher, first base, and outfield. For the next few weeks, he provided Verdi with yet another experienced weapon.

In the top of the sixth in his first game back with the Clippers, Werth broke a 0–0 tie with a single to left, knocking in Brown. It would prove to be the only run Wehrmeister and Griffin would need. The two combined on a four-hit shutout as Columbus won 4–0 to even its record at 12-12. The Clippers wouldn't see the underside of .500 again that season.

Known as Herbie, Werth was the resident inventor for whichever team he was on, fixing everyone's glove and helping Bruce Robinson create the "Robby Pad," a flap that protects catchers' right shoulders, now used throughout baseball. He'll tell you jokingly— well, maybe half jokingly—that he still wishes Robinson would send some of that "Robby Pad" money his way. These days Werth's ventures include making decorative lamps out of baseball bats. One of them appeared on an episode of *Seinfeld*.

Werth joined the Clippers with a groin injury, recovered enough from that to hit .341 over three weeks, then hurt his back lifting heavy boxes in the clubhouse. After struggling for the Yankees over the course of the '81 Major League season, and during brief duty with the Kansas City Royals in '82, he never returned to the Majors. He wasn't done having an impact on Major League Baseball, however.

In 1984 Werth married Kim Schofield, a former collegiate track star who'd made it as far as the Olympic Trials. He took her five-year-old son, Jayson Gowan, under his care and began teaching him the game of baseball, building a batting cage in the backyard and coaching Jayson's highly successful youth traveling teams. Dennis and Kim changed the young man's last name from Gowan to Werth.

"Jayson Werth" has a nice ring to it alright. During his senior year of high school, Jayson hit a ridiculous .652 with fifteen home runs in just thirty-one games. By the late aughts, he was one of the best players in Major League Baseball, and he helped the Philadelphia Phillies win the World Series in 2008.

As THE '81 CLIPPERS ascended, hopes for a breakthrough in Major League labor negotiations plummeted. With the May 29 strike deadline looming, negotiations between owner and player reps in New York were not going well.

A session on May 26 lasted for just ninety minutes. "On a scale of one to ten, as far as good meetings are concerned, I'd say it was about a one," reported federal mediator Ken Moffett. The next day's negotiations broke up after just seven minutes. A midseason work stoppage appeared inevitable.

The battle's multiple fronts included a union demand that the owners, some of whom argued that free agency would ruin them financially and sink their teams, open their financial records for the previous two seasons. Not surprisingly, the owners refused. The National Labor Relations Board took up the matter and ruled in favor of the union on May 28. The two sides agreed to delay the strike until a federal judge ruled on the dispute. Once that happened, players would have forty-eight hours to decide whether to strike.

Points of Reference

Balboni struggled mightily over the first six weeks of the season, aside from his stint with the Yankees in Brant's stead. Balboni only appeared in two games for New York that spring. He played a hero's role in both.

After tripling in his first Major League at bat on the night of April 22, Balboni came up in the seventh inning and drew a bases-loaded walk to break a 2–2 tie. The Yankees went on to win 7–2. Four nights later, again facing Detroit's Howard Bailey, Balboni broke a 0–0 tie in the seventh with an RBI double to the wall in left-center. The Yankees went on to win 3–1. In his two games, Balboni had doubled, tripled, walked twice, and delivered both game-winning RBIs.

The heroics didn't compel Steinbrenner and the Yankees to keep the big man around. On April 28 they reassigned him to Columbus. The call to the Majors had surprised Balboni. The early demotion, after his success in the two games, surprised him again. He was internally furious but externally humble, earning praise for taking the quick hook with quiet grace.

"It was definitely an outward appearance," he recalled three decades later. "Getting sent back down was horrible. But I couldn't

1981 Columbus Clippers
Infielder
STEVE BALBONI—37

FIG 10. Steve Balboni's 1981 baseball card. Courtesy of the Columbus Clippers.

go back down and feel sorry for myself. People were still watching. I had to prove them wrong."

Back in Columbus, Balboni struggled again. Part of it was adjusting to Triple-A pitching—he saw more breaking balls and more of them over for strikes. Part of it was pressing too hard as the slump got worse. Balboni's batting average dipped to a team-worst .195 after an 0-for-3 night on May 21 in Syracuse. He was seventeen for his last eighty-seven. He'd knocked in just eight runs and hadn't homered since opening night. But the next night, Balboni doubled, tripled, and homered. Vernon had tweaked Balboni's stance and had been coaching the big man to relax more at the plate. A week later came The Blast, a home run at Franklin County Stadium that Balboni still remembers vividly. I still remember it, too. I was there, once again with my dad, on a warm, late-spring night.

It came off Richmond's Steve Bedrosian, later an All-Star in Atlanta. In the bottom of the fifth inning, Balboni's three-run shot cleared not only the existing left-center-field fence, but the original brick wall, a good five hundred feet from home plate. It wasn't a towering home run. It was more of a line drive that still appeared to be headed upward as it left the park.

The rest of the International League had been served. The shot stunned the crowd. Stories were told of others—including Joe DiMaggio and Ralph Kiner—clearing that wall, but they were just stories. Only one other man is fully documented as having done it. The mighty Josh Gibson clubbed one over the brick wall in 1933, as a member of the Negro League's Pittsburgh Crawfords, in a game against the Columbus Blue Birds. Many consider Gibson to be the Babe Ruth of the Negro Leagues. Some consider the Babe to be the Josh Gibson of the Major Leagues. When Gibson hit his massive shot in Columbus, the crack of the bat was so loud the home-plate umpire went deaf in his left ear.

For Balboni, The Blast was prologue for a midsummer shredding of the league. He'd overcome his nearly homerless first six weeks of the season and finish the year with thirty-three homers, ten of those coming during a magical half-month stretch.

Balboni had many home runs in his future. He'd wallop 92 during his time with the Clippers and 181 over eleven Major League seasons. He'd win home run titles in six different Minor League seasons and finish his professional career with 420 total homers. Many were monstrous. None would top The Blast, though, in his memories. He'd never feel the ball hit the bat quite like that again. I haven't seen anyone hit the ball like that since.

The Clippers swept a doubleheader from Richmond that night for their fifteenth win in their last twenty games. They were 24-16, a game out of first place, and dominating my eleven-year-old spring.

• • •

It's September 5, 1988, and I'm a few warm nights into my freshman year at Gonzaga University, desperately seeking a point of reference.

Leaving the Bay Area for Spokane, a city far enough away that I couldn't run home every time something went wrong, is one of the smartest things I've ever done. And one of the toughest. I was off to a difficult start. Painfully shy. Lonely. Out of place.

Spokane is most of the way to Canada, near the Washington-Idaho state line, a medium-sized city with ponderosa pine trees and hot, dry summers. It's also the home of the Spokane Indians, a Class-A Northwest League baseball team. Tonight the Indians are playing at home in the third and deciding game of the league's championship series, against the Southern Oregon A's. I don't have a car, and I'm not feeling savvy enough to figure out a bus route to the stadium down by the fairgrounds. But I do have a radio, and KAQQ 590 has the game. Rich Waltz, a play-by-play man barely out of college himself, has the mic. I stretch out on my dorm-room bed and have a listen.

My newly adopted Spokane team ties the game at 2 all in the bottom of the eighth and has the bases loaded with two outs. I'm invested now, in need of something to cheer for. The Southern Oregon pitcher, a lefty with a big windup, named Tony Ariola, has stifled the Indians on two hits for a complete-game win in the opener. Now he's on in relief in game three, to close out the threat and help Southern Oregon secure the title. Spokane's Mike Humphreys—in his first season of professional baseball—dances off third base with the go-ahead and possibly series-winning run. Then he and Indians manager Steve Lubratich stun everyone, including the young broadcaster.

"From the windup," Waltz calls into the Inland Northwest night, amid cheers in the background, "Checks Humphreys . . .

"He's breaking for the plate! Here's the pitch! HE STEALS HOME! Humphreys steals home! Humphreys steals home! The Indians lead it!

"Humphreys steals home! Humphreys steals home! Indians lead it! He broke for the plate! Head-first slide! Humphreys steals home! Humphreys steals home!"

Spokane holds on for the 3–2 win and wins the Northwest League title. Well into the postgame show, Waltz is still out of breath. And I have my point of reference and another core baseball memory.

After that, things seem to get better.

I have a chance to meet Rich Waltz—now a Major League broadcaster—in the summer of 2002, before a Seattle Mariners game at Safeco Field. It's a brief, unexpected introduction by a friend who works with FOX Sports Northwest. I should thank Rich for that call, tell him how much it meant to me. But I inexplicably freeze up and botch the opportunity.

A few innings into the game, it's eating at me. Sitting behind home plate, I tell my friend what happened.

"That would have made that guy's day," he says, his voice thick with disappointment and disbelief. "Maybe his week."

He's right. I've blown it. And I'll regret it for a long time.

So Rich Waltz, if you're reading this, thanks. That call was one of the best ever.

A WEEK BEFORE RICH Waltz, Mike Humphreys, and the Spokane Indians lifted my spirits, my dad did his best to do the same. We sat together in the backyard on my last night at home before leaving for college. I was nervous and upset about leaving, scared about looming adulthood and entering a new phase of life, filled with unknowns. The advice he quietly gave me was simple yet profound. "Take life where you find it." In other words, quit trying to control everything so much, and make the best of whatever life circumstances you find yourself in. Oh, and for God's sake, relax.

Take life where you find it. I'd eventually get better at this. It would take a while, and I'd need a lot of help, but I would.

• • •

On June 11, 1981, a day after a federal judge nixed an injunction sought by the Major League players' union, Los Angeles Dodgers outfielder Jay Johnstone was one of many players who had given up hope for a last-ditch, strike-averting agreement with baseball's owners. Following a game at Busch Stadium, Johnstone posted a message on his locker, letting anyone who cared know that, if needed, he could be found at the Dunes Hotel in Las Vegas.

A few hours later, shortly after the clock struck midnight, exhausted union head Marvin Miller stood before a roomful of reporters and TV cameras on the second floor of Manhattan's Doral Inn, where the two sides had been mired in fruitless talks.

"We have been meeting most of the day," Miller said. "We have accomplished nothing.

"The strike is on."

The owners, via their player relations committee, announced that the season was canceled "until further notice." The Major Leagues went dark.

6

Hello, Baseball

I watched Andre Robertson's game-winning grand slam in person on the night of June 12, without a radio nearby, so I initially missed the Rick Rizzs call that captured the excitement so well. I was delighted to tune into a game from the start a few nights later and hear that clip lead off the broadcast, having replaced a more pedestrian call from earlier in the season, of Brant delivering an RBI single to give Columbus a 2–1 lead. The lead-in included a drumbeat, then a quick flourish of music from a peppy-sounding orchestra. "Heeere's the 1-2 on the way, swung on, fly ball to right field! Going back is Rajsich, near the wall, going, GOING, GOODBYE, BASEBALL! It's a grand slam home run! And the Clippers have won the ballgame, 9 to 8!" A flourish of trumpets and more music. Then a voice-over from a nameless announcer, paying the bills. "Col-UM-bus Clippers baseball is ON the air! This game brought to in part by Budweiser! For all you do, this Bud's for you! And by Gulf Oil! Who suggest you try Gulf Super Unleaded!"

"And now, here's the voice of the Clippers. WBNS sports director, Rick Rizzs!"

Rizzs sent the tape of that June 12 broadcast—along with that of an '82 Minor League pitching showdown between a demoted Righetti and former Major League star Mark "The Bird" Fidrych—to the Seattle Mariners following the 1982 season. The tapes helped him land a play-by-play job with the Mariners, completing his own odyssey to the Major Leagues. He settled in alongside Dave Niehaus, who had been with the Mariners since their first game in 1977 and was already becoming a legendary broadcaster in the Pacific Northwest. Rizzs politely yielded to Niehaus over the years, likening himself to Ed McMahon, to Niehaus's Johnny Carson.

The two of them suffered together through some terrible Mariner teams, particularly during Rizzs's first decade with Seattle. Toward the end of one particularly long season, Niehaus, announcing the end of the fifth inning, noted that he's seen the end of a lot of fifths that year. The two would be dear friends until Niehaus's death in 2010, at which point Rizzs took over the lead role, his heart heavy.

The 2018 season was Rizzs's thirty-third with the Mariners, a tenure uninterrupted save for three challenging years with the Detroit Tigers. During his first season with Detroit, in 1992, Rizzs was one of two announcers tasked with succeeding Ernie Harwell after the iconic broadcaster was ousted in a move that left fans infuriated. They took it out at least partially on Rizzs, unfairly. On his first Opening Day with the team, he was greeted with protest signs and a banner trailing behind a plane with the message, "Bring Back Ernie." Imagine dealing with *that* on your first day at a new job. The Tigers did bring Harwell back the following season but also held onto Rizzs, along with the other would-be Harwell replacement, Bob Rathbun. All three of them remained gracious. But many Tiger fans never warmed to Rizzs and his more enthusiastic broadcast style, nor to Rathbun, and following the '94 season, just before Christmas, the team unceremoniously fired both of them.

Rizzs's grandfather shortened the family name from Rizzitiello when he moved them from Italy to Illinois. That grandfather left the family when Rick's father, Don, was only eleven. As a tough Chicago kid, Don Rizzs struggled and drifted, getting kicked out of high school and leaving home at sixteen to build railroads in the Pacific Northwest for the Civilian Conservation Corps. They kicked him out too. He realized his life needed turning around.

Don Rizzs returned to Illinois, earned his high school degree, went to business school, married Rick's mother, Julie, and built a strong and stable life, working for a crane manufacturer called Whiting Corporation. He came home from work each day, tired, with his clothes smelling of steel from the factory. He still made time to play catch. Over the years, he worked his way up to head of shipping. His life lessons and work ethic were passed on to young Rick, who—to make it through years of arduous work as a Minor League broadcaster—would need every bit of them.

Rick Rizzs grew up in Blue Island, on Chicago's South Side. He adored the Chicago White Sox, but Chicago Cubs broadcaster Jack Brickhouse was his hero. From an early age, Rick turned down the volume on Cubs TV broadcasts and practiced calling the action. He played baseball himself, though not particularly well, and lent his still-lowering voice to a barbershop quartet. In high school, he wrote a letter to Brickhouse, asking for advice on how to become a Major League broadcaster. He received a handwritten response, with words he would take to heart: Get all the school you can. Broaden your education. Work hard.

After graduating from the University of Southern Illinois in 1975, Rizzs landed his first Minor League play-by-play job, with the Alexandria Aces of the Double-A Texas League. Broadcasting was only part of the gig. Rizzs called just three innings a game, and he was also responsible for washing uniforms, shining shoes, and other clubhouse duties. When it rained, he helped pull out the tarp. Along with the players, he endured long bus rides through Arkansas, Mississippi, and Texas, with journeys to El Paso taking sixteen hours or more. For all that, he earned $200 a month, plus tips. Sleep? There wasn't much of that, either, as Rizzs took a graveyard disc jockey shift to supplement his meager baseball income. He subsisted on dinners cooked for him most nights by the wife of the Aces' manager.

Minor League Baseball in South Texas and surrounding states was wild and unpredictable in those days, played on shifting infield dirt. The Alexandria franchise moved to Amarillo for the 1976 season and took Rizzs with it to sell advertising and call the action. Following the season, he'd also call the shots, serving temporarily as the team's GM. A brand-new, Class-A operation, the Gulf States League, had scrambled for a new team that spring after the New Orleans Pelicans folded just weeks before the season started. A team was hastily pulled together for Beeville, Texas. Rizzs, just twenty-two years old, was one of four investors, having plunked $300 on the table during a meeting at a Denny's.

When he wasn't running or investing in baseball teams that year, Rizzs handled play-by-play for the newly minted Amarillo Gold Sox. Promotions that season included visits by baseball "Clown Prince" Max Patkin and Bob Feller. On the Fourth of July, fans helped build the world's largest banana split. Another promotion, Short Night, involved Rizzs himself. He stood in front of the stadium, five foot six and three-quarters. Any adult shorter than him got in for free. The season ended with a title for the Gold Sox and the young broadcaster channeling Russ Hodges. "Popped up, right side, Delyon's under it . . . the Gold Sox win the pennant! The Gold Sox win the pennant!"

The season proved formative. Rizzs got a much-needed pep talk from Texas Rangers announcer Dick Risenhoover, who came through Amarillo as part of a Rangers caravan. Risenhoover's signature calls included "Gooood-byyyye, baseball!" for home runs, a call Rizzs modified and started using himself. It was in part a tribute to Risenhoover, paid after the beloved announcer died of cancer. Rizzs uses the call to this day.

Also in the Texas League, Rizzs crossed paths with the man who would eventually bring him to Columbus, Ohio.

Ken Schnacke grew up near Cleveland, attended Ohio Northern, got a degree in mechanical engineering and came to Columbus in the early '70s to work for the Environmental Protection Agency. His heart was always with baseball, though. Like Rizzs, he wasn't a star player himself, but there had to be a career in the game somewhere. Schnacke connected with Bobby Bragan, an influential Minor League figure, former Texas League president, and the prime mover in the creation of the Gulf States League. They attended baseball's winter meetings together. Schnacke ditched Columbus to pursue his baseball dreams in the Lone Star State.

When Rizzs arrived in Amarillo, Schnacke was the team's business manager, and they roomed together for ten days. Their paths diverged, at least temporarily, when one of the new Gulf States League teams, the Rio Grande Valley WhiteWings, of Harlingen, Texas, needed a GM. Bragan knew just the man for the job.

"Ken, this is what you got into the game for," Bragan told him while clutching a large cigar. Schnacke summoned up his courage, drove 750 miles through the heart of Texas down to the Gulf Coast, and started the WhiteWings out of the trunk of his car.

The Gulf Coast League lasted only one season, but Schnacke was just getting started as a baseball man. He returned to Ohio that winter and joined George Sisler's fledgling Columbus Clippers as an administrative assistant, then steadily ascended. Director of stadium operations. Director of business operations. Assistant GM, then GM, supplanting Sisler. These days, Schnacke is the team's president and GM, overseeing a multiaward-winning ballpark opened in 2009, and a two-time national championship team. The long partnership with the Yankees ended in 2006, and since 2009, the Clippers have been the Triple-A affiliate of the Cleveland Indians.

RIZZS FOLLOWED HIS YEAR in Amarillo with three in Memphis as the voice of the Double-A Memphis Chicks, then a year with the Nashville Sounds—another Double-A, Southern League team. When he got discouraged, he reminded himself that he was on a ten-year plan to reach the Major Leagues and that 1985 was still a ways off.

Following the 1980 season, with John Gordon promoted to the Yankees broadcast crew, WBNS radio and the Columbus Clippers needed a broadcaster. With Schnacke facilitating, Rizzs—now married with a one-year-old son—was brought on board. Short on money, he'd call Clippers games, then be back up for the station's early-morning sports reports. That meant waking up at 4:00 a.m., leaving home by 4:30, and arriving downtown by 5:00. He'd be on the air at 6:00 a.m., yukking it up with Columbus AM staples Jack Evans and Dick "Yeh boy!" Zipf, repeating that every half hour until 9:30. Then it was time go to the ballpark, get ready for the game, sell advertising, and work on promos before calling the action. He'd be up each night until at least eleven. Then he'd wake up at 4:00 a.m. and start over.

To my young ears at least, he never seemed tired. Quite the opposite. Rick Rizzs has always been known for his enthusiasm and positive energy, on and off the air. If you caught his eye from

FIG 11. Rick Rizzs called the action for the Clippers in 1981 and 1982. *Columbus Citizen-Journal*, Scripps Howard Newspapers/Grandview Heights Public Library/Photohio.org.

the stands and waved to him in the press box, he'd wave back. Listening to him that spring and summer, voicing my new heroes, accelerated my budding love for the game. He made each contest and the sport itself seem wonderfully important.

Plus, he looked kind of like Ron Burgundy from *Anchorman*.

Phil Neuman provided color commentary during Clippers homes games, then hosted a sports radio talk show on WBNS after the games. I often stayed up and listened through midnight and into Larry King's coast-to-coast, overnight radio program, unless my parents intervened. Neuman lost touch with Rizzs over the years but would recall him as genuine and easy to work with. "It was like watching the game with a good friend," he'd recall.

For me, too.

America's Team

June 12 was a wild night at Franklin County Stadium, and not just for Robertson's walk-off slam. A large crowd of nearly ten thousand had gathered, talk of the strike and the Tabler trade buzzed, ESPN cameras dotted the stands, and reporters from New York wandered around, trying to orient themselves. Jim Massie recalled one of them accidentally marching into the women's restroom, bumping into Elizabeth "Liz" Sisler, GM George's Southern belle-esque wife, and getting an earful of Scarlett drawl. "Can you forgive me, ma'am?" the reporter asked her. "Ahhh most certainly will not!" she responded.

Another story within that night's narrative involves Steve Taylor. The young pitcher hadn't woken up that morning expecting to be on national television, but that's exactly what happened.

Taylor had been one of those phenoms, a first-round pick of the Yankees four years earlier, out of the University of Delaware. His pro career began with promise. If only the Yankees could have cloned him. Actually, they sort of could. Taylor's identical twin brother, Jeff, also pitched in the organization. It made for some interesting situations. Like the time when Steve started a game for Nashville and pitched the first five innings, then Jeff pitched the final four innings for the save. The Memphis Chicks may not have been sure a reliever ever entered the game. The brothers did have different pitching styles. Steve had a good fastball and a knuckle curve. Jeff relied more on his slider. In later years they'd kid each other that if they'd put their two arms together, they might have had a great career.

Arm injuries sidetracked both Taylor brothers. By '81 Steve Taylor was already attempting a comeback. He was only twenty-five.

He didn't expect to pitch for Columbus that night. He was supposed to start the next night. He'd made the four-hundred-mile drive from Nashville that same day, called up to take Tabler's spot on the roster, arriving just in time to see Robertson end the first game with his walk-off homer. Between games, Taylor was able to get a Clippers uniform, which it turned out he would need, sooner than expected.

Paul Mitchell started the nightcap for Columbus, but his forearm tightened in the third inning. He'd strained it pushing too hard after the Yankees signed him in May, and the injury wouldn't heal. Mitchell's night was over. His baseball career would soon follow. Pitching-starved Verdi had been counting on Mitchell to go at least seven innings. Now Taylor was the only option he had left.

Taylor took the mound with the ESPN cameras rolling, family and friends watching at home. It didn't go well for him. The first five Tides he faced scored. He uncorked a wild pitch ten feet over catcher Brad Gulden's head. To Taylor's credit, he settled down somewhat and gave Verdi and the Clippers five innings they sorely needed, but those five innings came with seven runs—all earned—on nine hits. He didn't know he'd been pitching on national television until after the game, when he spoke to family and friends. You didn't see the best part of me, he told them.

It was Taylor's only appearance for the Clippers that season. After he was demoted back to Nashville, he asked for his release and signed with the Astros organization. He pitched briefly for their Triple-A team in Tucson, but after the season ended, Steve Taylor was out of baseball.

As a player at least. A few years later, Taylor was elected to Delaware's State House of Representatives, and his ten years of service included a tireless push for a new stadium in Wilmington and the return of professional baseball to the city after a forty-year absence. He was elected to Delaware's Sports Hall of Fame in 2003.

THE CLIPPERS OVERCAME MITCHELL'S injury and Taylor's struggles that night, rallying for an 8–7 win. With two outs in the bottom of the seventh, Brant and Balboni cracked back-to-back solo homers to tie the game at 7. A bases-loaded walk in the bottom of the eighth broke the tie, and Columbus held on. With Espino—the smiling catcher—warming up in the bullpen to pitch, dog-tired Jim Lewis heroically pitched the final two innings and earned the win.

By sweeping the showdown, Columbus boosted its lead in the IL standings to three games.

The baseball on display for the nation that night may not have been pretty, nor was it a treat for pitching enthusiasts, but it was exciting. The next day, the phones at the team's office on Mound Street rang off their rotors. Callers from across the nation wanted to find out more about the Clippers. They wanted to talk to Frank Verdi. They wanted merchandise. The Clippers had begun staking their claim as America's team, at least for baseball, at least until the Major League strike was over.

"The Whole Town Is Down"

The weather added to the crazed feeling in the Columbus front office that Saturday. With severe thunderstorm and tornado warnings issued, team officials decided to postpone Saturday night's game. The call was made around 3:00 p.m. That's awfully early, Tides manager Jack Aker thought, especially for a game on artificial turf. He even insinuated via his hometown paper that the Clippers made an early call on postponement to assure rest for their tired pitching arms. The night off certainly benefited Columbus in that regard. Verdi described the rain as a "godsend" when the decision was made.

The thunderstorms—and worse—did materialize, hitting the city around 5:15 that evening. There were lightning strikes, power outages, downed trees, and floods. It was the worst storm to hit Columbus that summer.

Not far from Franklin County Stadium, there were much more dire consequences. At least seven tornadoes touched down in Central Ohio that day. Around 3:45 that afternoon, just forty-five miles north of Columbus, three funnel clouds joined together to form what today would likely be classified as a devastating EF-4.

Evelyn Long lived in the tiny, tree-filled village of Cardington, population two thousand, along Route 42 in Morrow County. She was a reporter for the *Marion Star*, a paper once owned by eventual U.S. president Warren Harding. Evelyn was in nearby Marion that afternoon, about fifteen miles from home, buying furniture with her husband. She glanced at the sky to the east and knew something was wrong.

"There's something going on in Cardington," she said nervously. "Let's go."

In Cardington, volunteer fire chief Jim Ullom was working his regular job at a service station when the sky went dark. Morrow County hadn't been issued a tornado warning. There was no time to blare a siren, and barely enough time for Jim to reach shelter before the tornado hit. From his vantage point, Jim watched much of a trailer park, which had been north of town, rain down nearby. Gas meters, tree limbs, chunks of homes.

The tornado followed Route 42 right through Cardington, felling stately old trees and quaint three-story buildings "like they were matchsticks," Evelyn remembered. Nearly all of the nine-block business district was destroyed. The funeral home took a direct hit, leaving caskets strewn amid the wreckage. To the north, the storm cast trailers into the road like toys. Homes throughout the village suffered heavy damage. It all took less than two minutes.

A stunned amateur radio operator described the scene. "The whole town is down," he said. "I can't believe what I'm looking at. Downtown is wiped out."

Jim Ullom had grown up in Cardington. As a kid he sold popcorn and cold Cokes during movie nights in the park. In 1981 he was eighteen years into what would eventually be fifty years of service with the village fire department. But on this day, he found himself in the middle of town, unsure of which street he was standing on. No landmarks remained.

He called the disaster in on a radio, but a woman on the other end, at a 911 dispatch center, couldn't understand him the first few times. Finally Jim screamed, "A tornado just hit Cardington! Send all the help you can get!"

With his usual route to the fire station blocked, Jim ran through backyards. He arrived to find "half the fire station on top of the trucks." And of his usual thirty-some volunteer firefighters, about half were out of town at a firemen's' festival. Only two smaller trucks were available. Jim took the first through the door, then grabbed an axe and hacked away until the second truck was freed. He rallied rescuers as they arrived. First responders struggled with a five-mile drive to a hospital turning into twenty-five miles as they weaved their way through the devastation.

Like Evelyn, Jim's wife, Vickie, was in Marion when the tornado hit. Driving home, she heard the news on the radio and raced back to Cardington, desperate for word on her husband of eleven years. She arrived at the 911 dispatch center, terrified. Then she heard Jim's voice crackle through over the dispatch radio.

"I heard her on the other end, in the background, her high-pitched voice," Jim remembered, tearing up nearly thirty-five years later at age seventy-one. She was calling out, "That's my husband's voice! He's alright!"

The connection provided one moment of relief on Cardington's darkest day. Four people died. In a village like Cardington most everyone knew, or had known, everyone else.

"I cried," Jim recalled. "I ain't ashamed to admit it. I cried, and I cried a lot."

Fifty-three more were injured. Nearly two hundred homes were damaged, including twenty that were demolished. Looters moved in. Gov. James Rhodes, who at the time called the Cardington tornado "per capita, the worst we've had in the state of Ohio," brought in the National Guard.

Evelyn and her husband returned to learn their own home was

mostly intact. But the destruction in Cardington left Evelyn so shaken and the aftermath was so all-consuming that for three days, she forgot she had a job. When it finally occurred to her that she did, she called her editor at the *Star*. Relief poured through the phone lines. They'd had no idea whether Evelyn was okay.

The village of Cardington battled back. So many of the homeless were taken in by relatives and others that a shelter set up at the school wasn't needed for its intended purpose. It wound up housing National Guard members, volunteers, and others from out of town. The village of Mount Gilead, six miles away, had long been a bitter rival. But as Cardington dug out and recovered, Mount Gilead became a best friend. Government did its job. Loans were obtained. Some businesses didn't survive, but most business owners stayed and rebuilt, as did nearly every resident. Trees were replanted. Buildings were reconstructed, albeit single story. Cardington would never be the same, but it's still there.

"People just jumped in," Evelyn recalled years later. "There was no way they weren't going to. Everybody stayed, rallied, and rebuilt. And lots of people helped from the outside."

Drive from Columbus to Cardington on a spring day in this century, on a rising and falling ribbon of road, and you'll pass stands of trees, churches, farms, signs advertising raw honey. In the rebuilt town itself, there are no obvious signs of what happened on June 13, 1981. But to those who know, Cardington, Ohio, is a monument to resiliency.

Tornado warnings, accompanied by tv alerts with radar readouts and howls from an air-raid siren that scared me as a young boy, were not uncommon in Columbus. The following season, Franklin County Stadium provided the backdrop for as bizarre a baseball-weather story as you'll encounter. Clippers historian Joe Santry re-creates the scene in his unpublished book "Grazing through Columbus Baseball":

> On the evening of June 16, 1982, the skies darkened in the middle of the game between the Clippers and Richmond. Suddenly,

Columbus pitcher Lynn McGlothen pointed to the skies over the bleachers and cried, "TORNADO!" and bolted for the dugout. The rest of the Clippers glanced over their shoulders and didn't see anything. They looked at one another for a second, then not taking any chances, raced for the safety of the dugout.

An instant later, a thunderstorm hit. Fans scurried for cover. Adding to the confusion, a bolt of lightning struck the light tower over the third base grandstand, temporarily knocking out the lights and telephone lines. Suddenly, over one of the wire services flashed:

AAA.RICHMOND.AT.COLUMBUS.GAME.IS.POSTPONED.DUE.TO.A.FATAL.TORNADO.HITTING.

THE.STADIUM.RESULTING.IN.FATALITIES.AND.MANY.INJURIES.AMONG.THE.PLAYERS.

With the telephones out, no one could call and verify the story. CNN reported the story nationally. The storm was over in minutes and soon the lights were back on at the stadium. The game was suspended and the players from both teams stood in line in their uniforms to phone home on the only working phone in the neighborhood: The pay phone across Mound Street at the filling station.

There were also real tragedies around the Clipper teams of that era.

McGlothen, who starred at Grambling and pitched in the Majors from '72 to '81, died in a mobile home fire in 1984, in his native Louisiana.

In 1979 pitcher Rick Anderson helped the Clippers win their first IL pennant and Governors' Cup with a 13-3 record and an eye-popping twenty-one saves. He posted a miniscule 1.63 ERA. It was good enough for Anderson to be named MVP of the International League, but only good enough to earn him one brief appearance for the Yankees that September, and with no room on Steinbrenner's roster, he was shipped to the Seattle Mariners after the season. Still, it appeared Anderson and his devastating slider had finally made it after eight years in the Minors.

In 1980 Anderson made a handful of appearances for the Mariners. He also blew out his overworked arm. An attempted comeback the following season didn't last long, and Anderson's once-promising baseball career ended.

Anderson loved the game. And he loved the ride. But it was time to get off, and the transition didn't go well. Without baseball, Anderson drifted into depression and became increasingly withdrawn. He worked in construction and drove a truck to get by. But friends and family—including his wife, whom he'd met on a Florida beach one spring training—described a man who'd gone from living his dream to having his essence drained away. They saw him less and less frequently.

In June of 1989, Rick Anderson's body was found in a trailer in a Southern California boatyard. He'd been dead several days, his heart having given out. He was just thirty-five. Anderson's weight, just over two hundred pounds in his playing days, had ballooned to over four hundred. In his hand, he clutched a letter from a fan with a request for an autograph.

THERE ARE SOME PARALLELS between Anderson's story and that of Bob Kammeyer, another pitcher who starred for Columbus in '79 and '80.

Had Kammeyer stayed with the Yankees organization in 1981, Columbus might have won one hundred games that season. He was the reigning International League Most Valuable Pitcher, an ace who would later be inducted into the league's Hall of Fame. Add him to an already talented and gutsy staff, on a team that could hit like the Clippers, and you go from "exceptional" to "best-team-of-the-era" discussions, maybe higher. But Kammeyer wasn't there for the '81 season. That spring he retired in a cloud of frustration and practicality. He'd won forty-three games over three seasons at the Triple-A level. All three of those teams won championships. In the Majors, though, it had never come together for the tall right-hander out of Richardson, Texas.

Kammeyer pitched in seven games for the Yankees in '78, finishing with a lofty ERA of 5.82. In 1979 he made only one appearance for New York, and the opportunity turned into an epic nightmare. Against the Cleveland Indians, on September 18, Kammeyer gave up two homers, two doubles, and eight earned runs without recording an out, giving him an ERA of infinity for the season and ensuring that he'd never again pitch for Steinbrenner's Yankees. He also eventually landed—unfairly—on some "worst player of all time" lists. On top of all that, he was caught up in a small scandal. In the middle of Kammeyer's infamous outing, he plunked Cleveland's burly Cliff Johnson, who'd been traded from the Yankees that season after a fight with Goose Gossage. When the inning finally ended and Kammeyer slunk back to the dugout, manager Billy Martin handed him five twenty-dollar bills. Reports charged that Martin had paid Kammeyer to intentionally hit Johnson. Both Kammeyer and Martin denied any such arrangement. It was just beer money for after a rough outing, Martin said, to eye rolls and chuckles. A league investigation later cleared the Yankee manager.

Kammeyer enjoyed unquestionable success in the Minors, though his gaze was sometimes fixed elsewhere. Older than most of his teammates, the Stanford graduate pursued a CPA certificate during the season, sometimes pulling out a briefcase on the team bus for study time. Massie remembers Kammeyer as "the adult in the group," though he did have his wilder moments.

"Once in a while," former IL umpire Bill Emslie recalled, "he'd say 'Fuck it, I'm going with the derelicts.'"

By the spring of '81, Kammeyer had had enough. His outstanding work with the Clippers the previous season hadn't motivated the Yankees to boost his $20,000-a-year salary. No other teams seemed very interested, though the Padres offered yet another Minor League contract. Kammeyer was now thirty-one, and it felt increasingly late to start another career. His wife, Francine, had just opened a law practice in California. And that CPA exam was looking better and better. He gave up the game, far short of his dreams.

Eventually, playing in senior leagues and coaching youth baseball helped with the pain. He got that CPA certificate. He worked at a bank, a life insurance company, and as a tax consultant. He took care of his family. Still, Bob Kammeyer was never the same after his professional baseball career ended. He was never happy in any career after that. Everything he did worked out, at least financially, but he never enjoyed any of it.

On January 27, 2003, Bob Kammeyer collapsed at work and died suddenly at the age of fifty-two. Broken dreams aren't usually blamed for pulmonary embolisms, but Francine sees her late husband's sadness as a contributor to his death. She says she would never have changed him, though. If he hadn't loved baseball so much, he wouldn't have been the man she loved so much.

JOE SANTRY CAN TELL you all about these players and bygone eras of Columbus baseball. He can fill you in on *any* era of baseball, in Columbus or elsewhere.

The Clippers' bespectacled team historian and jack-of-many-trades since 1981 has an office at the Clippers' current home, Huntington Park, but good luck finding him in it. He'd rather be in the press box, or around the ballpark somewhere, sometimes to complete one of the many tasks he handles for the team, sometimes just to "be." For baseball fans who find themselves in Columbus, it's worth asking nicely to see if he's available to give a tour of Huntington.

The new park is more intimate than its predecessor, with about ten thousand seats compared to Franklin County/Cooper Stadium's fifteen thousand, and more of an old-timey feel. Huntington is also a museum of sorts, with nods everywhere to baseball in Columbus and beyond. On a walk around the park, you may see a Derek Jeter Clippers jersey, a retired Marshall Brant jersey, a bat used by Cleveland Indians great Rocky Colavito, a catcher's mitt dating back to 1900, baseball spikes from the Civil War era, and numerous photos of the city's greatest teams. It's lovingly done, and Santry provided a lot of that love after the team budgeted for the acquisition of numerous baseball artifacts.

If Santry is leading the tour, he'll fill your head with tales of Columbus baseball, relaying them as easily as he could recite the alphabet. The city's most epic home runs. Babe Ruth's visits. The numerous Hall of Famers who've come through. The time the grandstands at one of the city's old stadiums collapsed when everyone sat down after the national anthem. All that history lives inside Santry's head, and he loves to share it. He'll make you believe he's got the coolest job in the world, despite the long hours he keeps during the season. Some "shifts" top sixteen hours.

He grew up on the city's east side, in a family of twelve, and fell in love with the game early. Neither tickets nor time with his father—at least one-on-one time—were easy to obtain, so Joe savored every chance to combine the two. His dad taught him how to keep score, how to whistle down a vendor. He bought Joe his first media guide.

Young Joe once won tickets from a local barber, who let kids draw from a large bowl for a chance at box seats. The young man had just talked the barber's ear off about baseball, and in hindsight, Joe figures the barber made sure the tickets found their way into his young hands.

Another day, Joe opted to look at baseball cards instead of paying attention to a school lesson in long division. Rather than punish him, his teacher had Joe flip the cards over and explained that batting averages are calculated using long division. Interest kindled. Before long, the teacher had Joe giving weekly "who's hot–who's not" baseball reports to the class.

A lifelong love affair with baseball stories and stats was underway.

• • •

In the internet age, you can watch any number of Minor League Baseball games, or listen to the radio broadcasts, from pretty much anywhere. In 1981, playing on TV was a big deal for most Minor Leaguers. Playing before a national TV audience was unheard of.

When Tucker Ashford found out ESPN would be carrying Clippers games during the strike, he called his parents in tiny Covington, Tennessee. Now ubiquitous, ESPN wasn't so widely available back then. Nobody in Covington had it yet. Ashford advised his family to find a town that did. His parents found such a place in Dyersburg, hopped on Highway 3, and drove thirty-seven miles north. They stayed in motels with the cable network, just to get a chance to see Tucker play on TV.

During one of those games, Ashford drilled a ball down the left-field line but was thrown out trying to stretch a double into a triple. His brother Alan saw the whole thing go down on ESPN and provided this postgame encouragement on the phone:

"What are you, stupid? You've got Steve Balboni hitting behind you!"

ESPN wasn't the only place on TV for desperate, strike-time baseball fans. The USA Network picked up a few Minor League games and replayed highlights from big league contests. NBC rebroadcast parts of the '75 World Series.

Other outlets tried filling space with nonbaseball programming, with limited success. ABC tried a movie of the week on Monday nights. When the '75 Series failed to deliver ratings, NBC considered windsurfing coverage.

Around the radio dial, several Major League networks were about to get a dose of the Minors, with familiar voices calling the action.

7

"This Is Phil Rizzuto from Norfolk, Virginia"

HALF PAST JUNE, AND Phil Rizzuto had never felt more relaxed. The beloved Yankee shortstop, now beloved Yankee broadcaster, was taking full advantage of the Major League Baseball strike, vacationing in South Carolina, playing golf, working on his tan, and getting ready to celebrate his thirty-eighth wedding anniversary. The trademark "Holy Cow!" call, the bizarre tangents during broadcasts, the insightful and/or hilarious exchanges with broadcast partners Bill White, Frank Messer, and Fran Healy—all that could wait for a while. It was time to rest. Even if it weren't time, Rizzuto would have rested anyway. Doing as little work as possible and enjoying life—that was how the "Scooter" did things.

Rizzuto heard from the doubters as he transitioned to broadcasting nearly twenty-five years earlier. No less of an authority than Howard Cosell once told him he'd never make it. "You look like George Burns," Cosell told Rizzuto. "And you sound like Groucho Marx." But Rizzuto reinvented himself—or maybe he just allowed himself to be reinvented—and he became an icon all over again.

Rizzuto got away with a lot, on and off the air. He helped coach the Yankees during spring training, but he was known to slip away and head home early. Verdi once attempted to cover for him but couldn't prevent Steinbrenner from finding out and "firing" Rizzuto. The Scooter pulled similar stunts as a broadcaster, sometimes telling his wife, Cora, and the listening audience that he was heading home, before leaving an empty chair in the booth during the late innings. And when he *was* in the press box, Rizzuto was attention-span challenged. Among the K's, 6-3's, and F-8's on his scorecard, you might find a WW, which stood for "wasn't watching."

This time, baseball strike or not, Rizzuto wasn't able to wriggle out of his assignment. His South Carolina phone rang, and some huckleberry was on the line with word that the Yankees, WABC, and Adler Communications were reassembling the broadcast crew to fill the strike void with Columbus Clippers games and that they needed the Scooter. On the night of June 20, Rizzuto found himself three-hundred-some miles to the north, sitting alongside his broadcast partners in a row of tables in the open air behind home plate, signing on to call Columbus at Tidewater. "This is Phil Rizzuto from Norfolk, Virginia . . ." he announced in a surreal open. At least he and Cora got to celebrate that wedding anniversary in Norfolk, which oddly enough was the city in which they'd wed, in 1943.

The Yankees weren't alone in dispatching their varsity announcers to the relative sticks. Ralph Kiner and the rest of the New York Mets play-by-play crew sat at the next table over that night. On July 1 in Columbus, Rizzuto took notice of Cleveland Indians announcer Herb Score, in town as a new voice of the Charleston Charlies.

"Poor Herb Score is drooling over there," Rizzuto described to his listeners and broadcast partner Bill White. "You know he works the games all alone? Actually, all you need is one man to do the games."

"What are you saying?" White asked back.

"I'm saying we got three guys here," Rizzuto said.

"But what do you suggest to Adler?"

"That I take a trip home! Or one of us!"

"That's what I thought you were saying," White said with a chuckle.

Listeners along the Yankees radio network were treated to plenty of exchanges you wouldn't have heard from any other crew, perhaps even more so than during regular Yankees broadcasts.

"Didja ever hear of deer flies?" Rizzuto asked White later in the game, unprompted in any way.

"What?"

"These flies that are flying around, they're deer flies and they bite! And they were all over the golf course today. At least that's what they call 'em in Columbus, deer flies."

"Hmm," White responded, going with it. "D-E-E-R or D-E-A-R?"

"No, D-E-E-R," Rizzuto said.

"No deers down here in Columbus."

"Are you kiddin'? Oh no wait a minute, it was South Carolina I saw a lot of deer."

"So maybe that's where you saw the flies, too."

"Yeh . . . maybe you're right. Well, you know I hate anything that flies, except birds. Anything that crawls or hops."

During an earlier broadcast, Rizzuto wandered off into a story about his son-in-law's sojourns to Utah for a business venture.

Rizzuto: "They've got something going on out there that's unbelievable!"

Messer: "Can you tell us about it?"

Rizzuto: "YES I can certainly tell you . . . No-o-o-o-o, I might not be able to. Because it might drive the stock up and then I'd get in trouble. I remember Walter Winchell got in trouble like that once."

Amid those nontraditional moments, the big league broadcasters adeptly brought Minor League scenes to life. Messer described Verdi's reaction to Clipper reliever Jim Lewis coughing up a lead-off walk—"I thought that thunder cloud had come over." White likened the artificial surface at Franklin County Stadium to a pool table and shared a story about Charleston manager Frank Lucchesi once protesting an umpire's call by climbing a light pole. Healy broke down the issues he saw in the struggling Pacella's delivery and interviewed prospects from the stands. Rizzuto likened a particularly sweltering day in Norfolk to a time he, Yogi Berra, and Hank Bauer fried an egg on the roof of the dugout at Yankee Stadium. The Scooter even broke out one of his signature calls for a massive Balboni home run against the Charlies during the July 1 game, off an overmatched lefty named Rob Pietroburgo:

"The 3-0 pitch [crack of the bat] and he hit's one and IT's GONE. HOLEEE COW ON A 3-0 PITCH, HE HIT ONE NINE MILES over that left-field fence! Bill and I were hoping he'd give him the green light, HEEE got it!"

"That is awesome, raw power there!"

For a while at least, it worked from a commercial standpoint. WABC held onto 80-plus percent of its usual audience during the initial broadcasts from Tidewater. Executive producer Art Adler had his theories.

"My listeners were not all of a sudden starting to read hardcover books," Adler told the *Columbus Dispatch*. "As much as these people are Yankee fans, the people who listen are Rizzuto, White, Messer, and Healy fans. It's that warm, friendly umbilical cord every night."

At the outset, Adler and the Yankees radio network planned to carry Clippers games until the strike was over. But after the July 1 Charleston game, they pulled the proverbial plug, leaving listeners along the Yankees radio network in search of another umbilical cord for the next six weeks or so.

• • •

There were times that season when the Clippers' offensive array just didn't seem fair. June 19 was one of those times. Against the visiting Pawtucket Red Sox, Columbus rolled across eleven runs in the first inning. Patterson doubled and hit a grand slam in the first. Werth singled, doubled, and knocked in a pair of runs in the frame. Brad Gulden, the team's new catcher, chipped in a two-run triple.

By the time the score reached 13–0 in the second, someone in the PawSox dugout literally threw out a white towel.

The San Diego Chicken was in town, performing before a season-best crowd of twelve thousand plus. Pawtucket manager Joe Morgan should have asked him if he could pitch. Instead the Chicken mock-taunted the PawSox, sticking his big beak into their dugout and putting hexes on their pitchers, as if any were needed. Poor Keith MacWhorter lasted just a third of an inning and gave up seven runs. Wilhelmus "Win" Remmerswaal, Pawtucket's brilliant-but-eccentric Dutchman, stayed in the game for five and two-thirds innings but surrendered six more runs.

Perhaps Remmerswaal was tired because it was after 2:00 a.m. in Holland. He'd once asked Morgan to avoid putting him into games after the sixth inning due to the lateness of the hour in his native country, not cracking a smile as he did. Morgan just shook his head.

Teammates and fans have shared many more anecdotes about Remmerswaal, a textbook free spirit who somehow was not left-handed. There were paychecks Remmerswaal just never cashed. At one point during the '81 season, he simply left the team for several days before reappearing. "He went up to Rochester," Morgan said. "Somewhere he had never been. Maybe Niagara Falls."

Remmerswaal pitched for Boston during parts of the '79 and '80 seasons, becoming the first player born and raised in Europe to make the Majors. Red Sox manager Don Zimmer once called the bullpen to get Remmerswaal up and throwing. The pitcher was already up—in the stands buying himself a snack. Later that season, he had a pizza delivered to Boston's bullpen. On another occasion, in New York, he arrived at the stadium and went to the locker room, only to find the New York Jets were using it. He'd taken a cab but wound up at Shea Stadium instead of Yankee Stadium.

Remmerswaal was about as colorful a character as you'll find, but the larger story took a sad turn. He suffered through numerous arm injuries and increasingly turned to alcohol. His nickname of "Win" was supplanted by "Last Call Remmerswaal." The heavy drinking eventually overcame him, and in 1997 he was confined to a wheelchair in his native Netherlands, having spent time in a coma after cases of pneumonia and pleurisy led to severe brain damage.

IN PART DUE TO the efforts of Remmerswaal, Pawtucket actually *battled back* that night in Columbus, at least somewhat. Remmerswaal settled down and kept the Clippers off the scoreboard until the seventh. The PawSox pulled within five runs before the Clippers tacked on two more—on a two-run triple by Werth—and won 15–8. Columbus maintained a three-game lead against Tidewater.

• • •

Around this time, word came from the Smithsonian Institution in Washington DC that George Washington's false teeth were missing. It seemed that on or around June 19, someone accessed the basement of the American Museum of Natural History and swiped them.

They hadn't been made of wood, as many believed. This particular set included ivory, gold, and what appeared to be some actual teeth from others, possibly animals. The set included an inscription that read, "This was the great Washington's teeth." Museum curators were extremely upset to discover they were missing, an inside job was suspected, the FBI was brought in, and an investigation ensued.

The lowers turned up the following May in a Smithsonian storeroom. The uppers were never found and may have been melted down.

"It's better to have half the teeth rather than none," a Smithsonian spokesman said.

• • •

By late June, the Tides were fading and the Richmond Braves were emerging as the Clippers' chief antagonist. Richmond pulled within six and a half games of first place on June 25, clubbing Columbus 10–5 at Parker Field. Brant, my main hero and the reigning league MVP, was struggling. An 0-for-5 night dropped his average to .235.

His uncharacteristic hot start to the season had morphed into an uncharacteristic cold middle. He'd grown fearful of taking strikes and was swinging at bad pitches. The struggles in his head were raging, as they had throughout his career:

You gotta be kidding me. How do you miss that pitch?

Don't chase that slider. Don't go after that. Don't be fooled again.

What are you doing? I must have dropped my hands.

YOU BIG FUCKIN' . . . Okay, stay back. Be patient. I'm not going to let that happen again. I'm not gonna look stupid.

Brant's best chance to make an impression in the Majors may have come during the tail end of the 1980 regular season.

He'd had that monster campaign in his first season with the Clippers: .289, twenty-three homers, ninety-two RBIs, and an .898 OPS (a stat that combines slugging percentage and on-base percentage), the International League MVP Award, and Topps Minor League Player of the Year honors.

That's what it took for Brant to get the briefest of looks from the Yankees that October. The "look" would amount to six plate appearances in a handful of meaningless games, following weeks on the bench. But Brant, finally in the Majors, drank in the Yankees clubhouse.

He initially shared a locker with pitching coach Clyde King. After a quick glance at the name above the locker, Reggie Jackson offered Brant a welcome.

"How do you do, Mr. King," the slugger said, "I'm Reggie Jackson."

Brant's first encounter with Steinbrenner didn't go much better. "Hello Mr. Steinbrenner," Brant said to the Yankees owner in passing one day. "Hi, Bob," Steinbrenner said back.

For their part, the fans at Yankee Stadium didn't seem all that happy to see Brant. One Archie Bunker–type in particular, sitting close to the field as Brant played, complained loudly.

"Gimme the program," the man said. "Who is this? Where's Piniella? Where's Spencer? I paid all this money to see *these* guys?"

Some things would prove difficult for Brant to unsee, among them Goose Gossage and Lou Piniella in the clubhouse after New York clinched the division title and the booze ran out. Both naked, they chased down an also-naked and startled Luis Tiant, held him down and smeared milk, peanut butter, and jelly from the clubhouse fridge on the pitcher's hairy body.

Other moments were somber. Like the time Brant headed toward a seemingly abandoned locker, fully intending to claim it, before he was grabbed and stopped short by former Clipper teammate Roger Holt.

"What are you doing?" Holt said. "Look at the number above it. It's Thurman's."

The beloved Yankee captain's locker was frozen in time, untouched since Munson's death in a plane crash fourteen months prior, one of many corners of the clubhouse that oozed history. Iconic Yankees clubhouse attendant Pete Sheehy oozed plenty of history on his own.

"How long you been doing this?" Brant asked Sheehy one day.

"See that picnic table?" Sheehy said, glancing over at a modest-looking table with a couple of dozen balls, some pens, magazines, and newspapers on it. "I can remember watching Babe Ruth and Lou Gehrig playing cards at that table."

IN THE BOTTOM OF the ninth inning of the second game of a doubleheader, on the second-to-last day of the 1980 regular season, Brant led off with the Yankees trailing Detroit 7–6. He'd had two at bats as a Yankee, striking out both times.

Bob Sheppard, the Yankees' iconic public-address announcer, leaned into his mic. "The first baseman, Marshall Brant."

"Got a big league hit yet?" Tigers catcher Jim Wockenfuss asked Brant as he prepared for the at bat.

"Not yet," Brant responded.

"Okay," Wockenfuss said. "What do you want to hit?"

"Pardon me?"

"What would you like to hit?"

"Something straight?" Brant answered, unsure what to think.

Wockenfuss flashed the sign, and Tigers pitcher Aurelio Lopez grooved one for Brant. Right down the middle. But Brant didn't budge. Strike one.

"*What* are you *waiting for*?" Wockenfuss asked, laughing.

"I thought you were kidding," Brant said.

Now home-plate umpire Mike Reilly was laughing too.

Lopez served up another. Right down the middle, straight as a baseline. This time, Brant took a cut. But those fears—of failure, being made a fool of, looking bad—were still rattling around in the back of his mind. And his swing had a dash of tentative in it.

Brant flew out to the warning track in right. Another moment for the "what might have been" file.

The following day, in the regular-season finale, Brant went 0 for 3 with another strikeout. He did finish a 2–1 Yankee win, their 103rd of the season, by snaring a line drive and turning an unassisted double play at first base.

He wasn't part of the postseason roster. He'd never play for the Yankees again.

BRANT FIGURED HE NEEDED fifty Major League at bats to settle in and hit the ball like he had in the Minors. He even tried to negotiate a guarantee when he tested the waters with other teams like the Blue Jays and White Sox following the 1980 season. Just guarantee me fifty at bats, he asked. I don't care when they happen, late September, whenever. I just need fifty.

Necessary for his success or not, it was an unusual request that potential suitors weren't willing to consider. And of course, time to settle in was exactly the opposite of what the Yankees had in mind. The big club was infamously impatient with young players. Struggle early and you'd most likely be gonged off the stage before getting a chance to find your groove. Brant, perhaps unfairly, developed a reputation as a strikeout-prone, 4-A-ish player. The Yankees' patience with him was virtually nonexistent.

Former Yankees executive Bill Livesey described the situation many years later with a whiff of regret.

"I think Marshall Brant did about everything he could have done," Livesey recalled, "except get with a club that had patience with younger players. That wasn't us. In the end, you have to do what the group wants to do, and that group was led by George Steinbrenner.

"We didn't take the time to see people through. If you didn't hit the ground running . . . 'Next!'"

As JUNE OF '81 wound down, Brant heated up and helped fuel another Clipper surge. On June 27 he tied a game at Pawtucket's McCoy Stadium with an RBI double in the seventh, then put the Clippers up 6–3 with a three-run blast in the fifteenth. Columbus held on to win, overcoming four hits by Pawtucket's Wade Boggs. Brant homered again the next afternoon. Then again the following night. The Clippers started to put some distance between themselves and the rest of the league, flirting with a double-digit lead in the standings. Most of the games during Brant's hot streak were

1981 Columbus Clippers
Outfielder
GARRY SMITH—13

FIG 12. Garry Smith's 1981 baseball card. Courtesy of the Columbus Clippers.

broadcast on ESPN, WABC radio, or both. For players like Brant, buried in the Yankees system, it was a rare chance for exposure.

GARRY SMITH THOUGHT THE strike-fueled media blitz around the team was pretty cool. In the June 29 game at Pawtucket, another game broadcast back to New York on WABC, he provided a glimpse of why *he'd* been one of the Yankees' top prospects just a couple of years before.

In his first three seasons of pro ball, Garry Smith was a Minor League superstar. His first-season OPS was a hefty 1.045. In '78 with

Tacoma—then the Yankees' top farm club—Smith did it all, hitting .325 with thirty doubles, thirteen homers, seventy-three RBIs and twenty-one steals. He was one of the best defensive outfielders in the organization, known for his throwing arm. When he broke his wrist toward the end of the season in a collision at home plate, the Yankees flew him to New York for treatment. The Boss handed him $5,000 and told him he was slated to play for the Yankees by 1980.

A long series of setbacks followed.

In '79 Smith began having issues with his swing. He experimented but only made it worse. He was lunging at the ball. His confidence plummeted. Just sixty-one games in, he broke his ankle and missed the rest of the season. Smith was poised to bounce back the following year, hitting .400 in spring training and nearly making the big club. But after struggling at the plate with the Clippers, he found himself all the way down in Double-A Nashville. He struggled there too.

The Yankees insisted on an eye exam. Smith felt he could see fine but agreed to the test. He was diagnosed with astigmatism and fitted with glasses. Over the rest of the season he hit .369, and it appeared the old Garry Smith was back.

Now, like so many of his teammates, he found himself stuck at the Triple-A level with nowhere to go. A glut of outfielders, particularly in right field, hurt his chances even more. Playing time was elusive, as was getting in any sort of groove. He entered the June 29 game hitting just .225.

In the top of the third, Smith gave the Clippers a 2–1 lead with a two-run shot off the scoreboard in left-center, one of three hits he'd have on the night. In the bottom of the fifth, Pawtucket's Boggs—who'd already had eight hits in the series' first three games on his way to the IL batting title—drew a base on balls, bringing Julio Valdez to the plate. WABC's Frank Messer described what happened next.

"Ground ball right side, it's through, base hit into right field," Messer called. "Down to second goes Boggs, on his way to third, the throw to third and he . . . is OUT AT THIRD BASE! What a throw from Garry Smith into third baseman Dave Coleman, who put the tag on Boggs!"

"Couple seasons ago in spring training, the biggest prospect with the Yankee ballclub," color announcer Fran Healy noted. "Since then, he's suffered a number of injuries.

"Tough break. I tell you, so many things can determine your career."

For the one-time phenom, the game was the best of the '81 season, which he finished with a batting average of just .239. His once mighty OPS fell to .649, the lowest of his career. After putting up similar numbers between Nashville and Columbus the following season, he opted to retire.

"There are a lot of me's out there," Smith noted years later, having built a successful career in real estate back in his native Maine. "You know you'll need some breaks going in, but . . . a lot of good players never make it."

THAT NIGHT IN PAWTUCKET, the Clippers led 5–1 early before the Red Sox rallied. Pawtucket pulled within 8–7 in the bottom of the eighth inning and put the lead-off man on against George Frazier in the bottom of the ninth. Then it was Robertson's turn to star. Just inserted into the lineup for defense, Robertson made a diving stop of a Sam Bowen liner at short, sprang up, got the out at second himself, then threw to first for a double play. End of threat. The Clippers held on to win and extended their lead over second-place Tidewater to six and a half games. Before long, that lead would nearly double.

"Don't Start Anything You Can't Finish"

"Are you sure you want to do that?"

Harvest "Boe" Robertson heard that question more than a few times, either directly or indirectly. Most folks were well-meaning in asking. It was a legitimate thing to wonder about in mid-1960s Orange, Texas.

Are you sure you want to be the city's first black Little League coach? Are you sure you want your son, Andre, to be Orange's first black Little League player? He's only eight years old. Some people won't like it. There will be awkward moments, animosity, whispers, maybe outright slurs. Are you ready for that?

Boe and Andre were ready, and well-equipped. Each commanded respect in his own way. Neither left any doubt that he belonged. They had a way of neutralizing the integration issue, making it seem unimportant. That was no small feat in southeast Texas. Orange was further along on tolerance than most cities in the region, but you didn't have to go far for a full dose of segregation and hate. Andre still remembers the "colored only" signs in nearby Jasper. Up the road in Vidor, they burned crosses on the highway.

The Robertsons lived on a long lot on Barkins Street, with two enormous tallow trees out front, side by side. As Andre grew up, there were giants around, in stature and otherwise. Boe had played quarterback for Texas coaching legend Willie Ray Smith—Bubba Smith's father—at old Wallace High School in Orange. Boe's high school teammates included future NFL star and professional wrestler Ernie Ladd, and the two men were still friends. Andre's boyhood memories include the six-foot-nine, 330-pound Ladd gently lifting him high into one of the tallows.

Innocence marked the era. Young Andre and his siblings played basketball around the back of the house, where a wooden backboard had been nailed to another tree. They shot marbles. They played baseball on a big, empty lot in front of their house on countless warm afternoons. The Baptist church they attended was only a couple of blocks away. And the city's main drag, now seven lanes in spots, was just two at its widest back then.

Boe Robertson was only five foot six but tough and strong. Once when young Andre was struggling with a 110-pound weight set, his father grabbed the whole set with a laugh and lifted it repeatedly over his head with ease, with one hand. When discipline was needed, there was no laughter. Andre got the belt all the way up to age sixteen, the last one coming when some horseplay with his sister ended in a split lip for her. Their father rarely raised his voice. He didn't need to. The Robertson kids were known for being respectful, and their whole family was respected in the community, across racial backgrounds.

"Whenever Boe Robertson spoke, people listened," recalled Harold Fuqua, one of Andre's high school coaches and a family friend. "Shit, when he walked into a room, everyone knew who Boe was. And everybody respected him."

Boe worked for nearly forty years as a mechanic in a nearby chemical plant. He often disappeared into long shifts, sometimes even picking up extra holiday duty so coworkers could spend more time with *their* families. But Boe and his wife, Julia—another powerful force—always managed to show up at the games once their children started playing organized sports.

No one remembers Boe living out his own unfinished athletic business through his children, but it might have been understandable. After graduating from high school, he received a scholarship offer to play quarterback from Tennessee Tech. He had to turn it down, though, so he could stay home and work in a grocery store to help support his parents and siblings. He continued to provide without fail as his own family grew. "I'm going to give you everything you need," he'd tell his children. "You may not get everything you want."

WHEN ANDRE STARTED LITTLE League, he didn't see the different colors. He knew of Jackie Robinson and the breaking of the color barrier in the Major Leagues, but Robinson wasn't his hero. Andre was a bigger fan of Willie Mays. For the quiet young Texan, the slurs and other racially charged adversity didn't come until later. For now, he would take his place alongside the white Little Leaguers in the heat of Gulf Coast afternoons, the air almost tangible with humidity and fumes from a nearby paper mill. He'd outplay them all, and he'd keep the color of his skin a nonissue.

He did have a lot to learn about the protocols of the game, despite his father's instruction. The first time Andre took the mound to pitch, he launched into his delivery right as the umpire was bending over to dust off the plate, and nearly hit him in the rear end. Andre was a quick study, though. Before long, he stopped getting pitches to hit as he wore out opposing teams. He was increasingly focused on the field, where only the sound of his father's shrill whistling would distract him.

He'd excel at every sport he could find. Well, maybe not so much in basketball, but his father wasn't going to let him quit. "Don't start anything you can't finish," Boe would tell Andre and his siblings.

AT WEST ORANGE HIGH, Andre set a school record with a six-seven high jump, a mark he jokes can never be broken because West Orange no longer exists, at least not on its own since a merger with archrival Stark High School in 1978.

He played for two years on the varsity football team, during which time he starred, but his team only won seven games. Andre, just 150 pounds, replaced the coach's son at quarterback in a rivalry game against Stark during his junior year. He was one of the league's best defensive backs. He even kicked extra points. "But we didn't have many of those," he'd recall.

He was already magical on the baseball field. At West Orange, he wore purple and played on a field beside railroad tracks with dugouts made from creosote polls and fishing nets. Ronnie Anderson, his feisty coach, nicknamed him "Andre Magic" and "Silk." At shortstop, Andre gobbled up grounders and line drives and bad hops, and he made plays deep in the hole that should have been against the league rules, they were so far beyond what his peers were capable of. He was a slugger back then, sometimes clearing those railroad tracks with long home runs.

"Why do we *lead off* with Andre?" Fuqua drawled to Anderson one day.

"Because a lot of times after the first pitch, we're up 1–0," Anderson drawled back.

The soft-spoken shortstop was all-everything throughout his high school career. After his senior season in '76, he had a chance to play at the Houston Astrodome in the Texas High School All-Star Baseball Game, prior to the Astros' game against the powerhouse Cincinnati Reds. Andre took the opportunity to request an autograph from Reds star Ken Griffey Sr.

Griffey still remembered meeting Andre years later, when both of them played for the New York Yankees. It helped that Andre was the only black player on the field for the All-Star Game that day, and that he was wearing that garish purple uniform.

As Yankee teammates in the mid-'80s, Griffey and Andre lived in the same building in Guttenberg, New Jersey, along with another teammate, famed scatterbrain Rickey Henderson. Andre paid $1,100 a month for an unfurnished, one-bedroom apartment and had to handle his own cable hookup. Henderson, a superstar, had a fully furnished, fully loaded apartment.

"Look out the window," Henderson told Griffey and Andre one day. "Rickey got a view of the Entire State Building."

"That's great Rickey," Andre laughed. "You can see the whole thing."

Griffey's son, Ken Griffey Jr., was around in those days as a teenager. The younger Griffey crushed on Andre's wife, Lanier, and kept telling Andre how beautiful he thought she was. Ken Griffey Jr., of course, would become one of the greatest Major League Baseball players of all time and earn over $150 million in salary, plus millions more in endorsements. Andre would never get rich off baseball, and he'd return to modest means after his Major League career ended.

"I keep telling Lanier," he says with a laugh, "I think you picked the wrong one."

• • •

For many years, where Manhattan's Henry Hudson Parkway turns into the West Side Highway beside the Hudson River, there was a sudden, unmarked, reverse S-curve.

In 1970 the city made plans to place a diamond-shaped, yellow warning sign 346 feet before the curve. But years passed and accidents piled up. In 1977 plans were revised to add a thirty-five-mph speed limit sign as well. The following year, the warnings were finally posted.

But rather than 346 feet before the curve, as plans called for, the signage was incorrectly placed by city workers, right where the S-curve began.

• • •

It's 1996, summertime, and I'm watching an American Legion doubleheader at McEuen Field in Coeur d'Alene, Idaho. It's the Post Falls Cardinals versus the Atlas Building Center Lumbermen. High school kids filling their summer with baseball on a hot afternoon. I'm monitoring from a modest press box behind home plate, keeping score and trying to think of a good lede for my story in tomorrow's paper.

I've spent the first few years of my career writing for newspapers in the Inland Northwest. These days, I find myself at the *Coeur d'Alene Press*, a smallish daily with a circulation of about thirty thousand, in a resort town on a lake. My fellow sportswriters and I write up stories on events and athletes ranging from youth to high school to college, sometimes a regional pro event. We work desk shifts, taking phone calls from coaches, typing box scores, and laying out the next day's section. Past midnight we put the paper to bed, and we often follow that by closing out a local bar. We'll all wake up late the next day and start over again.

In many ways, it's a great place to spend my twenties. The friendships and life lessons are real. But I'm still struggling, looking for my place in life, too often consumed by fear. Not long ago, a friend snapped a picture of me sitting in a bar. I'm smiling, but I look heavy. There's a large glass of beer sitting in front of me, and a lit cigarette in my hand.

As I'm watching these kids play baseball, it occurs to me that I might have played too. I might not have been a star, but I think I could have contributed. I never did try organized baseball, settling instead for a few pickup-style games with a couple of neighborhood friends and a lot of ghost runners in a small field in front of my house in Columbus. I guess I was too timid to try Little League, and my parents didn't force the issue.

I try not to focus too much on regrets, but that's one I'm feeling. I've never really played the game of baseball. I've only watched.

• • •

The San Diego Padres won twenty-three straight games in the summer of 1981, three in real life followed by twenty in a fantasy world created by fans starved for baseball. The sixteenth win in the fake streak, cooked up by a local radio station, drew two thousand fans to the parking lot at San Diego's Jack Murphy Stadium on June 18. Real radio announcer Jerry Coleman called fake San Diego's 4–2 win over fake Pittsburgh, coming on a ninth-inning homer by fake Jerry Turner, while real fans cheered and dined on hot dogs and other snacks.

San Diego wasn't alone in conjuring up faux Major League action. Fake leagues with various methodologies sprung up across the country, often pushed by local newspapers desperate to fill column inches. In my hometown *Columbus Dispatch*, sportswriters created a tournament pitting thirty-two of the greatest teams of all time against each other. Games were simulated with stats, charts, and dice from a board game called Extra Innings. The *Dispatch* staff went all out, providing game stories and box scores. Readers were invited to pick the winners in a contest.

While no substitute for the real thing, it was fun for baseball historians. The entrants, selected by a panel of baseball experts, included teams like the Yankees of '27, '39, and '61; the Tinker-to-Evers-to-Chance Chicago Cubs of 1906; the "Gas House Gang" St. Louis Cardinals of 1934; Jackie Robinson's 1955 Brooklyn Dodgers; and more recent teams like the '75 Reds and '80 Phillies. The champions of sixteen-team fields in the American and National Leagues would face off in a best-of-seven World Series, with the winner of that emerging as the greatest team of all time, supposedly.

Dispatch writers did their best to have fun with the whole thing. The '75 Reds and the 1906 Cubs argued about which kind of ball to use. John McGraw, manager of the 1904 New York Giants, complained about playing the '75 Reds on artificial turf. Ty Cobb's 1909 Detroit Tigers pulled an upset against Babe Ruth and the '27 Yankees then lost to the '35 Tigers before a confused crowd in Detroit. Ruth tripled off Rollie Fingers. Goose Goslin played for both teams in a game between the 1924 Washington Senators and the 1935 Detroit Tigers. "You win some, you lose some," Goslin was quoted as saying after the Tigers won in fifteen innings.

The whole thing took six weeks to play out. And the winner was ... the 1968 Detroit Tigers, somehow. They beat Stan Musial's '42 Cardinals in the World Series, four games to three.

AFTER THE STRIKE HALTED real baseball, Righetti took his 3-0, 1.50 ERA start with the Yankees home to San Jose, where he stayed with his parents and threw with his ball-playing brother. The Yankee rookie hit the beach, played golf, and wondered how he'd stay sharp with no Major League hitters to face.

His unannounced rival, Valenzuela, returned to Mexico. The portly pitcher violated his contract by appearing in two semi-pro games, and he drew huge, adoring crowds wherever he went.

Most players received strike-shrunken paychecks on June 30 and didn't get anything two weeks later. Some needed to find nonbaseball work. Chicago Cub Mike Lum worked as a magician. Cincinnati's Ron Oester toiled in a daycare center. Lenny Randle put together a comedy review with eight of his Seattle Mariners teammates. Detroit's Richie Hebner returned home to Massachusetts and worked as a grave digger.

Steinbrenner dispatched his big league coaches to the Yankees' Minor League outposts to provide instruction. Yogi Berra ended up in Nashville, where he spent about ten days with the Double-A Sounds. Yogi showed up every day. When the Sounds took a road trip, Yogi joined the players for the long bus rides and stayed with them in hotels. He wore his Yankees uniform during games.

On his first day, Yogi approached Sounds manager Carl "Stump" Merrill. "Gimme somethin' to do," Yogi muttered. "I need somethin' to do. Who's that kid over at first base? He looks pretty good."

Merrill suggested to Yogi that he go over and hit some ground balls to the kid. His name was Mattingly, and he usually played in the outfield, but he was sharpening his skills at first.

Meanwhile, labor negotiations went nowhere. The day after the fake Padres ran their winning streak to sixteen, the real negotiations to end the strike collapsed. After another breakdown the following week, Moffett announced he wouldn't be calling anymore meetings, unless someone gave him a reason to do so.

FIG 13. Frank Verdi during his introduction as the Columbus Clippers' new manager. *Columbus Citizen-Journal*, Scripps Howard Newspapers/Grandview Heights Public Library/Photohio.org.

FIG 14. Frank Verdi was one of the original Columbus Jets in 1955. *Columbus Citizen-Journal*, Scripps Howard Newspapers/ Grandview Heights Public Library/Photohio.org.

FIG 15. Tucker Ashford starred for the Clippers in 1981 and won the league MVP Award the following season. *Columbus Citizen-Journal*, Scripps Howard Newspapers/Grandview Heights Public Library /Photohio.org.

FIG 16. Steve Balboni's thirty-three home runs led the International League in 1981. *Columbus Citizen-Journal*, Scripps Howard Newspapers/Grandview Heights Public Library /Photohio.org.

FIG 17. Frank Verdi provides instruction during the 1981 season. *Columbus Citizen-Journal*, Scripps Howard Newspapers/Grandview Heights Public Library /Photohio.org.

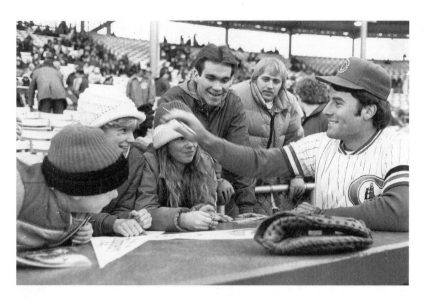

Fig 18. Marshall Brant was known for never refusing an autograph request. *Columbus Citizen-Journal*, Scripps Howard Newspapers/Grandview Heights Public Library/Photohio.org.

Fig 19. Shortstop Andre Robertson (*left*) wowed fans with his play at second as well as shortstop. *Columbus Citizen-Journal*, Scripps Howard Newspapers/ Grandview Heights Public Library/Photohio.org.

Fig 20. New York Yankees principal owner George Steinbrenner (*left*) confers
with Clippers general manager George Sisler Jr. *Columbus
Citizen-Journal*, Scripps Howard Newspapers/Grandview Heights
Public Library/Photohio.org.

Fig 21. Steve Balboni on deck at Franklin County Stadium. *Columbus
Citizen-Journal*, Scripps Howard Newspapers/Grandview Heights
Public Library/Photohio.org.

8

The Grind

Two-newspaper cities used to be common in the United States, and many large cities had three or more. That competition gave readers choices, fueled quality, and created a bundle of job opportunities for journalists.

A lot of that is gone now, and even papers lacking intracity rivals are struggling. The rise of internet media has stolen away readers and advertising revenue. Newsprint, the type of paper on which newspapers are produced, has soared in price. Newspaper readers are growing older and dying, less frequently replaced as younger consumers bury their faces in smartphones.

Columbus still had two papers in 1981: the morning *Citizen-Journal* and the afternoon *Columbus Dispatch*. Through a joint operating agreement, the papers shared a printing press, along with advertising and circulation staffs. The editorial teams were separate, with one always trying to one-up the other. There were competitions around numerous topics. Including Clippers baseball.

A pair of twentysomethings, the *c-J*'s Jack Torry and the *Dispatch*'s Jim Massie, covered the Clippers in the early '80s, clacking away on the manual typewriters of the day. Torry generally had the first shot at breaking stories, with the *c-J* plunking on porches early in the mornings. Massie had the afternoon paper, but his advantage was traveling with the team for all road games, which Torry usually didn't do, save for the shorter trips up Interstate 75 to Toledo, or down U.S. Route 33 to Charleston. The hours Massie logged on buses and planes, and in less-than-five-star hotels, endeared him to the Clippers players, at least somewhat. "They wanted to see you there," Massie would recall, "suffering along with them."

The rivalry between Massie and Torry was mostly friendly. The two men had a détente of sorts, including an unwritten agreement

that if one saw the other interviewing a certain player, he'd avoid
doing a feature story on that player the following day. During
spring training they stayed at the same hotel and sometimes had
dinner together. Both were friendly with players. Massie would
sometimes receive invites to join them for movies or other time
killers on the road. Torry and Wayne Harer once shared a condo,
where some epic parties happened.

Seasons dragged along painfully and filling downtime
on the road was difficult for media types like Massie as well as
players and coaches. Destinations like Richmond, Pawtucket, and
Rochester didn't have a lot to offer for young men in their twenties, outside of the bars. There were hookups for those who were
looking, but often just a lot of empty hours.

During his first season covering the team in 1980, Massie struggled to adjust to life on the road. He dared to complain to the grizzled Dave Coleman as one particularly rough, early-season road
trip dragged on. He can still recall the way Coleman looked at
him, as if he were an insect.

"Well," the veteran player lectured incredulously, "you better
get used to it."

With all that time to kill, Massie started tuning into *General
Hospital*. Before long he found himself hooked.

It was the "summer of Luke and Laura" for the famed soap opera.
A showdown brewed. Laura was married to Scotty but had fallen
in love with Luke, despite the rape at the disco. Luke shared her
feelings but was convinced he was in too deep with the mob to
ever have her. Instead, he would follow orders and marry Jennifer,
the mob boss's daughter, on a yacht. On the day of the wedding,
Scotty finds a love letter from Laura to Luke. Scotty calls Laura a
tramp! He storms off to kill Luke on his wedding day.

Massie watched alone in his hotel room. Along with millions
of Americans, he was glued.

Scotty jumps on board the yacht and attacks Luke. The two
men fight. Scott lands a left hook and knocks Luke overboard!

At that moment, Massie heard loud cheering—a roar—from

the other side of the hotel. It was the Clippers players, who'd also been watching. They were hooked, too.

TORRY LEFT SPORTSWRITING TO cover politics and joined the *Dispatch* staff after the C-J shuttered its doors at the end of 1985. He's written a couple of excellent books, including one on his beloved Cleveland Indians, and another on a tragic drunk-driving accident in a small Michigan town and its aftermath. The latter, entitled *Henderson's Light*, is sitting on my bookshelf, waiting for me to insist to my kids that they read it before they're old enough to start driving.

Massie left the Clippers beat, covered the Cincinnati Reds and other topics for many years and then returned to his roots, covering the Clippers again for several seasons after the team's new ballpark opened in 2009.

PLAYERS FACED THEIR OWN seemingly endless grind, particularly if they weren't going anywhere higher in baseball. In 1980 the Clippers had Roy Staiger, the aforementioned infielder playing in his sixth season in the International League. Staiger was a New York Met for about five hundred at bats in the mid-seventies, but he'd been stuck back in the Minors ever since. He'd just about had it with Minor League life, including being joined at the mitt with a bunch of dudes he otherwise might not have chosen.

"Man, I can't wait until I can go home and it's September," he once grumbled during a long road trip, "and I can pick my own friends."

During one at bat earlier that season, Staiger stepped to the plate in Charleston. The introduction crackled over the sound system.

"Now batting for Columbus . . . Roy Staiger."

An infamous Charleston heckler, known as Leather Lungs for his relentless taunts and bellowing voice, perked up more than usual. Remember, Charleston usually drew tiny crowds, and you could hear every word throughout the park. Not that the infamous heckler needed much help.

"Roy Staiger?" Leather Lungs asked aloud with mock shock. "ROY STAIGER?"

The taunts continued through the at bat.

"How long you been in this league, Roy?

"Staiger! You're gonna DIE IN THIS LEAGUE!"

Staiger backed out of the box and had to laugh. He retired before the start of the '81 season.

• • •

The Staiger-less '81 team lost 8–5 against Rochester on a soggy Fourth of July night at Franklin County Stadium. Max Patkin, baseball's "Clown Prince" and an old friend of Verdi's, was there to perform. Steinbrenner was there, too. He traditionally spent his Fourth of July birthday in Columbus, celebrating with loved ones.

The Clipper ship was already pretty tight, as was any outpost in Steinbrenner's empire. A visit from the Boss, on the Fourth of July or any other day, made everyone snap to attention even more crisply.

Verdi, not one to check his players' hair length or clean shavedness himself, put the onus on the players in delivering his warning.

"All of you guys know the rules," Verdi would say. "If it gets down to me, the shit is going to flow downhill."

Pacella had to lose his handlebar mustache after arriving in Columbus from that highway in Arizona.

Pitcher George Frazier joined the team just before the strike with long hair and a mustache, but both had to go, per Steinbrenner's rules. The young pitcher arrived at Franklin County Stadium, disappeared into the clubhouse and emerged for his Clippers debut, short-haired and clean-shaven. As he took the mound to warm up, his wife and their baby sat in the stands alongside the other players' wives. One of them asked Frazier's wife, "Who's this new guy pitching?" Mary took a good look.

"I don't know," she responded.

New-look Frazier would shine for the Clippers, adding depth to a tired staff.

As the Major League strike wore on, Steve Balboni wore out International League pitchers. On July 6, Balboni clubbed two home runs in one inning against Rochester. Columbus racked up ten runs in the inning on the way to a 14–4 win. He homered again the next night. In the first half of July alone, he collected ten home runs and twenty-five RBIs. A shot off Syracuse's Jim Wright on July 15 gave Balboni twenty-two for the season, one off the league lead. Baseball fans with no Reggie Jacksons or Mike Schmidts to follow had an alternative in Balboni, via ESPN. The surge had him leading the league in RBIs, with teammates Brant and Ashford right behind him.

There was precedent for Balboni's home run binge. Playing for Eckerd College in the '77 Division II World Series, he'd clubbed five homers in the first four games. He smacked seven in the first twelve contests of his second season with the Single-A Fort Lauderdale Yankees, on his way to a team-record twenty-six for the season. Then there was his start with Double-A Nashville in 1980: twenty-one round-trippers in the first thirty-nine games. He cooled off homerwise and ended up with *just* thirty-four, but he still won the Southern League MVP Award and put fear into its pitchers' hearts like no one else that season.

It wasn't just the number of home runs, though. It was the mileage.

Balboni hit four-baggers that traveled fast and far enough to forge legends at each stop in his baseball career. He slugged aluminum-powered moonshots at Eckerd. Opposing players sometimes wandered through orange groves the next day in search of Balboni's home run balls, some of which were never found. He hit a blast for Fort Lauderdale that flew out of old Miami Stadium, over the fence in left field. The fence was only 350 feet away, but the ball was halfway up one of the stadium's massive light towers as it passed. His manager, Doug Holmquist, was slack-jawed. He'd watched Maris and Mantle at Yankee Stadium during their primes, and he couldn't remember either hitting a ball that far. He couldn't remember *anyone* hitting a ball that far.

The towering shots with Nashville got the whole city buzzing. At least five hit the magical 500-foot mark, locals insisted. One of the homers sailed clear out of Nashville's Herschel Greer Stadium, over the wall in center, and through the windshield of a red sports car. That was a good 480. Coach Stan Williams saw the whole thing from outside the stadium, including the angry reaction from the car's owner, something like, "Who's the sumbitch who just broke my windshield?" Wrong attitude, counseled Williams. You don't want to find the guy who just hit a ball that far.

Balboni's time with the Clippers included a pair of memorable shots in Rochester, both of which may have traveled 500 feet. One of them, off Mike Boddicker, cleared the center-field clock. Another, hit into a high fog bank, completely disappeared from the view of anyone in the stands or on the field. No one, with the possible exception of Balboni, knew quite what had just happened. He began to trot around the bases. Seconds passed. One, one thousand. Two, one thousand. Three, one thousand. Four, one thousand. Then came a resounding OOOOM from far, far away. The ball had hit the metal roof of a factory well past the center-field fence, thirty feet up.

Multiple-homer innings. Grand slams in consecutive at bats. A shot onto the roof of a police station. Each homer added to the legend.

"Where we goin'?" Balboni used to ask his teammates most nights, wondering where the evening's drinking would take place. He generally didn't say much more. Despite his shy, quiet nature, Balboni was nearly as legendary in the bars as he was on the field. Whoever blessed him with powerful wrists, huge hands, and other home run helpers must also have blessed him with a gift for holding his liquor, impressive even for a man of his size.

He always loved having a few beers. Then, in A-ball, he was introduced to Jack Daniels by his teammate and buddy Paul Boris. Now, Balboni was known to do double shots of straight Jack like they were Dixie Cups filled with lemonade on a hot day. The hard drinking never seemed to faze him all that much, and he usually stayed in character, soft-spoken and humble.

At a West Virginia bar one night, a group of Charleston Charlies spotted Balboni and sent over a six-pack. They were playing the Clippers the next day. If you can't get him out, get him drunk.

Balboni sat there and calmly downed the whole thing. The next day, he hit two home runs. That's the last time we buy you anything to drink, he was told.

Other tales involve his brute strength, which he possessed without the benefit of weight training or particularly healthy living. His regimen included a lot of beer, coffee, and cigarettes. You wouldn't want to cross him, though. Pacella once remembered horsing around with Balboni and finding himself in a bear hug. "If he wanted to, he could break me in half right now," the pitcher thought. And at six foot three, 195, Pacella wasn't exactly a light wind blowing in from left field.

There's another story sometimes passed around when Balboni accounts are shared, about a callout from members of a local hockey team in a Nashville bar. Balboni was sitting alone, enjoying his solitude and a drink, when a group of other large young men decided to challenge his manhood. "C'mon, pussy boy, you aren't so tough"... things like that. After tiring of the abuse, Balboni did his shot, stood up, and knocked one of them to the floor, and all three of them were out of there pretty quickly. Or so the story goes.

Asked to verify many years later, Balboni pauses and looks downward. One, one thousand. Two, one thousand. Three, one thousand. Four, one thousand. Then he lifts his head with a faint smile.

"I don't remember that one," he says softly.

Likes and Dislikes

In early June, pitcher Mike Bruhert languished in the Texas Rangers system, stuck at Double-A Wichita, tagged with the dreaded "sore arm" label. He rarely pitched. When the Rangers finally released him, it appeared to most that his career was over, but he had one more call to make. Bruhert picked up the phone and dialed Frank Verdi.

FIG 22. Pitcher Mike Bruhert had a close connection with Frank Verdi before joining the Clippers. *Columbus Citizen-Journal*, Scripps Howard Newspapers/ Grandview Heights Public Library/Photohio.org.

The Clippers manager agreed to audition the sinkerball-throwing right-hander. Publicly, Verdi was all business. He was concerned about that sore arm. He'd have a look, but he wasn't about to put his own livelihood at risk to hire someone with an empty tank.

What didn't show up in the papers was that Verdi already loved Bruhert like a fifth son.

Back in spring training of '77, Verdi—in his first season managing at Triple-A Tidewater—had seen something in the six-foot-six, 235-pound right-hander, who'd been a son-in-law to the late Gil Hodges. Verdi decided to keep Bruhert, against the judgment of others in the organization. The two native New Yorkers had a father-son sort of connection right away. Both would arrive at the ballpark early. Both believed in playing hard. They played cards and talked baseball. Old school.

Bruhert struggled with his control that spring. Verdi nursed him through it. First pitch fastball, first pitch fastball. More generally, Bruhert learned from Verdi how to be a winner. He started the season 11-4 before arm trouble sidelined him. He returned but dropped his next five decisions. Verdi stuck with him.

The following season, Bruhert made it to the Majors with the Mets, appearing in twenty-seven games. It was a high point in a rollercoaster career.

Now, three years later, Bruhert needed somewhere to pitch and some help with his delivery. The Clippers needed a veteran pitcher who could gobble up innings. During their phone call, Verdi asked Bruhert about his alleged sore arm.

"Mike, what's wrong with you?"

"There's nothing wrong with me."

"Well, if you're telling me you're okay, we're going to fly you up here."

Paging Doctor Ellis. The Clippers pitching coach and Verdi watched Bruhert throw off the mound. Within five minutes, Ellis told Bruhert there was nothing wrong with his arm. His mechanics were the issue. Bruhert signed and started working with Ellis that very day. Before long, flaws were fixed, and Bruhert's pitches started sinking again.

By July 8 Bruhert had thrown back-to-back, complete-game victories for his new team. He was 4-0 with a 2.08 ERA, and had already logged thirty-four and two-thirds innings. The weary Clipper bullpen sighed collectively with relief. The rest of the league sighed in despair.

"They said he had a sore wing," Rizzs told his listening audience during Bruhert's Clipper debut. "He sure doesn't *look* like he has a sore wing."

The addition of Bruhert supplied another puzzle piece in the Clippers' dominant season. Bruhert would fight injuries and illness and would struggle as the season wound down. He would never return to the Majors, but his career had been extended thanks to a second chance provided by Verdi. He and the old man would remain friends for the rest of Verdi's life.

Many years later, Bruhert was leaving a buddy's butcher shop in East New York, heading home in a cab. Another driver cut the cabbie off.

"You cock-knocker!" the cabbie yelled to the offending party.

"One of my closest people in the world used to say that," Bruhert shared with a chuckle.

"Ya?" the cabbie responded. "Who's that?"

"Frank Verdi."

"Frank Verdi?" the cabbie said. "*That* cock-knocker?"

It turned out the cabbie and Verdi had grown up together in the pool halls of Brooklyn.

You know who Frank Verdi didn't like? Umpires.

There were exceptions. He could respect an ump who reached a certain standard, but very few of them did in his eyes. Even mentioning the profession could make Verdi cross. To hear him tell it, their incompetence threatened his livelihood. He resented them. He had years of practice doing so.

Even the mellower Verdi had some memorable confrontations with the men in blue. There was genuine anger in many of them, but also showmanship. During an '82 game, Bruhert nearly escaped a jam by throwing a perfect strike on a two-out, 2-2 pitch, but the umpire called it a ball. Ellis came tearing out of the dugout and was thrown out. Verdi followed, but with a calm, very slow walk. He shared a few choice words with the umpire and was himself tossed. As he walked away, he looked back at the umpire, waved his hand and said, "No, you're out of the game!" The fans loved it.

In '81 it took Verdi only six games to get ejected. It was the first of several times he got thrown out that season.

He managed to stay in the June 29 game at Pawtucket despite

blowing his stack in the top of the ninth. Columbus started the inning in a 6–1 hole, pulled within 6–4 on a three-run homer by Espino, and put two more men on base. It then appeared that Ashford gave the Clippers a 7–6 lead with a home run to left, but umpire Denny Craig called the ball foul. Fair by five to ten feet, Verdi yelled. Even Pawtucket's catcher agreed that Denny had missed that one.

Even before that call, Verdi was mad as a Durham bull. In the sixth inning, umpire Jack Lietz credited Pawtucket's Roger LaFrancois with a home run on a ball that appeared to go through a cyclone fence instead of over it. A similar call had given Boggs a home run the previous day.

"Umpires say they can't change the course of a game," an angry Verdi told reporters after the Ashford nonhomer game, which the Clippers went on to lose. "They can change the course of centuries. We've played seventy-three games and they've been involved in about thirty of them because of all the bad calls they've made.

"These guys are having a terrible century."

In fairness to the umpires, who also made plenty of good calls and rarely got credit, they weren't exactly living a plush life. In addition to abuse dealt out by managers like Verdi, Minor League umps had to deal with low pay, dressing rooms shared with lawn mowers, and the same oppressively hot or cold weather the players contended with. Players could go home, at least to their in-season apartments, during homestands. Umpires were on to the next city or town.

Columbus was a better place for umpires than most. Not only were the facilities better, but Sisler was known for having food brought in for them, and for having their clothes sent out and cleaned.

WHEN IT CAME TO running managers out of games, longtime International League umpire Bill Emslie didn't miss many guys over the years. He went nose-to-nose with Verdi a few times, but he never once threw Verdi out. Their exchanges often went something like this:

Verdi: "Aw, you little cocksucker, why don't you get your ass back behind the plate."

Emslie: "Go fuck yourself, Frank."

They liked and respected each other.

One steamy day in Norfolk, Verdi got Emslie pretty good. There were dragonflies all around the park. Verdi trapped one of them in the dugout and stealthily brought it with him to home plate for the exchange of lineup cards before the game.

When all were assembled, Verdi made his move. He glanced upward. "Huh," he said casually. "Look at that sumbitch up in the stands."

Emslie and the others turned around to have a look. Of course, there was no one particularly interesting up there. While they were distracted, Verdi opened one of Emslie's two ball bags and put the dragonfly in. Emslie turned back toward Verdi.

"I don't see anyone, Frank," Emslie said.

Verdi just shrugged.

A few minutes later, Emslie reached into the ball bag for the start of the game, got buzzed by the dragonfly, and must have jumped ten feet.

There was no doubt about who the culprit was. Verdi howled on the steps of the dugout.

"I'm gonna get you back, you fuck!" Emslie yelled.

VERDI ENJOYED ANOTHER LAUGH at Emslie's expense during a different game in Norfolk, when the umpire was suffering from, as Emslie gently put it, "the worst fucking diarrhea of my life." It got so bad they had to call in another umpire a few days before. Emslie eased back in with three games behind second base. By the fourth game, he felt well enough to handle the plate.

The game began. "I haven't shit for three hours," Emslie thought. "I think I'm good." He only made it to the end of the fourth inning. He needed someone to stall for him. Get it? Stall? The Clippers were due to bat against Tidewater pitcher Ron Darling. Emslie eyed Verdi in the dugout.

"Frank, I gotta take a shit," Emslie told the Columbus manager.

"Could you keep your guy on the bench for a minute? Tell 'em I have an equipment problem or something."

Verdi agreed. Emslie hustled down the right-field line, where a desperately needed toilet awaited in a small building. The radio broadcast was playing in there, and the announcers were doing their best to explain the delay. "We're told umpire Bill Emslie has an equipment issue."

After a few minutes, Emslie emerged and began walking back toward home plate, past the bullpen. He started to hear yelling. "Ems! Ems!" He wasn't sure what to make of it.

"I'm okay," he responded, waving toward the bullpen and the crowd.

The yelling increased as he approached home. The crowd began to cheer. Emslie continued to acknowledge them.

It was Verdi who broke the news to Emslie as he passed the dugout.

"You dumb sonovabitch!" Verdi yelled in between roars of laughter. "You cock-knocker! You've got about ten feet of toilet paper stuck to your pants!"

Digestive issues aside, Emslie was widely considered to be a top-notch umpire. He was voted International League Umpire of the Year in 1981, just as he had been in 1979 and '80 and would be again in '82. He should have realized his dream of umpiring in the Major Leagues, but like many of the Clippers, he didn't get the call.

EMSLIE GREW UP IN Hamilton, Ohio, near Cincinnati. He's believed to be a distant relative of Bob "Wig" Emslie, a Major League umpire famous for his longevity at the job (thirty-three years), for calling four no-hitters, for his role in the famed 1908 "Merkle's Boner" game between the Chicago Cubs and the New York Giants, and for the fact that umpiring caused him so much stress—particularly during the brawling, whiskey-soaked 1890s—that he literally lost every hair on his body.

Bill Emslie started umpire school in 1974 and rose quickly through the ranks, making it all the way to the Triple-A International League by May of '77. His reputation grew, and it appeared a shot at the Majors was near. Then in '79, Major League umpires went on strike. Emslie not only turned down an offer to umpire in the Majors as a replacement, but also publicly discouraged other Minor League umpires from doing the same. He believed supporting the union was the right thing to do. Officials in the American and National Leagues, on the other side of the dispute, wouldn't forget.

The strike was settled, and Emslie began collecting umpire-of-the-year awards. But no shots at the Majors were offered. Subpar umpiring reports on Emslie, which didn't jive with reality, were cited. None of the key figures ever admitted it, but common sense points to one conclusion: Emslie was blackballed for supporting the union. After the '81 season, IL president Harold Cooper fired Emslie, saying it wasn't for any lack of umpiring skills, but because Emslie wasn't considered a Major League prospect by either the American or National League. Cooper said it was a matter of policy, and that he was doing Emslie a favor. It certainly didn't feel that way to the young umpire.

A long struggle ensued between the Emslie-backing Umpires Association and Major League Baseball. Emslie would be reinstated with a promised shot at the Majors, let go again, then reinstated, then let go again. He took on full-time work as a house painter to make a living. The opportunity in the Majors never came.

After several years of fighting, Emslie decided he'd had enough and walked away from umpiring, in his midthirties, short of his Major League goals and bitter. By '85 he was working at a golf course in Tampa when karma struck. Emslie caught a break through his friend Rich Garcia, another umpire whom Emslie had painted houses with in Clearwater. Garcia had a friend he wanted Emslie to meet.

"Let's go see George," Garcia told Emslie.

"George?" Emslie responded. "As in Steinbrenner?"

The two men met Steinbrenner in his Tampa office at a table that Emslie found to be very large and very intimidating. Garcia began to tell Emslie's story. He didn't get very far before Steinbrenner put his hand up.

"I know all about it," Steinbrenner said. "I know how you stood up for the union.

"Bill, what would you like to do?"

Emslie figured Steinbrenner was talking about parking cars on the weekend or something similar. Nope. Steinbrenner offered him a job as the New York Yankees scouting director. Which was great, except that Emslie didn't know anything about scouting. So they had to walk it back a bit, but Emslie still landed a job on the scouting staff. That was just the beginning.

Following the '88 season, Yankees scouting director Brian Sabean let Emslie go. Emslie called Steinbrenner, just to thank him for the opportunity and wish him well. Steinbrenner rehired Emslie on the spot, this time as the Yankees' traveling secretary. Emslie didn't know what a traveling secretary was. He had that job for four years. He'd also work for the Yankees as a Major League scout and eventually become a baseball operations vice president, part of Steinbrenner's inner circle, during the team's return to dominance in the '90s. Amazingly, Emslie was fired four times from Yankees jobs, but never once by Steinbrenner, who became like a second father to him.

He never made the Majors as an umpire, but thanks in large part to the Boss, things worked out fine for Bill Emslie. He has the World Series jewelry to prove it.

"My God, We Need Pitching"

In 1981 the Clippers managed to keep winning through late spring and early summer despite their pitching shortage, which was rough even by Minor League standards. For about three weeks, Verdi and Ellis had only seven pitchers to work with. After Righetti's call-up, there were no left-handers on the staff. Lefty Tim Lewis was called up from Nashville but only appeared in five games before he was sent back down. Cochran was injured and out of the mix. McGaffigan was still on the disabled list. Steinbrenner whipping boy Mike Griffin, who was leading the Clippers in ERA and saves, got called up to the Yankees before a trade to the Cubs. Tom Filer pitched in just one game for Columbus before *he* was traded. Bill

Castro was sent back down to take Griffin's place, but that still only got the Columbus pitching corps back to seven.

Ellis and Verdi scratched their heads over why more Nashville pitchers weren't given a shot. Ellis dialed his friend Pat Dobson, who was Nashville's pitching coach.

"Dobber, my God, we need pitching," Ellis said. "Are any of these guys ready to come up and help us?"

"Hell yes," Dobson responded.

Why there were no additional promotions was still the source of some debate decades later. Ellis was convinced some sort of Nashville bias was involved, perhaps tied to Steinbrenner's friendship with Sounds owner Larry Schmittou. Years later, that was news to Larry.

"George loved Columbus," Schmittou said in 2015. "He had a goal of winning at every level. If he'd had a Little League team, he would have done everything he could have to win there too."

Bill Livesey, the Yankees' director of player development during the '81 season, concurred.

"We tried to win everywhere," Livesey recalled. "I can't tell you how hard we tried to play guys at the level they should have been playing at.

"We owed it to kids to pitch them and play them at the level they were going to have success."

Whatever the reasons, the Nashville staff remained relatively flush while the Columbus staff barely held together, at least in terms of availability. Pitching help would eventually arrive in the form of Frazier, Castro, Bruhert, and others, but not before some arms were seriously overworked.

If you watched a Clippers game that season, it was pretty likely you'd see either Jim Lewis or Paul Boris pitch. One or both of them appeared in a whopping 99 of the team's 139 regular-season games. Both were usually relievers, but Lewis pitched 150 innings, nearly tops on the team, and Boris tossed 131. Even for pitchers with "rubber arms"—a baseball term for the ability to pitch a lot of innings and on multiple days in a row—it was too much, and the strain on their arms likely damaged their Major League chances.

Verdi didn't have much of a choice. Many remember him as having a talent for handling pitchers, but there weren't enough of them to go around for a good chunk of that season. For Lewis, Boris, and others on the staff, that often meant making spot starts and pitching on little rest, as well as staying in games even while getting lit up by opposing hitters, because there simply wasn't anybody left in the bullpen who could go.

Take July 19, for instance. The whole staff was tired. A tired Jim Lewis relieved a tired Boris in the sixth inning, with Columbus trailing 7–4 against Pawtucket. Lewis got drilled, but with no more pitchers available, Verdi left him out there. By the time his outing was over, Lewis had taken one for the team but given up ten runs—all earned—on nine hits in two and a third innings. Verdi finally brought in Garry Smith, a right fielder who hadn't pitched in a game since his college days six years prior, in hopes he could finish. Oddly, Smith was the Clippers' most effective pitcher that day, shutting out the PawSox over the last one and two-thirds and even striking out a batter. It didn't help, at least not on the scoreboard. Final score: Pawtucket 17, Columbus 4.

If you take that one outing away from Jim Lewis's stats that season, his ERA goes from 4.98 all the way down to a more palatable 4.45. The 4.98 number more than doubled his ERA from the previous season, when he led the International League in ERA. The overwork was a main factor. His arm didn't hurt all that much, it just didn't have anything in it. He was also dealing with marital problems.

His career—and his life off the field—had an abundance of crazy. In 1979 Lewis made the jump from Single-A Stockton to Triple-A Spokane, as the relatively new Seattle Mariners didn't have a Double-A team yet. His manager in Spokane, Rene Lachemann, had his doubts Lewis could make it in Triple-A, and told him so. Lewis did better than prove Lachemann wrong. That September, the Mariners called him up.

"Well, I guess you stuck that up my ass," Lachemann said of his

PHOTO COURTESY OF TOM WATSON

Columbus Clippers
RH Pitcher
JIM LEWIS—21

FIG 23. Jim Lewis's 1980 baseball card. Courtesy of the Columbus Clippers.

earlier comments. "You're going to the Majors." It was Lachemann who nicknamed Lewis "Big Game Lew."

"Big Game" only pitched a couple of innings for the Mariners. He later got a handful more innings in stints with the Yankees, Twins, and the Mariners again, but like so many of his Clippers teammates, he never stuck in the bigs.

Around all that, there was winter ball in the Dominican Republic to help pay the bills. Lewis, his wife, and their young daughter spent time there with Marshall Brant and his young family, when the two men played for Estrellas Orientales in baseball hotbed San Pedro de Macoris. There were good parts, including housing right on the beach, and only having to play four times a week. Other parts weren't so good. Cars partially funded by the team were so old and broken down, Lewis and Brant tried to park them on hills to allow for a rolling start. There was the time Lewis accidentally hit local legend Miguel Diloné with a pitch and nearly started a riot. Also the times Lewis and Brant, on their way to the ballpark, got shaken down for whatever cash they had by armed guards, a semiritual that Brant described as "a little unnerving the first few times it happens."

More seriously, Lewis was involved in a bad car accident on the island in January of '82. He and teammate Steve Bedrosian had been out celebrating a league title. Lewis was driving them home when their car collided head on with another, sending Bedrosian through the windshield and sending the Braves into a panic about their hot young pitching prospect. Bedrosian would need some glass removed from his eyes and also suffered lacerations and a concussion. Lewis broke his foot. It could have been much, much worse.

"Too many Presidentes," Lewis confessed many years later, referring to the concoction of rum, curaçao, vermouth, and grenadine.

Indeed. Lewis partied plenty, at least after his divorce went through. He and many of his teammates enjoyed the perks of being ballplayers, especially around women, whose level of interest could border on scary. He recalls winding up at a Columbus bar on male strip night with some of his teammates.

"Women talk about being in bars and feeling like a piece of meat," he recalled. "Well, that was us that night. They almost got into fights. They got me up on stage and tried to take my clothes off."

The feeling was sometimes mutual, and hooking up was never too much of a challenge for Lewis, or any of his teammates who were so inclined.

"It was easy," he remembered. "You'd go out, and you were going home with somebody if you wanted to.

"It was power. For some reason, these women thought Minor League Baseball players had power."

Lewis and his wife had gotten married during his junior year at the University of South Carolina. During the '81 season, he'd had to pitch through the crumbling of that marriage. His wife wound up dating and eventually marrying one of his Clippers teammates, Brian Ryder. There may have been some overlap. Lewis was never sure, but there wasn't much doubt in his mind that his marriage just wasn't working out.

Lewis and his wife remained friends, and Lewis even became friendly with Ryder. By the late '80s, the two men were playing golf together. The first time they did, Ryder was in the middle of the fairway when Lewis hit a low liner. Ryder tried to move out of the way, but the ball trailed him and hit him in the leg. Left a big welt. Perhaps apropos, even if unintentional. "It was just an accident," Lewis says, with a grin.

Paul Boris, who grew up in New Jersey with a New York Yankees–loving mother, was traded to the Minnesota Twins organization in 1982. He was called up by the Twins that May, then roughed up by the Yankees in his Major League debut. Four runs on three hits and a walk, in just two-thirds of an inning. He hit a batter and gave up a two-run homer to Bobby Murcer. "You looked like shit tonight," his mother told him afterward. "But it's okay, because the Yankees won." Thanks a lot, Mom, he thought.

Boris didn't last long in the Majors, but for him just getting there was particularly improbable. His whole professional baseball career was improbable. Boris loved the game but wasn't a particularly strong high school pitcher. After graduating he decided to focus on his education and headed to Rutgers, where he'd earn a degree in applied mathematics and statistics, something you don't find often on professional baseball rosters. He also pitched for the Rutgers baseball team, again unremarkably, and didn't show up on the radar of any Major League organization.

Six months into his first job after college, an engineering gig with Exxon, Boris was tired of sitting behind a desk. He was gaining weight. He wondered if he'd focused *too much* on his educa-

1981 Columbus Clippers
RH Pitcher
PAUL BORIS—31

FIG 24. Paul Boris's 1981 baseball card. Courtesy of the Columbus Clippers.

tion, at the expense of baseball. Well, the sport's gods were about to give him another chance.

Boris had pitched for an open-age township team called the Woodbridge Woodies. The Woodies roster briefly included Gene Michael, who'd recently retired from the Major Leagues. Michael didn't hang around the league for long before joining the New York Yankees as a coach. Before he did, he took note of Boris. It was Michael who got the six-foot-two, 200-pound right-hander a tryout with the Yankees, alongside a hundred other undrafted, unsigned players, in Florida. It was the spring of 1977.

Boris scraped together a few thousand dollars and headed south a month early to get in shape. He was due back at Exxon by April 7, and he hoped to make a decision by April 1. His deadline drew near, with no contract offer, though he'd pitched well. On April 1, he approached Jack Butterfield, the Yankees' new director of player development and scouting.

"I have to have a decision from you," Boris told Butterfield. "If I'm not gonna make it, I have to go back to work."

"Well, Paul," Butterfield said, "we've only seen you pitch a few times. We can't sign you without seeing you pitch more. So thanks for coming down."

It might have ended right there, but Boris decided to push his deadline and stick around. The Yankees signed him on April 7, the day he was due to return to Exxon. They had found a gem. In his first season of A-ball, at Fort Lauderdale, Boris fanned fifty-three batters and walked only ten in ninety innings. Boosted by an improved fastball and a newly added forkball, he won sixteen games for Fort Lauderdale in '79 and then went 7–0 for Triple-A Nashville the following season. He'd settled in as a reliever. For the Clippers, he'd win ten, save nine, and perhaps most importantly chew up those 131 innings. The Major Leagues seemed like a real possibility.

In the spring of '82, the improbable story took another turn. Two days before spring training, Boris was jogging past a convenience store when he saw a car backing out of the parking lot . . . with no one driving it. A young girl, who mostly likely had released the parking brake, was sitting in the front seat. The car wasn't going particularly fast, but it wasn't stopping, either, and the little girl needed help. Superman Boris ran alongside the car, reached inside, and was able to stop it. He also wrenched his pitching shoulder, which would never be the same. The owner of the car came running out of the store, quite obviously inebriated. "What the fuck are you doing to my car?" he screamed at Boris, before stumbling in and speeding away. Boris would sometimes wonder over the years, whatever happened to that little girl? Was there more I could have done?

He pitched reasonably well for the Twins in '82, that first shelling by the Yankees notwithstanding. But he pitched through pain all season, and after forty-nine innings, his Major League career ended. After a few more years in the Minors, it was back to a desk job.

He remains a happy-go-lucky character. Every winter, Boris hosts a large gathering of his friends in Las Vegas, an event he calls "Barbary Boris." And guess who's joined the fun in recent years: Jim Lewis. The two hadn't been in touch for many years, but they reconnected through this book project.

IN 2005 ANDY McGAFFIGAN crossed paths with Steinbrenner at the Yankees training facility in Tampa. He'd barely known the Boss and had only spoken with him a couple of times, but he decided to approach Steinbrenner, then sixty-five years old and soon to fade from the public eye.

"Hi, I'm Andy McGaffigan," the former pitcher said.

"Andy McGaffigan?" Steinbrenner responded. "Andy McGaffigan? You had a great career. I shouldn't have traded you."

"You're right!" McGaffigan told the Boss with a chuckle.

The first half of the '81 season was mostly miserable for the right-hander from West Palm Beach. He had a good chance to make the Yankees out of spring training before his elbow injury, diagnosed as a strain, sidelined him. He rehabbed for a while in Sarasota—away from his wife, Jill—and spent time traveling with the Clippers, feeling like a fifth wheel. He hated waiting around but was fearful of coming back too soon.

"I was scared to throw," he explained. "I didn't want to hurt it again. All these things go through your mind. 'Will this be the last pitch I ever throw?'"

On June 14, in the fourth game of the showdown series with the Tides before a national TV audience on ESPN, it was time to give it a try in a live game. Verdi, still pitching-starved, gave McGaffigan the start, and would have been happy if the pitcher gave him a couple of innings. So he was delighted when McGaffigan went five strong and got the win. Also a little scared he was pushing things too far, with a strict pitch count in place due to McGaffigan's recovery.

"Frank," Ellis told Verdi before the top of the fifth, "if we screw this up, it's going to be both our heads."

McGaffigan was solid in his next two starts before his velocity issues caught up with him, and International League hitters started to knock him around. He dropped four straight decisions, rocked for sixteen earned runs in just nine and two-thirds innings. In a July 12 game at Rochester, he couldn't record an out. "Lunchmeat time," he'd describe it.

Then the turnaround. Helped by light tutelage from Ellis, improving velocity, and a different grip on his slider, McGaffigan won at Syracuse in his next start. He'd star for the Clippers down the stretch. A streak of five wins in six decisions, with an ERA of 1.41 in those games.

By 1983 McGaffigan was an established Major Leaguer with the San Francisco Giants, and he'd pitch in the bigs for ten seasons. Steinbrenner's Yankee teams of the mid- to late eighties probably could have used him.

• • •

Just before midnight on July 17, 1981, Phil Neuman wrapped up his WBNS radio talk show and grimly teed up the ABC News hourly update.

"There has been a tragedy," Neuman shared with what was left of his audience at that hour, "in Kansas City, Missouri."

About four hours earlier, some 650 miles to the west, Royals pitcher Rich Gale was tending bar at Kansas City's Hyatt Regency Hotel, picking up some extra money during the Major League labor strike and learning mixology. Gale was twenty-seven. He figured the skill might come in handy someday, as he'd considered investing in a restaurant or bar. Perhaps sooner rather than later, with the strike and all.

The hotel's ballroom was crowded that night, filled with 1,500 people for a tea dance, including two golfing buddies Gale had invited to stop by. Many more gathered to watch on walkways suspended above the dance floor. Big Band music had been playing all evening, "Satin Doll" by Duke Ellington at this particular moment. About sixty people were competing in a dance contest.

With a loud snapping sound and a chilling hiss, the upper walkway buckled, collapsed, and fell to the ballroom floor, taking a second walkway with it on the way down. There were screams, twisted metal, clouds of drywall powder and water raining down from broken pipes. It all happened right in front of Rich Gale.

He ran to the wreckage. Gale was a big man, six foot seven and 225 pounds, but unable to lift most of the debris, he felt helpless. "There's no way you can help them!" another man yelled. The pitcher cast aside any wreckage he could and provided comfort to victims. One of his golfing buddies survived. The other did not.

The design of the walkways in the one-year-old hotel had been flawed, with the lower walkway improperly suspended from the upper walkway. One hundred and fourteen people died. Scores more were injured.

It was the worst structural disaster in U.S. history, until September 11, 2001.

9

Flashing the *H*

THE CLIPPERS ROLLED THROUGH most of July, and Frank Verdi eyed the third pennant of his managerial career. The first had come with the Carolina League's Greensboro Yankees back in 1963, the second during a run of brilliance with the Syracuse Chiefs from 1968 to 1970, when Verdi was in his early forties.

The Verdi family was all over Syracuse baseball in those days. Dad managed. Mom played the organ. The Verdi boys pitched in as bat boys, scoreboard operators, members of the grounds crew, assistants to radio announcers—whatever was needed—under the guidance of Chiefs GM Tex Simone. Teenager Frankie Verdi, Frank's son, earned $5.00 a game, $7.50 for a doubleheader, to help the radio announcer re-create road games from a ticker that came off the wire. Frankie had always assumed the announcer was on the road with the team. It turned out he'd been calling the road games from Syracuse all along.

One night, young Frankie was at the controls for the scoreboard, which included a display with the letters *H* and *E* to inform fans whether a play had been ruled a "hit" or an "error." After a big home run for the home team, Frankie took the liberty of flashing the *H* repeatedly. The crowd loved it. But Frankie worried his father—the baseball purist and disciplinarian—would be angry.

The family of six rode home after the game, with the elder Frank driving, Pauline riding shotgun, and Frankie sitting alongside his brothers in the back seat. It was late, and very quiet in the car. Their father hadn't said a word. Finally, he broke the silence.

"Frankie, you work the scoreboard tonight?" he asked from the front.

Brief silence.

"Yeah, Pop," Frankie responded.

"Good, good. Get that money."

More silence.

"What was going on with that *H*? Something wrong with it?"

Frankie started bracing himself for a backhanded wallop from the front seat, which his father was known to wheel around and deliver with the best of them.

"Was it a malfunction, or d'chou do that?"

"I did it, Pop," Frankie said nervously. "I thought it would be pretty cool."

About ten more seconds of silence passed.

"I'll talk to Tex about it," Pop said. "But keep it up."

Frankie exhaled. "Flashing the *H* became a tradition at the stadium.

FRANK VERDI PLAYED FOR Syracuse in '53, '61, and '62, also managing the Chiefs for parts of the '61 and '62 seasons. A third of the way through the '68 season, he was promoted from Double-A Binghamton for another turn as Syracuse skipper. He arrived with the Chiefs mired in a long losing streak, as in they hadn't won an International League pennant since 1897, a span of seventy-three frustrating seasons. So far 1968 wasn't looking any different, with Syracuse already ten games below .500, when the Yankees organization fired Gary Blaylock and summoned Verdi.

The pennant drought didn't end that season, but Verdi helmed the Chiefs out of the International League basement to a relatively respectable fifth-place finish. He was brought back for another season.

The following spring, late on the night of May 14, a pair of teenage, would-be thieves attempted to burn through a safe at MacArthur Stadium—the Chiefs' home park—with a flare. They ended up burning through much of the stadium, sparking a blaze that took out the main entrance, a sizable chunk of the grandstands behind home plate, the press box, and about $6,000 worth of beer, among other items. Verdi's Chiefs were suddenly homeless, forced to temporarily move to smaller Falcon Park in Auburn, thirty miles away. When they returned to MacArthur a month later, there was a cavernous open space behind home plate where the fire had raged.

Another Syracuse season might have burned up as well, but the fire turned out to be a camaraderie-building clarion call for Verdi's team. When the blaze hit, the Chiefs were in sixth place with a 9-11 record. They went 73-57 for the rest of 1969, including the playoffs, finishing third, but then winning two series to claim their first Governors' Cup in fourteen years. In the deciding game five of the semifinal series against Louisville, the Chiefs trailed late before their center fielder, Jim Lyttle, seemingly came out of nowhere to make one of those game-saving catches no one in attendance ever forgets, and diminutive, twenty-two-year-old shortstop Frank Baker won it in the bottom of the tenth with a 430-foot home run over the scoreboard in center. He'd only hit one home run all season. The city went wild.

That first pennant of the twentieth century remained elusive. In 1970 Verdi and the Chiefs appeared to have it wrapped up before an eight-game losing streak, combined with nineteen wins in twenty-one games by the Columbus Jets, made it a race again. The Chiefs' eleven-game lead on August 12 shrunk down to a two-game lead, with three games left to play. Long-suffering Syracuse fans wondered, could this really be happening? Could we really miss out on the pennant, yet again, after holding such a huge lead so late in the season?

On the night of September 1, Syracuse clipped visiting Rochester 3–2. Seven hundred miles to the southwest, in Kentucky, Columbus and the Louisville Colonels were still playing. With a Columbus loss, the Chiefs would clinch the pennant and dodge epic disaster.

Verdi and his players huddled in their clubhouse, desperate for word. They called the ballpark in Louisville and reached Mary Straight, a front office employee. She propped her phone up against a radio carrying the Jets-Colonels broadcast. Back in Syracuse, Verdi held the phone to his ear and called out updates to his anxious bunch.

Louisville clung to an 8–7 lead in the top of the ninth. The Jets were threatening against Colonels reliever Ivy Washington. He needed just one more out to end it.

"C'mon, Ivy," Verdi pleaded, the room hanging on his every word.

Another moment passed. Verdi looked up at his team, dropped the phone, and planted a kiss on Simone. Ivy Washington and the Colonels had held on, Columbus was eliminated, and Syracuse had finally, *finally* won the pennant. For the Chiefs, the party was on. There was champagne and a lot of yelling. Local reporter Bob Snyder was caught up in the festivities, stripped naked and thrown into the shower. All in good fun. Snyder was friendly with Verdi and frequently drank with him, sometimes heavily. The old sportswriter still remembers closing out a bar with Verdi one Saturday night, then getting an icy glare from Pauline Verdi as she sat behind the organ in the bleachers the following day. Church and a doubleheader were on the schedule, and Pauline would have preferred her husband not stagger home drunk in the middle of the night.

After the Chiefs wrapped up the 1970 regular season and went on to win another Governors' Cup and Little World Series title, the local paper dubbed Verdi the "Resident Genius of the North Side Ball Orchard."

"And the guy who has made them look 'purty,'" read an accompanying poem, "Is none other than a Frank named Verdi. So hail to the Chiefs who've won their first pennant, they've finally become the league's Number One Tenant."

YOUNG FRANKIE AND HIS brothers had front-row seats—sometimes even better—for their father's exploits. Frankie recalls watching from the dugout as his dad demonstrated some managerial craftiness, with the Chiefs in 1970.

Early in the contest, Chiefs players in the dugout noted that their opponents, the visiting Winnipeg Whips, were batting out of order. The Chiefs players let their manager know, but the elder Verdi didn't want to hear about it. He turned to his players in the dugout.

"Shut up," he muttered under his breath.

The next time through the batting order, the Chiefs in the dugout were at it again.

"Skip, they're batting out of order."

"Shut . . . the hell . . . up," Verdi responded, again muttering quietly.

The manager had a plan. He waited until a key situation later in the game, in which Winnipeg had a run in and two runners on base with two outs. *Then* Verdi called the lineup error to the umpire's attention. The player who'd driven in the run, Boots Day, was called out, and the inning—and the threat—ended.

VERDI'S BEST CHANCES TO manage in the Major Leagues probably came during this period—and went. He'd had two and a half highly successful seasons in Syracuse, including the win-everything 1970 season. He coached winter ball and won there, too. The Yankees, the parent club for Syracuse at the time, were floundering, in need of better front office decisions, players, and field managers.

So what happened? Snyder may have put it best in one of his columns: "To the Yankees, Verdi was both a winner and a pain in the butt."

Verdi was already clashing with the Yankee brass, publicly criticizing their decisions, sometimes loudly and with colorful language. He ran his team the way he wanted, sometimes against the wishes of organization higher-ups. Verdi was a terrific manager. He never had been, nor ever would be, much of a politician.

Following the 1970 season, Verdi squabbled with the Yankees over his request for a meager $1,500-a-year raise, which he felt he needed just to keep up with the rising cost of living and take care of his family. Managing winter ball in Puerto Rico, he'd tear articles about worsening economic conditions out of the newspaper and send them to Yankees GM Lee MacPhail, sometimes with pointed comments added. The Yankees let him go, citing the comments he'd made.

Verdi struggled to find other baseball jobs his family could live on, worrying that he'd been blackballed. He spent much of the next six years out of the game, returning for heart-not-in-it seasons back in Syracuse ('72) and Denver ('74). Both teams finished in seventh place. He sat out the '71, '73, '75, and '76 seasons, while managerial peers such as Tommy Lasorda and Bobby Cox worked their way to the Majors.

During his time away from baseball, Verdi worked as a steamfitter, a car salesman, and a security man at race tracks, paying the bills but mostly miserable. His family watched him suffer and wasn't sure what to do. "He needed baseball," son Frank P. recalled. "It was his life from the time he could remember. Taking away baseball was like taking heroin away from a junkie.

"He was lost."

By 1977 Frank Verdi had pretty much given up on the game, figuring he'd never get another chance. He'd more or less settled into his race track job. Then the Tidewater Tides came calling, and for Frank Verdi, there was no saying no.

VERDI SOMETIMES MIXED WITH the players for a game of cards or other activities. One rare off day in Syracuse during the '81 season, Verdi joined a handful of players, Jim Lewis among them, for a round of golf. They were guests of a well-heeled Yankees fan at a local country club with a Mafia vibe. Adult beverages were consumed. Lewis can't remember much about the golf part, but he does remember someone kicking a huge divot high up into the air and having it land—and stay—on top of Verdi's head, causing everyone to double over with laughter. During that same round, one of Verdi's tee shots struck an unfortunate bird, which expired. Not without a fight from Verdi though. The inebriated manager attempted to revive the poor bird with CPR, and by blowing on it.

You had to laugh. As with any long Minor League season, you had to laugh.

Tucker Ashford had a reputation for joking around and keeping everyone loose. Bruce Robinson, the catcher who was injured all season but around the team, was the biggest practical jokester. *Columbus C-J* writer Jack Torry was one of Robinson's favorite victims. The catcher once put Atomic Balm in Torry's shoes. On another occasion, he gave Torry a hot foot at a bar. "I was trying to talk to a couple of women," Torry recalled, "and all of a sudden, my feet are on fire."

Righetti once spiked bullpen catcher Mike Barnett's hamburger with tobacco juice. A teammate took a dump in Joe Lefebvre's bed and made the bed up real nice, like all was normal. On another occasion, after Balboni drifted off to sleep on a training table, his teammates pulled a sheet over his head and added a few flowers, as if the big man had gone on to his great reward. Other jokes required more advanced planning. On earlier Clippers teams, at least one wide-eyed newcomer was driven out to the countryside with the promise of a rendezvous with "the farmer's daughter," only to run into someone pretending to be the farmer, toting a shotgun.

Sometimes it was what *wasn't* said or done. One night in Norfolk, Lewis—having emerged from his divorce—was attempting to reenter the dating pool and trying a few lines on a local hottie. A bartender took note.

"You might want to tell your friend," the bartender advised Wayne Harer and a couple of other teammates. "That good-looking girl? That's a guy."

Sharing a story like this, in a context like this, isn't exactly politically correct these days, and no offense is intended in sharing this one. But it bears mentioning, if for no other reason than to note the reaction of the straight and unsuspecting Lewis's teammates, who—after a very brief discussion—agreed it would be best to let this one play out.

After a mild romantic encounter in the parking lot, Lewis was finally given a heads up. Not surprisingly, the pitcher's testosterone-soaked teammates let him have it in the clubhouse the next day. And for quite a few days after that. Big Game Lew took it with one of his big grins.

• • •

While the Clippers dominated, Dave Coleman struggled. Driving a truck back in Dayton was sounding better and better. The season wasn't over yet, though, and Coleman continued to suit up, literally and figuratively. He still believed he could play in the Majors.

He'd been known for his durability for most of his career. He'd never once dealt with an injury, at least nothing significant. During the 1980 season, they started happening. Then they began to pile up. Coleman earned the starting left-field job and also saw playing time at third base. Halfway through the season, he injured his arm making an awkward, off-balance, sidearm throw from third. He returned to the lineup after two weeks then promptly broke his wrist attempting a diving catch on Franklin County Stadium's artificial turf. Even if he'd wanted to turn off the aggressiveness with which he played the game, he wasn't sure how.

The injuries healed slowly, with Coleman's push for an earlier return not helping. By the end of the season, he could barely lift his right arm, or swing a bat.

He recovered enough to play winter ball in Puerto Rico. That lasted eleven games. Coleman attempted another diving catch, this time making the play and preserving a no-hitter for Lamarr Hoyt in the seventh inning, but he reinjured his shoulder. The issues carried over into 1981, with Coleman making two more trips to the disabled list. He reinjured the wrist again in spring training, on yet another diving play.

When he wasn't on the DL that season, he usually rode the bench, despite his ability to play all those positions. There was just too much talent—younger talent—in front of him.

He'd hit a combined forty-four home runs over the '78 and '79 seasons. Just two seasons later, he'd finish 1981 with only six, and a paltry .231 batting average.

He committed an error at third base before a large home crowd that cost Columbus the game on the Fourth of July.

Through it all, he waited patiently for whatever opportunities he could get. Almost every day, even during stints on the disabled list, he came out early, taking ground balls and extra batting practice. He figured anyone who pouted over limited playing time might as well go on home.

Frank Verdi watched, and took note.

BACK IN 1977 COLEMAN had made as strong of a case as he could for sticking around with the Boston Red Sox. It was just a difficult—if not impossible—case to win. Coleman played an impressive six different positions, but the Red Sox were already loaded in all of them. The outfield included future Hall of Famer Carl Yastrzemski, alongside stars such as Fred Lynn, Dwight Evans, and Bernie Carbo. First baseman George Scott and third baseman Butch Hobson would hit thirty-three and thirty home runs that season, respectively. Future Hall of Famer Jim Rice was Boston's designated hitter. Carlton Fisk, yet another future Hall of Famer, was the catcher. Good luck making *that* team.

Boston manager Don Zimmer liked Coleman for his durability, athleticism, ability to play all those positions, and some heroics in spring training. On March 16, in Fort Lauderdale, Coleman hit a two-run homer in the tenth inning to spark Boston past the hated Yankees. It made a particular impression. Even spring training contests between the two teams were bitter, hard-fought battles in those years. Four days later, Coleman made a sparkling catch in center to steal a hit from the Cardinals' Charlie Chant. Still, Zimmer had no room on the roster for keeping Coleman around.

Then Coleman caught a break of sorts when Lynn hurt his ankle in spring training. Coleman beat out Jack Baker for Lynn's spot on the roster. A temporary spot, for sure, but a chance to show what he could do. He'd made it to the Major Leagues, on an Opening Day roster.

Coleman sat on the bench for the first three games of the regular season as the Red Sox, who began the season with great expectations, faltered. Two losses at home against the Indians, including a 19–9 drubbing in the second game. A 5–2 loss to the White Sox in Chicago. By the time Coleman came on to pinch-hit in the fourth game of the season, before just 5,344 fans at old Comiskey Park, the stakes for Boston felt unusually high, considering how early in the season it was.

Trailing 3–0 in the top of the seventh, the Red Sox awoke. At least they stirred. Evans tripled to center and scored on a single to left by Hobson. Rick Burleson sent Hobson to third with a double, and Boston, desperate for a win, had the tying runs in scoring position. With left-handed-hitting Denny Doyle due up, Chicago manager Bob Lemon brought lefty Dave Hamilton out of the bullpen. Zimmer countered with a right-handed pinch hitter, Coleman, who would never forget the feeling he had as he made his Major League debut. Scared shitless, to death.

It lasted one pitch. Hamilton threw Coleman a hittable fastball, head high. Coleman swung. He made contact, but millimeters away from where needed. His pop-out to Alan Bannister at short ended the inning. Boston went on lose its fourth straight, 7–3.

There were other opportunities, but Coleman couldn't settle down enough inside to play like he knew he could play. Nothing was easy. In his two starts, he faced two of the game's toughest lefties, California's Frank Tanana and Oakland's Vida Blue. His best chance for a hit may have come against Tanana, on a ground ball up the middle. Jerry Remy made a diving stop and nipped Coleman at first.

Lynn returned. Coleman was 0 for 12, with one costly defensive miscue in center, when he heard the words he'd been dreading.

"Zim wants to see you."

• • •

On the night of July 24, 1981, Dave Wehrmeister and Jim Lewis combined for a 2–0 shutout of Mike Boddicker and the visiting Red Wings. Midseason additions Patterson and Gulden each homered. The win was the Clippers' sixty-fifth of the season, moving them thirty games above .500. They'd won fifty-four of their last eighty games—a .700 clip—since their 9-11 stumble to begin the season, and their lead over Richmond in the IL standings was now a twelve-game chasm. For fans following around the nation during the strike, it was an impressive display.

Gulden—out of New Ulm, Minnesota—played a huge role, not just solidifying the catching position, but starring. He tripled and homered on Memorial Day in his second game back with the team, hit a pair of homers the next night and led the team in bat-

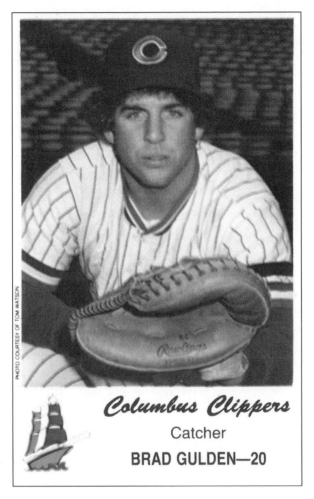

PHOTO COURTESY OF TOM WATSON

Columbus Clippers
Catcher
BRAD GULDEN—20

FIG 25. Brad Gulden's 1980 baseball card. Courtesy of the Columbus Clippers.

ting average for weeks. His three hits on June 7 helped the Clippers hold off Charleston 11–10 after Columbus nearly blew an 11–4 lead. He'd overhauled his hitting style during spring training with the Seattle Mariners, under the guidance of coach Tommy Davis. Now Gulden felt relaxed at the plate, and he couldn't remember a time when he was hitting the ball better.

Gulden starred in the field, too. While some on the pitching staff preferred Espino behind the plate, Gulden was an experienced pitch-caller who showed a flair for the dramatic that summer. On the night of July 30, in Syracuse, Gulden picked Greg "Boomer" Wells off first base to end the game in a 3–1 win. Wells had been the tying run. Gulden's play provided a needed boost for a Columbus team that was suddenly struggling, having lost four of its previous five games as hitters like Ashford, Patterson, and Balboni slumped at the plate.

Four nights later in Rochester, Gulden was a hero again. The Red Wings scored three in the bottom of the ninth to tie the game at four and force extra innings. Gulden snapped the tie with a two-out homer in the top of the tenth. In the bottom of the tenth, he ended the game by throwing out LaRue Washington on a steal attempt. Final score: Clippers 5, Red Wings 4.

Despite Gulden's success during the '81 season, the Yankees didn't recall him. He played briefly for the Expos in '82, the Reds in '84, and the Giants in '86. He unfortunately may be most remembered for a takedown of a much older Zimmer—then coaching for the Cubs—in 1984, during an epic bench-clearer that lasted for thirty minutes. Zimmer was arguably the instigator and wasn't done scuffling with younger men. At age seventy-two, as a coach for the Yankees, Zimmer famously tangled with Red Sox pitcher Pedro Martinez during the 2003 American League Championship Series.

Less famously, Gulden and Clippers coach Howard "Hop" Cassady fought in an airport before the team's final flight home in '81. A fair amount of drinking had been done, a playful Gulden punch didn't come across as all that playful, and the next thing everyone knew, Cassady, forty-seven, had charged the twenty-five-year-old Gulden and found himself in a headlock. Teammates scrambled to break it up, with Balboni getting a big arm in between the two men to end it. Gulden and Cassady each came out embarrassed.

"It never should have happened," Ellis recalled. "They were both good people. But there were two piles of rocks right there."

• • •

On July 29 my family joined nearly a billion people watching and listening to the "wedding of the century" between Britain's Prince

Charles and Lady Diana Spencer. In the U.S. alone, millions rose early on a Wednesday morning to tune in.

Lady Diana, who'd just turned twenty a month earlier, arrived at London's St. Paul's Cathedral in a glass carriage, wearing a Victorian-style dress made of silk taffeta and lace, embroidered with ten thousand pearls and followed by a train that stretched twenty-five feet, long even for a royal wedding.

Much of the world was captivated.

Resolved

Reps for Major League Baseball's players and owners negotiated through the night and announced a settlement just after 6:00 a.m. on Friday morning, July 31. The strike was finally over. Warm feelings were hard to come by after the announcement, though. Miller refused to have his picture taken with Ray Grebey, the owners' chief negotiator. Player rep Rusty Staub of the Mets dodged a handshake from Grebey and called him a liar to his face.

The owners came away with compensation for lost free agents, but not the direct compensation they'd hoped for, and not enough compensation to hobble the free agent market, as they set out to do. Among the many details of the new system, teams could now "protect" twenty-four to twenty-six players on their rosters. Unprotected players would go into a pool, from which teams that lost top free agents could draft. The players, for the most part, had won, helped in part by the fact that the owners' strike insurance money was about to run out.

Major League Baseball would return with the All-Star Game in Cleveland on August 9, followed by the resumption of regular games the following day.

The strike cost the players about $28 million in lost salaries. The owners lost about $116 million but recouped about $44 million of that via the insurance policy. Others connected to baseball, such as stadium workers and owners of nearby bars and restaurants, may have taken the hardest hit, pound for pound.

Now there was the matter of how to finish the season. Should play resume with the standings where they were on June 11? Should the season be divided into two parts? The owners settled on the latter. In each division, winners of the first and second halves would face off in a playoff series, with the winners advancing to their respective league championship series. That meant new pennant races as well as an extra layer of playoff baseball, which the owners hoped would lure fans back through the gates. It also meant first-half winners like the Yankees were already guaranteed a postseason spot. In the "second season," what would Steinbrenner's Yankees have to motivate them?

The playoff system created some excitement, but it was deeply flawed. The Cincinnati Reds demonstrated just how much, finishing 1981 with the best combined record in the Majors, but failing to win the National League West in either half and missing out on the postseason.

As for the Columbus Clippers, the last of that special attention they'd received that summer was about to disappear. The end of the strike, combined with the approaching college and pro football seasons, would hinder attendance the rest of the way. They were back to relative anonymity.

AFTER THE STRIKE ENDED, Major League players didn't have much time to get back in shape before play resumed. The Yankees summoned Frazier and Castro to Yankee Stadium for a simulated game. The two pitchers suited up for rookie-level Bradenton and faced the big league lineup. Admission was free, and fans of little means had a chance to sit in prime seats.

Frazier and Castro both looked prime time. They combined with another young pitcher named Ken Smith (a different Ken Smith than the one who played for Richmond that season) to shut out the big leaguers on seven hits. Frazier stood out after coming on in the sixth with a runner on third, one out, Dave Winfield at bat, and Reggie Jackson in the on-deck circle. Frazier struck out both to end the inning.

Yankees GM Bill Bergesch approached Frazier as the pitcher emerged from a postgame shower. "You're not going back to Columbus," Bergesch told Frazier. "You're staying here." Frazier had just come off a long trip with the Clippers and had nothing but dirty clothes, so he started looking for somewhere to do his laundry.

Then the Yankees abruptly changed their minds and sent him back to Columbus where, he arrived around 5:00 p.m., at which point Verdi told him he was going back to New York, again.

"For what?" Frazier asked.

"To pitch in the big leagues," Verdi said.

"Are you kidding me?" Frazier said. "Do I have time to do some laundry?" His flight left two hours later.

Frazier stayed in New York this time. He was awed by the Yankee locker room, having grown up in Missouri dreaming of wearing pinstripes, but he wasn't awed on the mound. Frazier had an advantage. He was in shape after playing through the strike. In his Major League debut on August 11, the Yankees' second game back after the strike, he pitched three scoreless innings against visiting Texas, allowing just one hit. He posted a 1.63 ERA with three saves down the stretch, and he'd be doing his laundry in the big leagues for a while.

MIDSEASON EXHIBITION GAMES BETWEEN Major League teams and their Minor League affiliates used to be common, with many big clubs coming to Minor League cities once a season, giving fans there a look at big league stars. For fans who lived far from Major League cities, it was a rare treat.

The tradition faded over the years, and the exhibitions were eventually banned as part of the working agreement between Major League and Minor League Baseball. Big leaguers generally hated the contests, which meant another day of travel on what they figured should have been a day off. And even though the results were meaningless, Major Leaguers would just as soon not lose to Minor Leaguers, especially if Steinbrenner was in charge.

When the Yankees came to Columbus in '79 and '80, my dad got us tickets. The games provided my first glimmer of professional baseball, and though my love for the sport wouldn't really take hold until a couple of years later, my imagination was on its way to being captured. Franklin County Stadium was packed for both games. I still have the programs from the two contests.

The '79 Clippers, managed by Gene "Stick" Michael, were a Triple-A powerhouse. Columbus was a Yankee affiliate for the first time that year, and the Clippers won ten in a row to start the season. Later in '79, they won sixteen straight games.

That season's exhibition game, won by the Yankees 8–5, featured a pair of home runs each by Chris Chambliss and Jim Spencer. Dennis Werth hit a three-run shot for the Clippers, who nearly rallied to win the game in the bottom of the ninth. Michael managed to get himself thrown out (of an exhibition game!) in the ninth after arguing a call at second.

In 1980 New York beat Columbus 8–6. Here's how serious manager Dick Howser and his Yankees were about the contest: Bullpen catcher Dom Scala played right field. At one point, Howser sent pitching coach Stan Williams to the mound. Williams was only forty-three at the time, but he was nine years removed from the Majors and hadn't pitched in a Minor League game in six years. Williams went four innings and didn't pitch badly, though he did serve up a three-run homer to Joe Lefebvre.

• • •

On August 1 of '81, a new television network for music videos launched, with footage from launches of Space Shuttle Challenger and Apollo 11, followed by images of an astronaut planting the new network's flag on the moon. MTV would revolutionize music and pop culture, as well as eventually bring *Beavis and Butt-Head* into U.S. living rooms.

You probably know the first video ever played on MTV: "Video Killed the Radio Star" by the Buggles. But do you know the second? Pat Benatar's "You Better Run." Rod Stewart's "She Won't Dance with Me" was third.

Two days later, most of the nation's air traffic controllers—about thirteen thousand of them—walked off the job, demanding higher pay, better benefits, and a shorter work week. In addition to fairness, the union argued, it was a matter of public safety. Unfortunately for the controllers, for the future of labor unions in America, and for anyone who'd booked a flight around that time, President Reagan stepped in, and he wasn't in a negotiating mood.

Citing a twenty-five-year-old law banning strikes by government unions, the Gipper threatened to fire any of the controllers not back on the job in forty-eight hours. Through numerous labor disputes since the law was passed, it hadn't been leveraged in this way, and the entire air traffic control system hung in the balance. It was hardball to say the least, and it turned into one of the defining moments of Reagan's presidency. The two days passed, only about a thousand controllers returned to work, and the rest were given the heave ho. Reagan banned those fired from ever working for the FAA again.

Military controllers were brought in to help cobbled-together crews. Chaos initially reigned, and thousands of flights were canceled in the middle of the summer travel rush. The system would buckle but not break as replacements were hired. It took years, but prestrike employment levels eventually returned.

In addition to busting the union and changing labor relations in the U.S. forever, Reagan's move also left the Columbus Clippers grounded in Rochester.

On the night of August 5, the Clippers beat the Red Wings 8–5. Gulden hit a pair of home runs, scored five times, and even stole a base. Brant and Stenholm homered. Frazier ran his record to 4-1 with two and a third perfect innings of relief. A long road trip was ending, and things seemed to be looking up. Unless you were Mike Patterson, who had just gone 0 for 5, was mired in an epic 3-for-42 slump, and still 2,700 miles away from Oakland. In some ways, further than ever.

With no flights available, the Clippers faced a four-hundred-mile bus ride back to Columbus. To help the trip go down easier, they were supplied with a tremendous amount of beer for the way home. They drank it. At least most of them, and most of it.

It turned into one of the rowdiest nights of the season, increasingly raucous as the bus rolled through New York, the northwest tip of Pennsylvania and back into Ohio. Eventually, exhaustion took over and players began settling down and drifting off. Gulden, apparently the last player standing, made his way to the front of the bus and talked through tears about how he'd always dreamed about playing for the Yankees. "Is this guy ever going to pass out?" Massie wondered, hoping he, too, might eventually get some sleep.

It turned out that at least one other Clipper was still awake, and after Gulden finally closed his eyes, in the late stages of the trip, Patterson made his move. He'd been fuming all night, in desperate need of rest but unable to get any as his teammates carried on.

Patterson quietly rose from his seat and retrieved a bat from his luggage. He proceeded to walk up and down the aisle, unloading on the back of his teammates' seats like they were hanging curveballs.

"Rise and shine!" Patterson yelled. "Rise and shine, motherfuckers!"

To paraphrase Tom from *The Glass Menagerie*, and also Garfield the cat, the Clippers rose but did not shine. Patterson made sure of that.

10

Time to Get Up

It's July of 1997, and I'm sitting down the first-base line at Warner Park in Madison, Wisconsin, getting ready to watch the hometown Black Wolf play the Fargo-Moorhead Red Hawks in a matchup of teams from the independent Northern League. It's a stopover in a one-man, Idaho-to-Indiana road trip for a family reunion. I'm trying to channel Kerouac. But mostly I'm feeling tired and scattered, clobbered in waves by sadness over a particularly rough breakup two months earlier. My time on the road has left me feeling free, but also rudderless.

My seat is close to the field. Very close. I feel like I could stand up, take a few steps, and coach first base.

Then she appears. A stunning young woman, midtwenties, dressed elegantly, looking more ready for a high-powered job interview than an evening at the ballpark. She's walking down the first base line toward right field, in some sort of official capacity. Somehow, she seems out of place and right at home, at the same time.

I'm astonished. I even turn to the stranger in the seat next to me, who appears to be a regular, and mutter something along the lines of "Oh my God." He responds with a "Yah. I know."

For a few minutes, I project everything I've been looking for onto this unknowing woman who has something to do with an independent Minor League team in Wisconsin. Everything I'd hoped my shattered relationship would be. The direction in life I've been desperately searching for. All of it. I don't even consider attempting to speak to her. Best to leave her alone to go about her life.

The game begins, and I'm glad to be watching Minor League Baseball on a beautiful evening in the Midwest at a nice little ballpark. It helps some. The next day, I hit the road and complete my trip to the small Indiana town where my mom was born and grew up.

IT'S SIXTEEN YEARS LATER. I'm reading Neal Karlen's *Slouching Toward Fargo*, a great read that will turn into one of the inspirations for this book. Karlen spent the '96 and '97 seasons hanging with the Northern League's St. Paul Saints, perhaps the wildest show in baseball at the time. Comedian Bill Murray was a co-owner, along with Mike Veeck, of the over-the-top-baseball-promotions Veecks. The book's cast of characters also includes deposed Major League star Daryl Strawberry, attempting a comeback from drug problems; Ila Borders, a pitcher who would become the first woman to start and win a men's professional baseball game; Dave Stevens, who played baseball without the benefit of having legs; and "Sister Roz" Gefre, a nun who gave out massages in the stands.

They weren't the only ones to stick out. Karlen also wrote about the rival Madison Black Wolf's director of community outreach and promotions, a woman he'd gotten to know those two summers. In the book, he dubbed her the "Most Beloved Woman in the Northern League."

I'm reading Karlen's description and it dawns on me. Oh my God. That's her. The woman who made my jaw hit the fold-up seat down the first base line all those years earlier. Her name was Monica.

I read about her dreams of someday owning her own team, and the stir she created when she attended baseball's nearly all-male winter meetings. About the numerous roles she filled for the Black Wolf and the way she basically ran the team herself. About her refusal to date players and her earning of their respect, and how she dressed so nicely out of reverence for the ballpark. I learned about her devotion to baseball history and to Christy Matthewson, the gentlemanly Major League pitching great who had died more than seventy years earlier, and how she hoped to find her own "Christy Matthewson" someday.

It's May 25, 2016, and I'm speaking with Monica on the phone, having tracked her down to explain my book project and politely request an interview. She's a bit bewildered but gracious and happy to talk about her time in Madison. I leave out the whole "I loved you for five minutes in 1997" thing. Mostly I'm interested to know how a twentysomething woman wound up running a Minor League Baseball team in Wisconsin, her memories of that time, and what she's been up to since.

Monica explains that she was headed to law school, but she fell in love with baseball and took a detour.

She still loves the sport, but she no longer dreams of owning her own team. Following the '97 season, she moved to Connecticut and found other work. She's uncomfortable with her portrayal in the Karlen book and had a hard time reading it. She prefers her well-worn copy of Christy Matthewson's 1912 book *Pitching in a Pinch*. It's barely holding together these days.

Not all of her Madison memories are fond ones. It was hard work for little money. She felt very lonely at times. Handling box scores, press notes, and other baseball chores amid men who were used to other men doing all those things was often a steeper climb than she'd expected. Most players were respectful, but not all. One night, when she was cleaning out the press box, she found a note left by a visiting male beat writer to the next beat writer due in. The note was all about her, with comments on her clothes, her body, the color of her lipstick. It invited other reporters to add their own thoughts.

But for all of the moments like that, there are numerous others she gladly recalls, of her love for the team and the fans, of quickly replacing kids' dropped hot dogs, of negotiating a cable TV contract for the Black Wolf and providing color analysis for the broadcasts. She doesn't seem to have any regrets.

"Watching the sun set in those ballparks when you're in your twenties," she shares, "there's nothing quite like that."

Monica did eventually find her own "Christy Matthewson" and got married. She sounds happy about the way her life has turned out so far, and I'm glad for her.

Sometime after that night in Madison, as the pain of my breakup faded, I resumed the search for my own "Christy Matthewson," female version. It turned out that as I was sitting in the ballpark that night, she was 1,900 miles away, in the early days of a new life in Seattle. It would take me another seven years to find her.

IT'S APRIL 12, 1998, early on Easter morning. I open my eyes in a small tent, in a campground in Springfield, Missouri, in the middle of another solo, soul-searching, cross-country road trip. The sun is up. As its light hits the nylon fabric at the top of the tent, it's splaying into a large, bright cross. I stare at it for a while.

It's time to get up and go to church.

• • •

Like Mike Patterson, Marshall Brant wasn't part of the wild bunch. In many ways, Minor League life just wasn't for Brant. It wasn't that he disliked his teammates. Quite the opposite, in most cases. He just wasn't very social, and ballplayers' usual methods of killing time didn't suit him. Brant didn't carouse or play cards or gamble. On the road, he was more likely to call home, order a pizza, and eat it in his room, alone. He watched a lot of Johnny Carson. Some nights he'd wander around the various towns, sometimes ending up in cemeteries, just looking at the names and dates. He didn't even sleep in on the mornings after games, for fear doing so would make him feel groggier at the ballpark. It didn't. But any potential threat to the success he needed so much for validation was intolerable.

He didn't drink alcohol. It wasn't a choice born out of his religious convictions. It traced back to a preteen night in Penngrove.

About twelve people crammed themselves into the Brants' small, three-bedroom home. Kenneth's siblings were visiting from Minnesota, and the party was on, an epic drunk fest. One of Marshall's older brothers, about fifteen at the time, took advantage of the chaos to guzzle as much as he could. From a top bunk that night, young Marshall listened to—and smelled—his brother throwing up into a bucket for what seemed like forever. Younger brother decided at that moment that he would never touch the stuff. To this day, he can still smell the alcohol, the puke.

BRANT ONCE STRAYED FROM his personal prohibition for about two weeks. In 1977 he visited Tulsa as a member of the Double-A Texas League's Jackson Mets. Game-time temperatures approached a million degrees. After one brutally hot game, Brant staggered into the clubhouse in search of something—anything—cold and wet. A huge tub filled with ice and beer was the only option.

Brant grabbed a beer, cracked it open, and took a swig. He hated it. He passed the rest to teammate Mike Scott, the future Cy Young Award winner for the Houston Astros.

The next night, Brant got three hits. Perhaps he was onto something. After that game, he took another swig and passed the rest to Scott. He hit safely again the next night.

A player on a streak has to respect the streak. The ritual continued. Take a swig, hate it, hand the rest to Mike Scott, repeat. It continued after every game until Brant's hitting streak ended at eighteen, one of the longest of his career. He can't remember drinking any other time in his life.

Brant didn't take any illegal drugs, either. At least not on purpose.

During the '81 season, on a muggy July night at Franklin County Stadium, Brant launched a walk-off home run in the bottom of the eleventh, giving the Clippers a 4–3 win against Rochester. Many of those in attendance noticed the slugger was unusually animated, for him at least. Brant smacked Verdi's hand so hard rounding third that the manager quipped it had to be iced. Arriving at home plate, Brant leaped in the air and high-fived teammates.

Years later, Brant's daughter watched a videotape of the home run and her dad's reaction.

"Wow, what got into you?" she asked him.

What got into him were some "greenies" that a teammate had added to his pregame iced tea. The pills, a type of amphetamine, were ubiquitous in Major League clubhouses—and many Minor League clubhouses—until Major League Baseball banned and started testing for them in 2006. Taking them without a prescription was a federal offense. But for decades, greenies were commonly used by players to boost energy and alertness, particularly after a rough night out, or during the exhausting stretch drives of long seasons. They were new to Brant, and they had quite an effect on him.

When he came to bat in the bottom of the first inning, he realized something very strange was going on. The bat felt awfully light. The ball looked pretty big. "Okay, I know what happened," he thought to himself. "I know what somebody did."

Instead of trying to amp himself up, Brant spent the game trying to dial himself back. In the fourth inning, Rochester starter Tom Rowe brushed him back with a close pitch. It wasn't malicious and not even that close, but Brant had a flash of "You motherfucker" in his mind. For a brief moment, he wanted to do something he'd never done, nor ever would do, in his career. He wanted to charge the mound.

Greenies were one of baseball's dirty secrets. Pete Rose is one of the former superstars who has acknowledged taking them. Brant recalled a spring training rain delay in '78, when Rose was with the Reds, and Willie Mays was coaching for the Mets. Rose came into the Mets clubhouse and started playing cards with Mays. "Let's play for these," Rose said, producing a handful of greenies from his back pocket, to big laughs.

• • •

Like any baseball players, the '81 Clippers had their nicknames. In addition to "Bonesy" (Balboni), "Big Game Lew" (Jim Lewis), and "B.B." (Brown), the Clippers had "Whermy" (Wehrmeister) and "Cocky" (Cochran). Mike Patterson was referred to as "Buck." The erudite Paul Boris was sometimes referred to as "The Professor." Mike Griffin was tagged as "Muffin Head."

Dave Coleman had a few: "Coley," "Moe Bagger" (because of his haircut, which called to mind a certain Stooge), and the least fortunate of the three—"Dick Nose." The origin of that last one is less clear. But Harer remembers it being used widely, even by Coleman's Minor League coaches, one of whom came from the South and spoke like Foghorn Leghorn. "Ah say, ah say, ah say, Dick Nose?"

Harer played with Coleman in the Red Sox farm system and will forever be known to former teammates and baseball friends as "Hanger." Gary Allenson gave Harer the moniker when they played together in the Red Sox organization. At the time, Harer

1981 Columbus Clippers
Outfielder
WAYNE HARER —22

FIG 26. Wayne Harer's 1981 baseball card. Courtesy of the Columbus Clippers.

had particularly broad shoulders and an otherwise skinny body. "Take the hanger out of your shirt," Allenson quipped.

"Why these things stick, I'll never know," Harer said many years later.

Like his good friend "Dick Nose," "Hanger" suffered a crushed heart in 1977, into 1978, courtesy of the Boston Red Sox. His sparkling .350 average for Pawtucket had earned him an International League batting title and seemed to secure at least a look from the big club. The following spring, the first baseman/outfielder not only didn't make the Boston Red Sox, but he wasn't even invited to spring training. "They took my spirit," he'd describe. "They broke my heart."

Back with Pawtucket instead of up with Boston, Harer wasn't the same player. His average dipped to .247. His lack of power had already hobbled his chances to advance, especially in the Red Sox organization, and they parted ways at season's end. The following year, Harer was back in Double-A with the Yankees' West Haven club. A bounce-back performance got him a bump to Triple-A Columbus, but as previously noted, the Yankees weren't exactly the org to be with when it came to promotions to the Majors. Plus, Harer was tagged with the wrong labels. Arm not up to Major League standards. Inconsistent at the plate. Insufficient speed. With the Clippers, though, he made one last kick. The team's moment on the national stage during the Major League strike afforded him some exposure he wouldn't have seen otherwise. Unfortunately for Harer, ESPN and WABC audiences tuning in during June and July wouldn't see or hear him at his best.

HARER STARTED THE '81 season as hot as ever. On May 3 he helped Columbus snap a four-game losing streak with a two-out, two-run double in the top of the ninth at Norfolk. His batting average stood at .343, best on the team. Then that inconsistency struck, along with a hand injury, and he cooled considerably. A 3-for-26 stretch in July dropped his batting average to .267. As teammates like Balboni and Ashford made an impression before a national TV audience, Harer's Major League hopes faded further.

It wasn't for lack of dedication or effort. "Rookie" Letendre, the team's trainer, remembers Harer as the "consummate pro." The Clippers outfielder was known for doing his share of carousing and joking around off the field, even at the then ripe old age of twenty-nine. On the field, it was different.

"This wasn't 'Slapshot,'" Rick ("Rock Head") Stenholm remembered. "This was a professional baseball player. He wasn't a great athlete. For him to play as well as he did at that level . . . that's saying something."

Harer wasn't going any higher in his baseball career. The Major League strike ended. The ESPN cameras packed up and left. He didn't do either of those things. As the season wound down and the Clippers found themselves back in a pennant race, he very much showed up.

In late July, the rest of the International League was choking on the Clippers' base-path dust. Columbus had built that twelve-game lead in the IL standings and showed no signs of letting up. The Richmond Braves weren't quitting, though, and they made it a race with an unbelievable tear. The Braves rolled into Columbus on August 10 having won five straight games, fifteen out of their last sixteen, and twenty out of their last twenty-four. Richmond had pulled to within six games of the Clippers, and the atmosphere at Franklin County Stadium during the three-game series was electric.

After the teams split the first two contests, Harer delivered his biggest game of the season in the rubber match.

In the top of the fourth inning, Harer, playing left field, snared a sinking liner to rob Ken Smith of a base hit. In the seventh, Harer leaped high and reached over the fence to rob Matt Sinatro of a home run. Then in the bottom of the ninth, Harer delivered a two-out RBI single that dropped just in front of speedy Braves center fielder Brett Butler, capping a three-run rally as the Clippers won, 4–3. As Butler lay on the artificial surface with his face to the ground, Clipper teammates mobbed Harer. Those dashed big league dreams weren't so important right then.

Columbus had snatched momentum back from Richmond in one of the season's biggest moments. For Hanger, there were more heroics to come.

Friendly Confines

"Col-um-bus Clippers, our team is number one . . . Col-um-bus Clippers, our fans are half the fun . . ."

The team's two jingles, "Hometown Heroes" and "Ring Your Bell," are inescapable. The lyrics for the hokey, polka-inspired tunes are simple, by design. The fans never seem to tire of them. Opposing players do. Subjected to the tunes endlessly, and often amid their own misfortune, opponents must figure there's a special place in hell for whoever wrote the damn things. "If it bothers the opposition," Schnacke says, "so much the better."

An Indianapolis jingle company crafted the songs. Team officials listened to a hundred different options before settling on the two winners and paying $2,000 for the rights. The songs would be phased out, at least mostly, by the time the Clippers moved into a fancy new ballpark in 2009. But for now, "Hometown Heroes" and "Ring Your Bell" are as big a part of the experience as a hot dog and a Coke, or a beer, if you're old enough.

Most fans in attendance carry their own Victory Bells, modeled after the big bell sounded after each Clipper victory. The mini bells, $2.50 a pop, are top sellers at souvenir stands. Fans ring them throughout each game, exhorted by messages from the scoreboard. The titular lyric in "Ring Your Bell" is followed by the biggest flurry. "No matter who they're playin', they'll always play 'em well," the song informs, "Col-um-bus Clippers ring your bell."

On any game night at Franklin County Stadium, there are at least several thousand in attendance. Joe Hill, also a public-address announcer for Ohio State football, introduces batters in stern, grandfatherly tones. That hot dog–beer combo—with some Cracker Jack thrown in—will cost you $3.00, up from $2.50 last season. A bag of peanuts will really set you back relative to last year at 80 cents, an 89 percent increase, due to bad weather and poor crops in the South.

Take a walk around the ballpark, and you might hear the loud cheering and bell ringing of Henrietta Webster, one of the team's biggest fans, known to bake cakes for grateful players. Henrietta lost her eyesight to glaucoma at age fifty-three and nearly lost her will to live. She'd wander into the street, hoping to get hit, before realizing that God just wasn't done with her yet. Now, twelve years later, she's found a new calling in counseling others facing impending blindness. After the game tonight, she'll stay close to her phone, ready to field calls from others in the early stages. She'll talk with them, pray with them, help them prepare for life with little or no sight.

You might run into Caryl Starkey of nearby Grove City, known as "the bubble gum lady," handing out some of the fifty pieces she brings to every game for young fans.

Check the box seats down the first base line, four rows up, and you'll find superboosters Pat and Betty Mahoney. After the game you'll probably find Pat Mahoney at a bar called Patton's, and he'll probably be picking up the tab. Pat works in the steel business. The Mahoneys look after Clippers players, providing beer and occasional meals, and stepping in to help if someone gets into a jam.

You might run into Glenn Stout. Before he became an award-winning author, Stout sold ticket packages for the Clippers during the '81 season. He worked in a boiler room in the visitors' locker room, down the first base line, earning ten dollars for every twenty-dollar ticket package he sold. There wasn't much to like about the job, except for getting to attend a lot of games while eating nachos with double jalapenos. And for having any job right out of college in a craptacular economy. It mostly beat working the overnight shift in a grocery store, which he did previously.

For some reason, Stout had his best luck selling tickets to Catholic priests and motorcycle gangs. A courier once delivered some of the tickets Stout sold to a gang house in a rough part of town. "Just climb in the window," a gang member had instructed. "The money's on the table."

Back at Franklin County Stadium, a developmentally disabled young man named Jeff helps out with the grounds crew. Like Henrietta, he is known and beloved by the players.

Young Lindsay Brant has wandered away from her seat behind home plate again. Mom Diana is home tonight with baby Matti, listening on the radio. A shrill whistle from Lindsay's dad, who is standing in the on-deck circle, sends her scampering back. Regulars sitting nearby will keep watch as well, making sure she doesn't wander too far.

New Heroes

Yet another hero for the Clippers' stretch run emerged during the Richmond series.

After making the big club out of spring training at age twenty, pitcher Gene Nelson wound up on the disabled list with an intestinal virus, then looked less than sharp on the mound. He hadn't pitched all that badly, and the Yankees remained high on him, but they thought better of rushing him to the Majors. As big league play resumed on August 10, they sent him to Columbus, making room for Frazier.

The Braves entered game two of the showdown series that night with six straight wins, including a victory in the opener that shrunk the struggling Clippers' lead in the standings to five games. Richmond had every bit of the momentum at a crucial point in the season. Nelson, who hadn't pitched in two months, save for one exhibition inning, arrived in Columbus just one hour before game time.

Verdi tossed the young pitcher right into the intensifying heat of the IL pennant race. In the sixth inning, the Braves pulled within 5–4 when Bo Porter led off with a homer off Castro. Nelson, his mustache just shaved off per Steinbrenner's rules, came on in relief. He allowed a bunt single to Matt Sinatro. Then he struck out Chico Ruiz, retired Paul Runge on a grounder to first, and fanned eventual league MVP Brett Butler on a dramatic 3-2 changeup that demonstrated poise well beyond Nelson's years. Remember, this guy was still just twenty years old. He finished the game with four shutout innings, allowing just two hits and striking out six. To Verdi's particular delight, his new star didn't walk a batter.

The Clippers went on to an 8–4 win and reestablished themselves in the IL race. Nelson went on to a long Major League career, after starring for Columbus as a starter down the stretch.

The ever-evolving, previously shaky starting rotation had turned into arguably the league's best. Wehrmeister missed stretches due to injury and a brief call-up to the Yankees, Ryder was slumping and Bruhert had faded somewhat. But rapidly improving McGaffigan and Pacella were becoming anchors. Castro remained a strong option as a starter or out of the bullpen. Now the Clippers had Nelson, too. And Wehrmeister would be back before long.

• • •

The Lord had taught Rick Stenholm patience. He wasn't sure what else could be getting him through the '81 season. There weren't many Clippers, if any, who had a tougher time that spring and summer.

"Rock Head" (nickname courtesy of an opposing coach) had been in the Minors for six seasons, never hitting below .270. He also hit for power, smacking forty-nine homers in his first three seasons, including an impressive nineteen-homer, 102-RBI campaign with Double-A West Haven in '78. The Yankees loaned him to teams in Maracaibo, Venezuela, and Mexico City for portions of the '79 and '80 seasons. The ball really flew off his bat in the thin air of Mexico City, seven-thousand-plus feet above sea level. The locals in the stands, many of whom were very poor, passed the sombrero after home runs to reward their heroes. A homer could fetch the equivalent of $400 U.S. Stenholm was one of the heroes, and it was the best time he ever had playing baseball.

Stenholm helped Columbus to its first two pennants and Governors' Cup titles in '79 and '80. At the outset of the '81 season, like most of his teammates, he figured it was past time he broke through.

Looking back, he'll tell you that if it weren't for his faith, the '81 season might have broken him.

An injury during batting practice provided a microcosm. Stenholm had just walked up and leaned on the batting cage when Tucker Ashford sent a screamer right at him. The ball hit the net but continued right into Stenholm's lip, which exploded. Team doctor John Stephens told Stenholm he couldn't numb him up before stitching him up. If he did, the lip wouldn't come out right. Stenholm had entered the clubhouse with a dry T-shirt. By the time Stephens was done, the T-shirt was so soaked with sweat that Stenholm could have wrung it out.

More seriously, Stenholm got beaned by Tidewater's Tim Leary on August 9, spent three days in Mount Carmel Medical Center, the hospital where my dad worked as an administrator, and didn't rejoin the team for a week.

FIG 27. Outfielder Rick Stenholm never hit below .270 in the Minors until a difficult 1981 season. *Columbus Citizen-Journal*, Scripps Howard Newspapers/ Grandview Heights Public Library/Photohio.org.

But Stenholm's main source of frustration was a losing battle for playing time amid the glut of talented outfielders. Without that playing time, he struggled for the first time in his career. His batting average dipped below .200. More outwardly than most, Stenholm resented the Yankees' "stock-the-Minors-but-sign-free-agents" approach. He was tired of feeling like a spare tire. After winning a game with a pinch-hit home run, then finding himself out of the lineup the next day, Stenholm confronted Verdi. The veteran manager explained that he was just doing his job, trying to put the best team on the field each day. Stenholm then laid into Verdi for a good fifteen minutes. Verdi sat there and calmly took it. Then he buried Stenholm on the bench for about two weeks, until the outfielder apologized.

Stenholm's real beef was with the organization. It was Steinbrenner and the Yankees, though, who first gave Stenholm a chance when no one else would.

A NATIVE OF BROOKSVILLE, Florida, Stenholm played baseball for the University of South Florida in Tampa. When he started, the program was less than stellar. The coach, Hubert "Beefy" Wright, had taken on another job and often wasn't even there for the first few innings of the team's games. A well-meaning graduate assistant filled out the lineup cards, but he didn't exactly inspire confidence among the players. "Ya right, Davis," they'd tell him.

Enter Jack Butterfield, who replaced Wright in '75. Butterfield brought an impressive coaching résumé from the University of Maine, including a third-place finish in the College World Series eleven years earlier. Any issues with discipline or seriousness were toast. "He jerked the 'slacker' right out of us," Stenholm would recall.

Stenholm starred at USF but wasn't drafted. He began to drift again, smoking a lot of pot and wandering around the country like Caine in *Kung Fu*. After spending some time as an iron worker in Wyoming, Stenholm found himself back in Tampa late in '75, at Christmastime. Butterfield was now scouting for the New York Yankees, having been hired by Steinbrenner.

"If you clean up your act, I can get you a tryout with the Yankees," Butterfield told Stenholm. "But you'd better shave off that beard, son. And all that long hair."

Stenholm and Garry Smith, his former teammate at USF and future teammate with the '81 Clippers, went to meet with Steinbrenner at the Old Hillsborough Building on Florida Avenue. Smith was from Maine and knew Butterfield from there. The coach hoped Steinbrenner would give Smith a chance, too. At the meeting, the newly shorn Stenholm was so nervous that he bobbled a cup of coffee and knocked it over.

"Son," Steinbrenner said, "I hope your hands are better than that."

The Boss asked them if they thought they could play for the New York Yankees. Their "yes" and Butterfield's recommendation was all it took. "See you at spring training," the Boss said.

The following year, the Yankees elevated Butterfield to a new post, director of player development and scouting. He became a beloved and important figure in their organization, a gung ho, father-figure type and a great baseball man. In November of '79, still deeply hurting from the death of Thurman Munson three months earlier, the Yankees received another horrible blow when Butterfield died in a car accident on an icy night near Paramus, New Jersey. He was just fifty years old.

Smith was a sophomore in high school when Butterfield, then the head coach at Maine, first recruited him, and Butterfield became a second dad. Smith and his wife were driving home from the Florida Instructional League, stopped for the night, turned on the TV, and heard the news of Butterfield's death. They sat there in their hotel and just cried for an hour. A statement from Steinbrenner read, "He was the epitome of what you'd look for in a teacher of young men."

STENHOLM LOST THE BUSHY hair but remained a wild man during his early years as a Minor Leaguer. Fort Lauderdale, West Haven, Maracaibo. The hard living left him increasingly unfulfilled. It reached a head in South America. He felt that when he stepped on the baseball field, he could do no wrong. Off the field, nothing felt right anymore. There was also the matter of a pregnant young woman back in West Haven. Stenholm wasn't sure what to do.

He had never been particularly religious, but before a game in Maracaibo one day, he knelt in the outfield, amid unmowed blades of Bermuda grass, and told God he couldn't take it anymore and needed help. He made his way back to the dugout, checked the lineup card, and didn't see his name listed. He checked under "Extras." His name wasn't listed there either. He didn't have much time to wonder what was going on. Manager Luis Aparicio appeared and told him he'd been recalled. Stenholm was headed back to the states. He took it as a sign, and from that point on, he dedicated his life to Jesus Christ.

Stenholm returned to the U.S. and got his life in order. He went to West Haven, sat down with his pregnant girlfriend's parents and begged for their forgiveness. It wasn't an easy sell. "If I were thirty years younger," her father told him, "I would kill you right now." Stenholm eventually married her, and it would last, as would his newfound faith.

Stenholm never did regain his prowess with Columbus, finishing the '81 season with a batting average of just .220. He returned to Mexico City for the next two seasons before deciding to retire. These days he owns a construction business, builds dream homes in the Tampa area, and shares his story of a life turned around.

11

"I Guess I'm in Charge"

DAVE RIGHETTI RETURNED FROM the strike showing no ill effects from the two-month break. In the Yankees' second post-strike game, he suffered his first loss of the season as New York fell to visiting Texas 1–0, but he allowed only the one earned run and fanned nine in six innings. Frazier, making his Yankee debut, pitched three scoreless innings in relief.

Righetti went 1-2 during the abbreviated August schedule with a sparkling 1.89 ERA. Over in the National League, Valenzuela struggled in his first two games back before righting himself. On August 27 at Dodger Stadium, the other hot young lefty ran his record to 11-4 with a ten-strikeout, four-hit shutout against the Cubs. Both young pitchers were closing in on Rookie of the Year honors.

Up in San Jose, Leo Righetti's pain was eased somewhat.

HE CAME WITHIN ONE hour of the Major Leagues. The man who would be Dave Righetti's father figured he'd made the Boston Braves' roster in the spring of '52. A middle infielder, he struggled with the bat for most of his career but was known for outstanding defense. It apparently had been enough this time, and Leo suited up for the Braves' Opening Day game against Jackie Robinson and the visiting Brooklyn Dodgers.

Just sixty minutes from game time, Leo learned he was headed back to the Minors. The Braves had decided to instead keep Jack Cusick, a light-hitting shortstop they'd acquired in a trade with the Chicago Cubs. Leo, never known for keeping his emotions in check, did not handle the news well. There are different accounts of the incident, but all of them involve a chair, either kicked or thrown, at either Braves manager Tommy Holmes, or at the team's GM, John Quinn. However the chair was delivered, and to whomever it was directed, Leo was not long for the Braves organization. He never again came so close to achieving his Major League dreams.

Leo Righetti was born in 1925 in San Francisco, where his mother had grown up next door to Yankees great Tony Lazzeri. Leo took to athletics early on, starring in basketball at San Jose's Bellarmine Preparatory. Legend has it that he once heaved a football eighty yards, but he didn't play football for Bellarmine, as the sport just didn't interest him. Baseball did. He got his start playing sandlot ball before joining the St. Patrick's CYO (Catholic Youth Organization) team, managed by Father George Francis. A pitcher back then, fiery Leo grew into one of the best prep players in California, finishing his Bellarmine career with five one-hitters and a no-hitter in his last six games. Yankees scout Joe Devin took notice. Leo became a "bonus baby," signing a $10,000 contract with the Yankees. He was only seventeen.

The Minor Leagues were mostly unkind to Leo, whose nickname was "Pinky." In 1946 he tripped on a glass bottle in Binghamton, fell, and sliced off the tip of his right index finger, ending his pitching career. Leo shifted his focus to playing in the infield, loudly criticizing himself on the field, externally as well as internally. He frequently clashed with umpires, among others. With the Texas League's Beaumont Roughnecks in '50, Leo had a run-in with the legendary Rogers Hornsby, the team's manager. Get your face out of your racing form and teach us some hitting, Leo told Hornsby, adding that Hornsby could take his racing form and stick it. The outburst earned Leo a suspension. Later that season he quit the team, ending his time in the Yankees organization.

He spent the last five years of his baseball career in the Pacific Coast League. As his playing days wound down, he married a woman named Sandra Jean Smith. Son Steve came along in '57, followed by Dave in '58, fourteen months later. The family settled in San Jose, where Leo worked in his father's tallow factory. Tallow is made by rendering leftover animal parts into a substance used to make candles, soap, shortening, and other products. It was hard, mostly unpleasant work, hauling large containers of meat scraps, among other tasks. Leo was usually out the door for work by 5:00 a.m.

Steve and Dave emerged from the Leo Righetti School of Baseball and took different paths. After three frustrating, injury-riddled seasons in the Minors, Steve wound up back in San Jose, working at the tallow factory. Dave became a Major League Baseball star. In 1983, the same year Dave tossed a no-hitter against Boston on the Fourth of July, Steve nearly died in an accident at the factory. Dave struggled with guilt. A few years into Dave's Major League career, the two men argued in a parking lot outside a bar, loudly enough that the police were called. It ended with Dave in tears and Steve understanding for the first time how badly his brother felt about their reversals of baseball fortune.

"I feel like he should have made it," Dave said years later. "He was better than me."

As for Leo, Dave can't remember his father complaining directly about falling short of the Major Leagues, but it ate at him. Leo lived vicariously through Dave, and watching his son succeed where he hadn't succeeded helped Leo some.

"He talked about it filling an emptiness," Dave said. "It meant a lot to me."

"Was That a Changeup?"

As impressive as Andy McGaffigan's turnaround was, it couldn't match the reversal of pitching fortune enjoyed by John Pacella.

Pacella had once pitched a no-hitter on Opening Day in the Texas League. He'd briefly tasted the Majors in '77 and '79 before sticking in 1980, when he outdueled Hall of Famer Steve Carlton for his first Major League win. Pacella threw as hard as anyone in the Yankees organization not named Goose Gossage, so hard that his cap flew off his head with almost every pitch.

Yet there Pacella was, well into 1981, not only back in Triple-A, but getting shelled by opposing hitters most outings. His confidence had been beaned. He was confused. But his issues were no mystery to Sammy Ellis.

The coach would describe the big right-hander's delivery as "all

FIG 28. John Pacella credits pitching coach Sammy Ellis with his 1981 resurgence. *Columbus Citizen-Journal*, Scripps Howard Newspapers/Grandview Heights Public Library/Photohio.org.

tensed up." Pacella's mechanics were a mess, and he wasn't finishing his pitches or finding the plate with them. His mid- to upper-90s fastball had lost its pop. His cap stopped flying off.

Ellis needed to loosen Pacella's delivery. "Go down to the bullpen," Ellis told the struggling pitcher one day. "I want you to air it out. I don't care where the ball goes."

Another drill, which Ellis borrowed from baseball coaches in Japan, involved repeatedly folding a hand towel over and cracking it like a whip. "Great," Pacella thought. "I'm struggling and this guy's got me snapping a frickin' towel."

The Ellis regimen started working, though. Pacella's arm unwound. The two men studied films of Pacella's delivery. Ellis adjusted Pacella's grip on his slider and got him driving off the mound properly to recoup some of that missing power.

Pacella's cap started flying off again, which for him, at that time, was a good sign. But his struggles continued as he adjusted. On June 4, in Columbus, he took a thrashing from the Charleston Charlies and endured boos from the home crowd. He followed up with another bad outing. And another. On the night of July 4, Pacella coughed up six runs on twelve hits in just five innings against visiting Rochester. His ERA was a rotten 6.39, and his career was teetering.

Then on July 9, a hot night at Franklin County Stadium, Pacella started turning his season around. Perhaps all the tips from Ellis finally came together. Maybe a pregame switch to a new locker on the other side of the clubhouse made a difference. Whatever the reasons, Pacella looked like a different pitcher. He threw six and a third solid innings, allowing a run on four hits. He struck out three, and more importantly, he walked only one.

Pacella beat Pawtucket in his next start. He shook off one more shaky outing, then evened his record at 8-8 with a win at Syracuse on July 30. The following month, his turnaround went from impressive to stunning. No pitcher in the league was hotter. In four August starts, Pacella posted a 0.53 ERA with thirty-three strikeouts and just six walks.

Verdi may have been happiest after a three-hit shutout against Toledo on August 25. Pacella retired the first thirteen Mud Hens in order and struck out nine. To Verdi's particular delight, Pacella didn't walk a batter.

After the game, Verdi approached Pacella by his locker, grabbed the pitcher by the sides of his head and looked him in the eye.

"No walks!" Verdi beamed. Then the old coach pulled his hands back and into the air, as if he were performing a magic trick, and shuffled away.

OF ALL PACELLA'S IMPRESSIVE outings late that summer, his August 4 start in Rochester was special.

More than he had all season, Pacella was able to locate his pitches, which consistently topped 90 mph. Heading into the eighth, his fastball had literally been unhittable. He'd faced the minimum and had a no-hitter going. Rochester's only base runner to that point, Floyd Rayford, walked in the third, but Espino threw him out on an attempted steal.

In the bottom of the eighth, Pacella briefly abandoned his fastball and tried a changeup on Rochester's Tom Chism, who promptly broke up the no-hitter with a single to center field.

Verdi was up and out of the dugout immediately. He made his way out to the mound, waddling somewhat. Pacella could tell that his manager wasn't pleased.

Verdi calmly arrived. He looked at Pacella.

"What the fuck was that?" he asked the pitcher. "Was that a changeup?"

"Ya, uh . . ." Pacella responded.

"You got a changeup?"

"Ya, I've . . ."

Verdi removed his cap, and in front of seven thousand people, whacked Pacella on the head with it.

"What the hell are you doing," Verdi said, in more of a statement than a question. "I'll be a sonovabitch." With that, he waddled back to the dugout.

Pacella completed nine innings, allowing just the one hit and the one walk. He had struck out eleven batters. It was a masterpiece. Unfortunately for Pacella and the Clippers, Rochester starter Brooks Carey had been almost as stingy, shutting out the Clippers on just four hits and striking out seven. The game went into extra innings tied at 0–0.

Carey added one more scoreless frame in the tenth. In the bottom of the inning, Pacella looked slightly more human, allowing a lead-off single to Dallas Williams and falling behind Cal Ripken in the count, 2-0. Verdi opted to bring Jim Lewis in from the bullpen. Lewis completed the walk to Ripken. Then pinch hitter Chris Bourjas bunted down the third base line. Ashford fielded the ball and attempted to force Williams at third, but his throw to Robertson covering was too late, and the Red Wings had the bases loaded with nobody out.

The next batter, Dan Logan, hit a high chopper toward Ashford. It was a tough play. Ashford's throw home was wide, Williams scored, and the epic game was over. Rochester 1, Columbus 0.

Pacella took the loss, but no one—with the exception of Pacella himself—was talking about that afterward. It may have been the best pitching performance in the International League that season, and Rochester manager Doc Edwards said after the game that Pacella "was a Major League pitcher tonight."

Pacella was quick to share credit. "I'm a better pitcher now than I ever was," he told reporters after the game. "And it's because of Sammy Ellis."

Verdi may also have had something to do with it. Even days later, though, Pacella could hear the manager muttering as he walked by.

"Changeup. What the hell."

FEW—IF ANY—MINOR LEAGUE TEAMS back then had a pitching coach as gifted as Ellis. Some teams didn't have a pitching coach at all, at least not fulltime. Some Minor League managers even ran a one-person operation, which meant lonely lives on the road for them, as well as less help for developing players.

Steinbrenner and the Yankees took a different approach, stacking their teams with more and better coaches, in addition to better players. It was another perk of playing in the Yankees organization. In this case, it probably saved Pacella's career.

In addition to Ellis and the experienced Verdi, the Clippers coaching staff included former big league catcher McNertney, an able bench coach and a foil for some of Verdi's wilder ideas. They debated baseball scenarios well into the night during long bus trips. "Why can't I bring my stopper in if I'm in a jam in the earlier innings?" Verdi would ask. "He's my stopper, isn't he?" McNertney and Ellis would talk Verdi down if they could.

Johnny Oates (the baseball man, not the Daryl Hall sidekick) spent some time as a Clippers coach that season, in between his playing days and very successful managing career. Showalter and Oates became the closest of friends, and Showalter will tell you there was no one better in terms of positive things to emulate. Oates died of a brain tumor in 2004. When Showalter took over as the Baltimore Orioles manager several years later, he chose to wear number 26 in Oates's honor.

Clippers strength coach Howard "Hopalong" Cassady was already a legend, just not in baseball. "Hop" was a former Ohio State running back who won the Heisman Trophy in 1955. Steinbrenner knew Cassady from their Ohio State days, and the Boss set him up with the Clippers job.

The Columbus coaching staff also had Mickey Vernon, a quiet gentleman from Marcus Hook, Pennsylvania, who'd won two batting titles during a long Major League career. Vernon, a smooth-fielding first baseman and fan favorite, first broke into professional baseball way back in 1937. An assistant GM for the Baltimore Orioles once called Vernon the "only man I know of in baseball who could play first base in a tuxedo, appear perfectly comfortable, and never wrinkle his suit."

Vernon was now twenty-plus seasons into coaching and managing. He didn't say much, but he was known to tell a story or two from way back, including this one: Vernon first made the Washington Senators roster coming out of spring training in 1939. In those days, you didn't fly up from Florida to start the regular season. You barnstormed your way back, playing exhibitions against other Major League teams along the way. Jacksonville, Savannah ... wherever the train would stop.

Vernon, just twenty and wide-eyed at the time, remembered facing the powerful New York Yankees during one of the stops. He watched as Lou Gehrig, a superstar known as the "Iron Horse" for record-breaking durability, manned his usual position at first base for New York. A throw from one of the infielders came Gehrig's way, but glanced off his glove.

"God dammit, get those throws up!" Gehrig screamed at the infielder in frustration. "You know I'm having trouble with the lower ones!"

Something was wrong and rapidly getting worse. Just eight games into the regular season, Gehrig pulled himself out of the Yankee lineup before a game in Detroit. All in attendance were stunned. He'd played in a record 2,130 consecutive games and hadn't missed one in fourteen years.

Just over two months later, Gehrig was at the mic in Yankee Stadium delivering his "luckiest man on the face of the Earth" speech, his body already ravaged by the disease that now bears his name. His career was over; and less than two years later, he was gone.

ON TOP OF HIS skills as a pitching coach, Sammy Ellis—he preferred to go by Sam later in life—was a players' coach, closer in age and temperament to those early '80s Clippers teams than Verdi, or Joe Altobelli the previous season. Ellis, who himself had won twenty-two games for the Reds in 1965, wasn't much of a disciplinarian, as evidenced by an incident in Richmond during the 1980 season.

The team was preparing to leave Parker Field for a bus trip to Norfolk. Altobelli had decided to skip this particular bus ride. He left Ellis and McNertney in charge and planned to meet up with the team later.

The team was on the bus, waiting for a few stragglers, when a policeman walked on.

"Who's in charge?" the policeman asked. There was a brief silence.

"I guess I'm in charge," Ellis said.

"We had three of your players under the stands, smoking a little reefer."

The three players—Ellis asked years later that names be left out—had apparently been soothing themselves for the hundred-mile trip. Their careers hung in the balance. Ellis, the policeman, and the accused ended up in the office of the Braves' general manager.

The policeman agreed to let the players go if the team provided the discipline. Ellis said the team would. But Ellis didn't report the incident to Altobelli or anyone else in the Yankee organization. The players might have been released on the spot, their careers derailed. Instead, two of them eventually made it to the Major Leagues.

"To this day, Altobelli still doesn't know what happened," Ellis said in 2015, less than a year before he died of cancer at age seventy-five.

Ellis was "called up" to the Yankees during the '82 season. Righetti was suffering through a sophomore slump, and Steinbrenner angrily shipped the reigning American League Rookie of the Year back to Columbus. When Righetti rejoined the Yankees, the team took the unusual step of promoting Ellis, too. The two men made the drive from Rochester to the Bronx in Ellis's car.

For Ellis, it was the beginning of a three-year stint as a pitching coach with the big club. He'd spend nine more seasons as a Major League pitching coach, sprinkled amid other gigs.

• • •

The Richmond Braves stayed hot for the rest of the '81 regular season, slowing the Clippers' march to the IL pennant, despite losing Brett Butler to the Majors. Butler got the call on August 19 and got off to a hot start in Atlanta, where they played the theme from "Gone with the Wind" before his at bats, as if his first name were Rhett instead of Brett.

My family packed up and drove to California with the pennant race still unsettled. Good-bye, Columbus. Hello Davenport, Kearney, Rock Springs, and Elko along the way. At each stop, I wondered how that pennant race was going.

The Clippers put together a six-game win streak of their own, capped by a 5–2 win at Richmond on the night of August 21, with Ashford going 5 for 5 and turning in another dazzling play at third base. Then Richmond bounced back and won the next two games of the series, including a 1–0 pitchers' duel between McGaffigan and Larry McWilliams. Richmond's lone run was set up by a Coleman throwing error in the third inning.

But the Clippers' lead in the standings proved too much for Richmond to overcome, despite the Braves ending the season with thirty-two wins in their final forty-two games. Columbus clinched its third straight IL flag on the night of August 29, downing visiting Charleston 8–7 before a jacked-up crowd of nearly nine thousand. Balboni clubbed his league-best thirty-second home run. Robertson knocked in the decisive run with a single in the bottom of the eighth. A few now meaningless games remained on the regular-season schedule. After that, it would be on to the Governors' Cup playoffs.

The Clippers passed cigars and champagne around the locker room after the game. Wehrmeister gave Verdi a champagne shower. Patterson, who'd caught the final out in center field, talked afterward about never playing on a winning team before this, and how this team was the greatest he'd ever been a part of. He wasn't much of a drinker, but he grabbed a nearby bottle of Jack Daniels and guzzled a good amount of it. "I've never seen a guy get so drunk, so fast," Brant would recall.

Despite their struggles in August, Columbus finished the regular season with a record of 88-51, five games ahead of second-place Richmond.

ON SEPTEMBER 1, DURING the final days of the regular season, the International League handed out awards voted on by players, coaches, front office personnel, and members of the media. The Clippers had three legitimate candidates for MVP of the league. Balboni would finish with a league-best thirty-three home runs and ninety-eight RBIs. Brant would end up with twenty-five homers, ninety-five RBIs, and fewer strikeouts. In a *Dispatch* column, Massie made the case for Tucker Ashford.

The Columbus third baseman would finish the campaign hitting .300 with a team-record thirty-two doubles, plus seventeen homers and eighty-six RBIs. He did pull somewhat of a reverse–Ted Williams, opting to sit out the meaningless regular-season finale to preserve the batting average. Verdi understood. "He's done his job," the manager told Massie. "Nobody remembers what you did in your last game, they remember what you hit. If you hit .300, it's like being one of the top ten sexiest guys in the world."

Ashford added to his sexiness that season by saving at least a few games with terrific plays at third base. And unlike Brant and Balboni, he'd been consistent at the plate throughout the season.

It turned out none of them won the award. It went instead to Richmond's Butler, who hit .335, swiped forty-four bases, and ignited the Braves' offense night after night, before his call-up to Atlanta.

Ashford came back to win the International League MVP Award in 1982. In spring training of '83, he made two errors in the city game against the Mets, unforgivable as far as the Boss was concerned. After uttering the famed "We've seen enough of Tucker Ashford," Steinbrenner traded Ashford to the Mets that very day.

Ashford briefly returned to the Majors at the beginning of the '84 season with the Royals. When George Brett returned from an injury, though, Ashford was expendable. He spent most of '84 playing for the terrible Rochester team managed by Verdi, then—after some short-lived struggles with the Pacific Coast League's Portland Beavers the following season—he decided to retire.

Among the other awards announced September 1: Richmond's Eddie Haas beat out Verdi for manager of the year, deservedly so. Unlike the Clippers, Richmond had a roster loaded with Triple-A rookies. Pawtucket's Bob Ojeda was named the league's top pitcher, and Ripken earned top rookie honors. Bill Emslie won his third straight IL umpire of the year award.

VERDI AND THE CLIPPERS learned after their game on the night of September 2—an 8–6 loss at home to Toledo—that they'd be playing for the Governors' Cup without Robertson, their defensive Gibraltar and good luck charm. He was hitting .259 with a career-best nine homers, on top of all those plays at short that made the whole team better. Now the Yankees needed him for their stretch run, particularly with Bucky Dent sidelined by a fractured hand. Robertson packed his belongings and said good-bye. It felt strange to him, not seeing the season through with the Clippers. He'd get over it. Just shy of twenty-four years old, Andre Robertson was headed to the Major Leagues. His ascent had been quick, his journey long in its own way.

• • •

The Texas Rangers were the first team to draft Andre Robertson, right out of West Orange High School in 1976. Most kids in similar situations would have gone pro right then, especially with $7,500 on the table, but to Andre it didn't feel right. Despite all the remarkable plays he'd made in high school, he didn't think his fielding was good enough yet. Plus, he'd already committed to the University of Texas, a powerhouse program that had never signed a black player before. The unprecedented move didn't go unnoticed by the media. "UT Inks Black Shortstop," the Abilene paper specified. Nor would it go unnoticed by baseball fans in the heart of Texas, some of whom weren't ready for a black player wearing Longhorn burnt orange and white, no matter how talented he was.

Despite his shortstop credentials, Andre spent his Texas career at second base, the only position not already locked down by an established college star. He showed up at UT wearing a heavily decorated high school letterman's jacket. Eleven varsity letters. As if Andre weren't humble enough already, he heard about it from his new teammates. "That's a nice jacket," Longhorns All-American outfielder Charlie Proske told Robertson. "But you know, that don't mean nothin' here."

The Longhorns, coached by the legendary Cliff Gustafson, were already the best program in college baseball, arguably at least. They'd won a national championship as recently as 1975. They fell short of expectations in '76 but still won the Southwest Conference title. In '77, Andre's first year with the team, Texas ripped off thirty-four straight wins to start the season. Andre sat out the first fourteen of those games with a broken hand but emerged as a star after his return. After two relatively down seasons—in which they *only* went 89-25—Texas emerged as conference champion during Andre's junior year and returned to the College World Series.

Throughout his Longhorn career, he worked on that fielding with an assistant coach named Bill Bethea. Andre learned footwork. "Get your feet quick," Bethea would tell him, "and your hands will be quick." The young man learned quickly and began making plays even he couldn't have touched in high school.

By all accounts, Andre never let his success at the college level go to his head, and his work ethic impressed Bethea, Gustafson, and the rest of the coaching staff.

"He was the kind of kid that if you asked him to stack greasy BBS, he'd ask you how high," Bethea recalled.

"They don't stack well."

The Toronto Blue Jays came calling in the '79 draft. This time, Robertson felt he was ready, and he signed his first pro contract. He began his pro career that summer in A-ball at Dunedin, Florida. Within months, he found himself all the way up in Triple-A, playing for the Syracuse Chiefs, in the middle of the Governors' Cup finals.

He'd arrived at the University Texas as a shy, skinny kid. He left Texas as, well . . . a less shy, skinny kid, but he'd grown up in so many ways, off the field as well as on.

PROSKE AND THE OTHER Longhorns had welcomed Robertson from the start, treating him like any other teammate, maybe a little better. They looked after him, and he did his best to reciprocate. Jim Cisarik, a player from Houston who met Andre during a state high school All-Star Game, asked to room with him. The arrangement continued through all three of Andre's seasons at UT. The two men are close friends to this day. There were places the Longhorns went where it wasn't advisable for a young black man to go on his own, but it didn't come up often. Throughout his time at Texas, Andre was usually "either in class or with my guys."

The slurs Andre endured usually came from the relative anonymity of the stands at opposing ballparks. Baylor, Texas Tech, Houston, and Arkansas were particularly rough for that, and there weren't exactly a lot of other fans in the stands delivering rebukes. More like keeping quiet or laughing along. Andre used the tunnel vision he'd learned from his father to stay focused, but he did hear many of the comments. He took pride in quieting his abusers with his play on the field.

"N——, you ain't worth a shit."

Make another diving stop, Andre would tell himself. Make someone else make a right turn at first base.

"Stupid n——. Why you hittin' ninth?"

Just hit a double off the wall. That will shut him up.

"You're a no-good n——."

Start a double play and end this game, like you did the last time we played at Tech.

Of the many slurs Andre endured at UT, one stands out. It came at him when he had his guard down, from a friend.

He found himself taking a car ride to a club for some disco dancing, just him and the Longhorns' head cheerleader—Pam from Mesquite—and another cheerleader named Allison. "Look at lil' ol' me," he thought, "from lil' ol' Orange, Texas."

In high school, he'd made it to prom once but never had a girlfriend. He was always too busy with baseball, and he had his shyness to deal with. He was so reticent around girls, then around women, that some friends assumed he was gay. He was known for being soft-spoken. Then came Austin and fifteen-cent beer night. "I haven't shut up since," he'll tell you.

Pam's friend is driving. Pam is riding in the front seat. She's white, blonde-haired, and blue-eyed. Andre is sitting in the back seat. They arrive at The Keg, a few streets west of campus, and circle in search of a place to park. Two promising spots are taken, grabbed by someone whose car is taking up both. Pam is frustrated, and at least a few beers in, when something ugly slips out.

"Oh, some n—— parked there," says Pam from Mesquite.

The car is suddenly very quiet.

She otherwise hadn't seemed to have a racist or spiteful bone in her young body. Perhaps it was an odd, awkward attempt at humor. Perhaps there were deep-seated feelings, products of her upbringing on the outskirts of Dallas that she hadn't been aware of. She wasn't sure. She felt terrible.

Andre's thick skin, toughened through abuse from anonymous others, had been broken. He was shocked and hurt and unsure how to handle the situation. Pam and Allison were his ride home. He went ahead and went inside with them, danced and processed. He got his ride home. Then he wouldn't speak to Pam for the next month or so. What she'd said wasn't okay, even in the absence of spite. He needed her to know. It wasn't okay.

She was deeply sorry. They reconciled. They'd been friends before, but they became the best of friends.

• • •

With our family relocated in the Bay Area, Dad and I continued attending the occasional baseball game over the years. We drove up the freeway to Candlestick Park to watch the San Francisco Giants, who supplanted the Clippers as my favorite team. We checked out the A's at the Oakland Coliseum. We took in a couple of San Jose Bees games at Muni Stadium, though regrettably none in 1983, the year Frank Verdi managed there.

We were growing apart, though. Dad was out of town often, traveling to St. Louis or Los Angeles or elsewhere for his hospital administrator job. When we were together, neither of us were particularly comfortable discussing the struggles I was facing growing up, some of them garden variety, some of them tougher fueled by anxiety and depression that I didn't yet have the words for. Dad had his own inner struggles. He'd been heavy since I could remember. More and more as I grew up, he turned to food—the unhealthy kinds and too much—to cope. I began to do the same. It was our drug of choice, a way we both checked out when life felt too difficult.

I loved him, and I know he loved me. But it felt at times like there was a large pane of clear glass in between us and that we could see each other but never truly connect.

Our family didn't lack for anything. I had some very good friends. There were glimmers of success as I headed for manhood, small victories that nudged me in the direction of self-confidence. Going through with a concert trombone solo I'd literally been frantically still learning that morning, and pulling it off. Being picked first—for once—when my sixth-grade class broke into teams for a writing contest. Good grades. Getting recruited to help with my high school yearbook and starting to zero in on journalism as something I might be good at.

The feelings of "less than" continued, though, largely unchecked, for many years.

IT'S APRIL 20, 1990, spring of my sophomore year at Gonzaga, and I'm still scuffling my way through. When I'd first decided to go to college in the Pacific Northwest, I was delighted to discover that good ol' Rick Rizzs was not only still broadcasting, but that he was doing so for the Seattle Mariners. I'd get to listen to him again, regularly. It would be a welcome dose of familiarity.

On this Friday night, I've returned to my dorm room around 10:00 p.m. The Mariners broadcast, on tape delay in Spokane that night, is just starting. I flip it on, with no idea how things will turn out. Tape-delay any game, and I'll listen to it. I've always enjoyed listening to sports on the radio late at night. There's a relaxing joy to it that likely springs from my formative summer as a Clippers fan.

Dad took me to a game at Seattle's Kingdome several years earlier when we trekked to the Northwest to check out possible colleges. The Mariners have since been pushing the Giants as my favorite team. This spring, Seattle has lost seven of ten to start the season, but I am undeterred. They have to break through and have their first winning season *some* year. Their starting pitcher tonight is Brian Holman, a young right-hander out of Wichita.

In the fourth inning, I take note: Holman hasn't allowed a base runner yet. There's such a long way to go at that point, but the minds of many baseball fans start to entertain that possibility of a perfect game. Going the distance without allowing a base runner, twenty-seven up, twenty-seven down. Just like Len Barker had back in 1981. At this point in Major League history, only fourteen pitchers have done it. Only three in my lifetime. California's Mike Witt threw a perfecto in 1984. Cincinnati's Tom Browning threw one in 1988.

The Mariners break a scoreless tie with two runs in the top of the fifth. For Holman, the outs continue to pile up, in order. Oakland masher Mark McGwire leads off the bottom of the fifth with a fly ball to deep center field. Ken Griffey Jr. tracks it down. Whew. Ron Hassey flies out to left. Terry Steinbach strikes out swinging. In the Oakland sixth, three straight groundouts. Eighteen batters up, eighteen down.

It's getting serious now.

I'd gotten home relatively early for a Friday night. My roommate isn't around. It seems like no one is around. Just me and my radio, tuned to Spokane's KXLY 920, keeping vigil in my dorm room at Dooley Hall with a candle burning. Barring a lot of extra innings, the game has already ended. He's either done it or he hasn't. I have no idea.

Bottom of the seventh. Fastballs, cutters, sliders, changeups. Rickey Henderson pops out to short. Stan Javier grounds out to second. Jose Canseco strikes out swinging. Wire services were sending out advisories at this point: "Brian Holman of the Seattle Mariners has been perfect through seven innings." If the young pitcher pulled this off, sports editors across the country would need to tear up their front pages. Past midnight now. McGwire comes up again in the bottom of the eighth and flies out to right this time. Hassey strikes out looking. Steinbach grounds out to second. I'm hanging on every Holman pitch.

He starts the bottom of the ninth by striking out Felix Jose, swinging. Two outs to go. Walt Weiss hits a ground ball to second. Harold Reynolds ranges to his left, scoops it up, and throws to first. Holman is one out away.

Oakland's Ken Phelps, a Seattle native in his eleventh and final season in the Majors, steps to the plate as a pinch hitter for Mike Gallego. Phelps is hitting just .214 at that point, his career nearly over. Here we go. One out away from baseball immortality for

Holman, from the first no-hitter and perfect game in the history of my Mariners.

Holman starts Phelps with a fastball.

Thwack.

Deep to right field. Cotto going back. To the warning track. Gone.

There's no signature "Good-bye, baseball!" call from Rizzs this time. Just an "Oh no!" With one swing, Phelps has wrecked Holman's bid for baseball immortality, his no-hitter, and his shutout. It's the last home run the bespectacled Phelps will ever hit. I sit there alone, stunned. Yes, there are more important issues in the world, but for a young baseball fan, this is a tough moment. I've never seen or heard of anything quite like it, and I haven't since.

The young righty strikes out Henderson on a slider to end it, settling for a one-hitter. The Mariners, still a year removed from that first winning season, will go on to finish in fifth place.

An arm injury will derail Holman's career. The following season with the Mariners will be his last in professional baseball. The night of his almost-perfecto, he wasn't able to sleep. Around 4:00 a.m., fully realizing just how close he'd come, and how unlikely it was that he'd ever get that close again, he sat up in bed, and let out a scream.

IT'S FOURTEEN MONTHS LATER. Dad is just back from the hospital, having undergone triple-bypass surgery, a scary byproduct of all that extra weight he's been carrying around for so long. I can hear him in the kitchen. He's fumbling around with a jar of mayonnaise and a stack of lunchmeat, building himself a second dinner.

I'm furious. I want to march into the kitchen, confront him, and demand to know what the hell he thinks he's doing. I imagine grabbing the jar and throwing it, as hard as I can, into the wall. I envision the breaking glass, the mayonnaise oozing down.

It wouldn't have helped anything, my also frustrated mom explains to me later, as I'm tearing up over it. It would only have made things worse. I'm beginning to understand. It's not that my dad won't stop. It's that he can't. At least not without help, help that he isn't—and never will be—willing and able to get.

Food addiction and compulsive eating seemingly lack the same street cred as their counterparts involving alcohol and drugs. Left unchecked, though, they'll kill you just as dead. They're more insidious, and getting "clean" is more complicated. With alcohol and drugs, you either use or you don't. You've got to eat, though, and learning to do that in a healthy way—as someone with addiction layered in—can be a lifelong struggle. It's a full-on disease that was in the middle of robbing my father of his spirit, his vitality, and eventually his life. It drove a wedge between us. Especially since I, as I'd realize in the years to come, was struggling with the same addiction.

It doesn't discriminate. Go to support groups where they talk about these issues, and you'll find people of all different weights, from all walks of life. You might find me. I've been blessed to get that help my dad never would, and helped it has, in a life-changing way. It was—and continues to be—worth the effort and the fear-facing.

12

Postseason

IN THE FIRST ROUND of the 1981 Governors' Cup playoffs, the Clippers faced fourth-place Rochester, a team that had played them just about even that season and mounted its own late-summer surge to sneak into the postseason. The series was best of five. Columbus dropped the first two games on the road amid numerous rain delays and rainouts, and the Clippers were on the verge of being swept out of the playoffs. Loved ones, home, and the International League pennant seemed far away. Most if not all on the team were anxious for the long season to be over. Just not like this.

The Red Wings, tired of hearing about how great the Clippers were, brimmed with confidence despite the series shifting to Columbus. Even if Rochester dropped the third game, the Red Wings had Brooks Carey—who'd owned the Clippers that season with a 3-0 record and 2.20 ERA—and ace Mike Boddicker lined up to pitch the final two contests. Plus, the Clippers were without Robertson, who had been called up to New York. Robertson's spot on the Clipper roster was filled by a young speedster named Otis Nixon, just up from Nashville. In fairness, though, the Red Wings had lost Ripken to Baltimore a few weeks earlier.

"The pressure's on them," Rochester outfielder Dallas Williams told reporters. "They have to win three in a row, not us. And we've got our two best pitchers going. I really don't think it's going to be a problem."

Rochester newspaper columnist Greg Boeck had called a Red Wing series victory ten days earlier. After Boddicker outdueled Pawtucket's Bruce Hurst 1–0 on August 31, clinching Rochester's spot in the playoffs, Boeck himself brimmed.

"And you know they'll beat the Clippers—Tucker Ashford, Steve Balboni, Marshall Brant and all of them," Boeck wrote. "They've got

Columbus's number, have now for two seasons. The Red Wings' 20-20 record against Columbus these past two years might not look impressive but the Red Wings are the only IL club the Clippers have not owned these last two pennant years." Boeck did add that Major League call-ups could change all that.

Now it appeared the columnist had been spot-on. While the Red Wings crowed after taking a two-games-to-none series lead, Balboni sat in the Clippers clubhouse with his balding head in his hands. Others joined him in moping. This was no way to end their pennant-winning season. Hopes of a third straight Governors' Cup appeared lost.

Coleman surveyed the room. "Gitcher head up, Bones," he told Balboni. "We're going back to Columbus."

ON THE NIGHT OF Thursday, September 11, the teams reconvened at Franklin County Stadium. Players chattered before the game. "Have you heard who's here?" Steinbrenner showed up and would watch the rest of the series in person.

Werhmeister pitched the Clippers to a 10–2 victory. The Red Wings learned after the game that Boddicker had been called up by the Orioles. The next night, the Clippers finally solved Carey in a 7–0 win. Pacella and Bill Castro combined on a six-hit shutout, and Brant and Balboni each blasted four-hundred-foot home runs. The series was even at two games apiece.

On Saturday, the Ohio State football team opened its season by manhandling Duke in front of 86,000-plus. Only 6,400 turned out that night for game five between the Red Wings and Clippers. Those who did were treated to a classic.

With Boddicker gone, the Red Wings turned to Larry Jones, a .500 pitcher who'd started the thirty-three-inning game with Pawtucket five months earlier and been moved to the bullpen in July. He'd never appear in the Majors. Jones had pitched three and two-thirds scoreless innings in the series, however. Columbus rolled the red-hot Gene Nelson.

Jones was battling a virus and filled to his brim with penicillin. He pitched gamely, tossing seven innings with nine strikeouts and three walks, but a dramatic Balboni blast in the sixth inning gave the Clippers a 1–0 lead.

Nelson and his slider were cruising, and it appeared the one run might be all he needed. But in the top of the seventh, Rochester's Floyd Rayford turned the drama up higher with a solo shot of his own, tying the game. The Clippers loaded the bases in the bottom of the ninth, but reliever Tom Rowe got both Ashford and Balboni to pop out. On to extra innings, with the loser going home.

Nelson kept the Red Wings off the board in the tenth. His numbers for the game: ten innings pitched, one run on just four hits, six strikeouts, and a one walk.

Glenn Stout remembers the performance well. Seated between home plate and the dugout on the first base side, just a few rows up from the field, the author had a perfect view of Nelson's slider. Stout hadn't seen a break that late or sharp all season. And he'd watched dozens of games.

"He exuded confidence," the author recalled. "Head up, chest out, the arrogance of a pitcher who knows he's on and in command and pitching without fear. He couldn't wait to get the ball back from the catcher after every pitch."

THROUGHOUT THE GAME, DAVE Coleman had paced back and forth in the dugout, pissed off that he wasn't in the lineup. For all the struggles he'd had that season, he'd been playing better lately. Verdi had tried several pinch hitters late in game five, but not Coleman. "Why is Verdi letting a veteran sit on the bench?" he wondered to himself.

In the bottom of the tenth, with one out and the game tied at 1, Stegman reached on an infield hit. Rochester manager Doc Edwards brought in lefty Pete Torrez. With the winning run at first base and runs at a premium, Verdi needed to counter with a right-handed hitter. He looked to his bench and chose Coleman over Garry Smith.

Coleman, fired up over finally getting his chance, grabbed a bat and walked to the plate. The crowd buzzed. After all those frustrating at bats, games spent on the bench, injuries, and miscues, here was an opportunity that might never come again.

Against Torrez, he battled, fouling off six pitches. Stegman took his lead off first. Steinbrenner watched intently from the press box. At 9:57 p.m., with the count at one ball, two strikes, Coleman turned on a Torrez pitch and drilled it high over shortstop Bob Bonner's head, into the left-field corner. Williams, playing left field, tracked the ball down but bobbled it, just for a moment. Verdi, coaching at third base, saw the miscue. The grizzled coach energetically waved Stegman around third and toward home.

Bonner took the throw from Williams and gunned the ball toward the plate. But his relay was high, and Stegman slid under, head first. Safe. Columbus had won, another spot in the Governors' Cup finals was secured, and the celebration began. With a cloud of dust still hanging in the air near home plate, Coleman's jubilant teammates stormed the field, lifted him off his feet and into the air, and patted him on the back. Verdi made another quip about needing to ice his hand, after the celebratory slap he received from Coleman. Harer grabbed a bottle of cheap champagne, sprayed some on the crowd, took a few swigs himself and then passed the bottle around.

Following the game, Ellis rounded up a handful of the team's career Minor Leaguers, including Coleman, Harer, and Schmitz. The Boss wanted to see them.

In an office at the stadium, Steinbrenner expressed his gratitude. As a reward, he asked the group to join the Yankees and live the Major League life for a couple of weeks, all but the playing part, after the Minor League season ended. It was a generous—and uncommon—offer. Schmitz politely declined. He stayed behind to make sure he'd be around for the birth of his first child, which happened on September 29. It was the right call, especially since his wife ended up being in labor for fifteen hours. The others joined the Yankees in Cleveland, took early batting practice, shagged balls in the outfield, stayed at fancy hotels, and ate at fine restaurants.

"Just like big leaguers," Coleman remembered.

He called his game winner against Rochester "the biggest clutch hit" of his career. It would also be the last hit of his career. In his own way, Dave Coleman would go out on top.

The Clippers sorely needed rest following their extra-inning thriller with Rochester, but there was no time. The next day, Richmond came to town for the start of the Governors' Cup finals that night. The Braves were relatively well rested, having finished off Tidewater two days earlier in the other semifinal. They'd arrived in Columbus that morning on an early flight, confident, and—like the Red Wings—sick of hearing about all that Clipper talent.

The season-ending, best-of-seven matchup felt appropriate, first place versus second and the rivalry *de l'année* in the International League. *Columbus v. Richmond* had intensified a year earlier, when the Clippers rallied from a 2-0 series deficit to eliminate the Braves in the semifinals. The '81 season series was nearly even, with Columbus winning eleven of twenty contests. The Braves had the best pitching in the league over the whole season, statistically at least. And of course, Richmond had nearly pulled off a miracle comeback after Columbus positioned itself to run away with the pennant. Wayne Harer's heroics helped the Clippers hold off the Braves then, and he'd deliver again in game one.

The opener pitted McGaffigan against Bob Walk, who had started a game for the Philadelphia Phillies in the World Series less than a year earlier. On this night, Walk didn't make it out of the first inning, which ended with Columbus up 4–0. Richmond clawed back from the early deficit and tied the game at 5-all on a Jim Lewis wild pitch in the ninth.

With one out in the bottom of the twelfth, more than four hours after the first pitch, Stegman lined a Carlos Diaz pitch into right for a base hit. Without hesitation, Stegman motored into second base, just beating the throw from Steve Hammond. Stegman's aggressive base running placed the winning run in scoring position.

After Schmitz flew out to right, Nixon legged out an infield hit, sending Stegman to third. That brought up Harer, who was looking for a slider from Diaz and got one. The Clipper left fielder hit a grounder past a diving Ken Smith at first base and into shallow right. Second baseman Chico Ruiz fielded the ball. Now Harer and Diaz—attempting to cover—were in a dead sprint for first base. Harer needed to reach safely to allow Stegman to score from third with the game winner.

Ruiz had broken for the bag a millisecond too late. Harer beat him there with a head-first slide, Stegman scored, and the weary Clippers had a 6–5 win, and a 1-0 lead in the cup finals.

A THUNDERSTORM BLEW THROUGH Columbus the following night, resulting in yet another rainout. When the teams met for game two on the night of September 15, Wehrmeister faced off against Richmond's Ken Dayley.

In the third inning, Wehrmeister threw a slider to Terry Harper, who lined the ball back up the middle and into the pitcher's face. The ball ended up at first base, where Brant recorded the out before heading to the mound to check on Wehrmeister. For Brant and many others, the moment was eerily similar to a horrifying incident at Franklin County Stadium the previous season.

On July 14, 1980, Roger Slagle had taken the mound for Columbus. The former first-round draft pick from Kansas had sniffed the Majors in '79, pitching two scoreless innings for the Yankees and appearing on the first-ever broadcast of ESPN's SportsCenter. The lanky right-hander was surprisingly relaxed for a Major League debut, which came on a rainy night in Detroit. Teammate Goose Gossage asked him if he needed any tips on the Tigers he'd be facing. Slagle responded that he had no idea which Tigers he'd be facing. No matter. Slagle retired all six of them, two on strikeouts.

The following season, Slagle hurt his arm and wound up at Double-A Nashville. He earned his promotion back to Triple-A in July, red hot, with nearly a strikeout an inning and an ERA under 2. Unfortunately, he arrived in Columbus with a case of pinkeye, having grabbed a teammate's towel to wipe his face. His eyes swelled shut, and when they first reopened, he felt like he was looking through Plexiglas. When he came on in relief that July night against Charleston, his vision was still blurry.

Slagle hung a screwball against Charleston's Danny Walton, who lined the pitch back up the middle. Before Slagle could react, the ball drilled him directly in the face. He crumpled to the ground and lay face down near the mound.

Rick Stenholm, who was playing right field, thought Slagle had been killed. The sound of the impact was chilling, "like somebody dying," Stenholm recalled.

The pitcher never lost consciousness. When he rolled over, he could feel the blood. He felt like someone had put a shotgun inside his head and pulled the trigger. He was having trouble breathing. Teammate Dennis Sherrill, who was playing shortstop, got a look at Slagle's face and retched. "Oh God," Slagle thought. "I must look like hell."

The ball had ricocheted off the pitcher's face and out to Brant at first base. Brant stepped on first to record the out, as he would on the Wehrmeister play, then joined everyone else in running to the mound. Walton, horrified, raced directly to Slagle. He left bruises on the pitcher's arm from squeezing it so tightly. "You're gonna be alright," Walton said repeatedly.

Slagle's mug had been hit so hard that *the ball* came out of the exchange with a one-inch gash, torn open on the exposed cartilage of the pitcher's nose, which was crushed. As he was carried into an ambulance, he managed a small wave to the anxious crowd and joked to his teammates about how it was a good thing he had such a big beak. Reconstructive surgery, including thirty stitches on the inside and outside of his nose, awaited at Mount Carmel. Slagle was done for the season. He missed losing an eye by millimeters.

Slagle kept the blood-stained ball as a souvenir of sorts, a reminder of something that doesn't happen to many people, and of how much the human body can take. The following spring, he was back for Nashville, using the same glove, also stained with blood. Looking down at it helped him concentrate. In his first outing, though, he heard a pop. The gruesome injury hadn't ended his career, but a torn rotator cuff would.

Years later, back in Kansas, he reflected on his career and wished he'd had more of a chance in the Majors. He figures he could have

FIG 29. Pitcher Roger Slagle returned in 1981 after a gruesome injury. *Columbus Citizen-Journal*, Scripps Howard Newspapers/ Grandview Heights Public Library/Photohio.org.

made it. But he doesn't have any regrets. Slagle held onto that blood-stained ball for many years, but he's not sure he has it anymore. At some point, mice got into his house and gnawed on it.

WEHRMEISTER'S INJURY WAS NOT so serious, but substantial. The ball off the bat of Harper hit him in the side of the face. Like Slagle, he crumpled. But Wehrmeister, in one of the toughest performances by a Clipper all season, was able to get his bearings and stay in the game. He learned afterward that the ball had cracked his jaw. "As much guts as anyone breathing," Ellis would say.

Wehrmeister took the loss in Richmond's 6–3 victory. Dayley, who had been 1-5 against Columbus that season but 12-3 against the rest of the league, picked up the win. Oddly, when Dayley was pitching years earlier for the University of Portland against Gonzaga, he took a line shot off his forehead. The ball ricocheted into the outfield and went for a triple. The phrase "hit a triple off his forehead" became part of the lexicon around Gonzaga baseball.

With the Governors' Cup finals tied at a game apiece, the Columbus Clippers and the Richmond Braves headed back to Virginia for the next round.

GAME THREE THE FOLLOWING night was a microcosm of the Clippers' season. Columbus piled up nine runs in the top of the first inning, no doubt helped by the Braves being dead-on-their-feet tired. The Clippers had taken a chartered flight to Richmond. The Braves had endured a ten-and-a-half-hour overnight bus trip and hadn't arrived until ten o'clock that morning. With all the rainouts throughout the playoffs, there was no off day in between.

The Braves' fatigue showed. Columbus sent thirteen men to the plate in the first, which included five walks (two with the bases loaded), a run-scoring wild pitch, and four RBIs from Ashford. Braves starter Tony Brizzolara had returned to Richmond early to rest up, but it didn't seem to help as he lasted just a third of an inning. Reliever Rick Matula wasn't able to record an out. The top of the first took so long that Pacella, the Columbus starter, had to warm up in the bullpen for a second time. When he finally took the mound, he was warm alright. Pacella was outstanding, striking out the first four batters he faced on the way to ten, walking three and allowing just three unearned runs over seven innings. Balboni homered. Brant homered, singled twice, and knocked in four. Jim Lewis finished it with two scoreless innings of relief, and the Clippers had a 2-1 lead in the series. The final score was 13-3, and it was more final than anyone realized at the time.

The Braves looked to square the series on Thursday night, sending Jim Acker to the mound against Gene Nelson. The teams dressed and warmed up, anxious to get the game in. Then, as the organist at Parker Field began playing the national anthem, the rain returned. Richmond didn't have much of a grounds crew, at least in terms of numbers, and what the team did have was caught off guard by this particular downpour. Soon the tarp was inundated and too heavy to cover the field. The rain had its way.

It was the Clippers' sixth rainout of the playoffs, and it was way past getting old. A combined nine players on the two teams who were slated for late-season call-ups missed out on another day of Major League pay. Coaches and managers worked one more day *without* pay. What seemed to be an endless cycle of poker game after poker game resumed. To many of the weary, having a Governors' Cup playoff at all seemed less worth it.

THE FOLLOWING AFTERNOON, RICK Rizzs was killing time shooting pool at a Richmond bar when Jim Massie walked in the door.

"It's over," Massie announced.

"Not yet," Rizzs said, eyes downward as he lined up his shot. "Not until I sink the eight ball."

"No, the Governors' Cup," Massie explained. "It's over. The Clippers won."

The parent clubs, along with IL and team officials—at least most of them—were through waiting for better weather. With no end to the rain in sight and boggish Parker Field unlikely to be playable anytime soon, the remainder of the series was canceled, a first in the league's long history. League officials discussed declaring the Clippers and Braves co–Governors' Cup champions, with some claiming that had been agreed to by all parties, including the owner of the ultimate decision, IL president Harold Cooper. If Cooper had agreed, he changed his mind. The Columbus native and baseball godfather ruled that the Clippers, by virtue of their 2–1 series lead, IL pennant, and head-to-head advantage during the regular season, would be crowned champions on their own.

That's how Columbus secured its third straight Governors' Cup, completing the three-peat of both the cup and the IL pennant. It hadn't been done before, and it hasn't been done since. Add an asterisk if you like, but you won't find one here.

Hammerin' Hank Aaron, the director of Atlanta's farm system, was furious—not that the series was called early, but that Richmond hadn't been declared a co-champion. He complained to the press that Cooper had gotten "cold feet" and reneged on an earlier deal. Cooper said the decision was about the integrity of the game. A few Richmond players joined Aaron in wearily but angrily questioning Cooper. "It's unfair to everybody on this team—the players, the coaches and the manager," Braves reliever Tony Alvarez told reporters. "They've taken this thing right out of our hands."

For their part, the Clippers spoke of not having anything else to prove. Some wished they'd been able to play all seven games, at least publicly. Privately, many were just glad to have the damn thing over. The movie *Groundhog Day*, in which Bill Murray finds himself trapped living the same day over and over again, wouldn't come out for another twelve years, but it captures pretty well how the Clippers were feeling. Now it was time to end the boredom, get some clean clothes, and get on with their lives. "I want to go home," a tired Verdi told Torry. "The only thing is I wanted to go home a winner."

That he did. Verdi collected the third cup of his managerial career. Letendre, the Clippers' trainer and jack-of-all-trades, hastily arranged a celebration in a local hotel. The party was relatively muted, but Verdi's happiness wasn't. As the players sipped beer and savored the victory, their manager surveyed the room and beamed like a proud father.

In the Bigs, a March to the World Series

To George Steinbrenner's consternation, the poststrike, "second-half" New York Yankees were lackluster at best. The Yankees had posted the best record in the American League East before the strike, ensuring themselves a spot in the playoffs, under the strange format settled on by Major League Baseball. But in the season's second act, New York hovered around the .500 mark.

The team's uninspiring play in the second half cost manager Gene Michael his job. After micromanaging and otherwise tormenting Michael all season, Steinbrenner put him out of his misery on September 6, and brought one of his many former managers, Bob Lemon, back on board. Lem didn't fare any better, and after dropping twelve of their last seventeen games, the Yankees finished with a 25-26 record in the second half. As the "winners" of the American League East in the first half, they'd face second-half "winner" Milwaukee in a divisional playoff series. In the American League West, Billy Martin's Oakland A's would face the Kansas City Royals.

Four members of the '81 Clippers made the Yankees' postseason roster. Righetti, of course, was becoming a bona fide star. Had he pitched another one and two-thirds innings, he would have qualified for and likely won the American League ERA title. Frazier earned a spot by posting a 1.63 ERA in sixteen appearances with the Yankees down the stretch. Robertson stuck around after hitting a respectable .263 following his September 1 call-up. And Brown, despite hitting just .226 for the Yankees in '81, also made the postseason cut.

For another group of late-season call-ups—including Balboni, Patterson, Ashford, and McGaffigan—the season was over.

THE YANKEES WON THE first two games in Milwaukee, with Righetti tossing six shutout innings in the second contest. The Brewers, a slugging team with Robin Yount, Paul Molitor, and Ben Oglivie among their stars, weren't finished, though. Milwaukee took the next two games in New York, evening the series and sending Steinbrenner into a panic. In the Yankee clubhouse after the fourth game, the Boss tore into his players—especially catcher Rick Cerone, who'd made a crucial base-running error, and struck out to end the game. Before long, Cerone was done hearing about it. He erupted.

"Fuck you, you fat son of a bitch," the Yankee catcher yelled, in front of the whole team. "You don't know what you're talking about. You've never played the game." Steinbrenner told Cerone he'd be done as a Yankee once the season ended. The Boss would soon relent.

The series stayed in the Bronx for game five. Steinbrenner preached focus and warned that anyone caught out on the town—even eating out at a restaurant—would be fined $10,000. That proclamation cost Frazier and his wife a chance to see *Cats* on Broadway. The Fraziers cashed in their tickets, went home, and instead dined on bologna sandwiches.

There's no telling whether Steinbrenner's approach altered the trajectory of the series. Something did. The following night, in the bottom of the fourth, the Yankees arose from their two-game nap. Reggie Jackson delivered a Mr. October special, a dramatic two-run blast off Moose Haas to tie the game at 2–2. Oscar Gamble followed with a solo shot, and the Yankees were back on top, their fans jubilant.

Cerone, whose stock had already gone up with teammates after his showdown with Steinbrenner, contributed a big home run of his own in the seventh. With red-hot Righetti tossing three solid innings of relief and Gossage finishing, the Yankees staved off disaster with a 7–3 win. New York had won the American League East, just after the regular season had ended, due to that strange playoff structure that had so many baseball purists fuming.

There was no champagne in the Yankee clubhouse. The Boss had banned the stuff, noting that his players "haven't won anything yet." Steinbrenner had won something recently, though. He'd just been voted one of the year's ten sexiest men in a Playgirl poll, joining the likes of James Garner, Gene Kelly, and Dan Rather. "I'm too old to be a sex symbol," the fifty-one-year-old

Steinbrenner told the *New York Times.* "I'm gonna get a lot of flak from my friends for this."

IN THE WEST, THE Oakland A's dispatched Kansas City and earned a shot at New York in the American League Championship Series. Oakland had become somewhat of a home for refugees from Steinbrenner-land. Manager Billy Martin was by far the best-known Yankee castoff now wearing Kelly-green and gold, but he wasn't alone. Pitching coach Art Fowler and six of the A's players were former Yankees. Oakland PR director Mickey Morabito had also toiled under King George. Few things would have satisfied that bunch more than clinching a berth in the Series with a New York knockout.

It wasn't to be, and it wasn't close.

Graig Nettles drove in nine runs in a three-game sweep. Frazier tossed five and two-thirds scoreless innings in game two, striking out five. Righetti, pitching in his own backyard against a team he'd loved growing up, in his first big league game with his parents in the stands, threw six more scoreless innings as the Yankees took game three and earned a spot in the World Series. In three postseason games, he was 3-0 with seventeen strikeouts and a 0.53 ERA. Can you pitch in the big leagues? Hell yeah. After the final out, Righetti had old friends from home jumping on the field.

All that, and the debut of the Wave, the cheer that would soon sweep the nation. Professional cheerleader Krazy George Henderson introduced it at that very game.

The only real drama happened after the series concluded. Nettles and Reggie Jackson came to blows in an Oakland restaurant, at a postgame celebration. Some members of Jackson's entourage had dissed Nettles's wife, and the two stars had never cared much for each other, anyway.

THE LOS ANGELES DODGERS—WHO like the Yankees had won the "first half" before stumbling in the second—vanquished the Montreal Expos in the National League Championship Series, earning their place alongside New York in the 1981 World Series. The

Yankees and Dodgers had met ten times previously in the Series with the Yankees winning eight, including back-to-back titles in '77 and '78. It was, historically at least, as good a matchup as any, as one weird baseball season drew to a close.

Brown, Frazier, Righetti, and Robertson would all see action against the Dodgers on baseball's biggest stage. Three of the four would play crucial roles.

Unfortunately for them, and for the New York Yankees, not the good kind.

THE WORLD SERIES RETURNED to the Bronx on the night of October 20, the Fall Classic's latest start ever, thanks to the strike. You wouldn't have known it from the game-time temperature, a relatively cozy fifty-one degrees. Public-address announcer Bob Sheppard made his introductions, Yankee fans booed L.A. manager Tommy Lasorda and his Dodgers heartily, Pearl Bailey belted out the national anthem, and Joe DiMaggio tossed out the first pitch.

Righetti blew a large, pink bubble as he stepped forward for his pregame introduction. Robertson, who'd had just one at bat in the Yankees' two playoff series, also did his best to dodge the hype and stay loose. Just before he was introduced, he drawled to Goose Gossage, "If I don't get as much applause as you, I'm gonna be very mad," drawing a laugh from the Fu Manchu–wearing ace reliever. Any awe the young shortstop felt around the stage he was on, or the Dodgers, didn't last long. Steve Garvey was shorter. Davey Lopes was the same height. "I can play with these guys," Robertson told himself.

He wouldn't get much of a chance. Robertson would ride the bench, appearing only once in the Series, as a pinch runner in Game Four.

The Yankees didn't need any defensive help from Robertson, at least not in Game One. Third baseman Nettles set the tone on the fourth pitch of the game, with a diving stop and laser throw that barely beat Lopes to first. In the eighth, Nettles snuffed out a Dodger rally with a leaping grab of a Garvey liner. Bob Watson clubbed a three-run homer off Jerry Reuss in the bottom of the first. Ron "Louisiana Lightning" Guidry went seven strong, Gossage closed it out, and the Yankees had a 5–3 victory and a 1-0 Series lead.

It seemed easy again the following night, with Yankees starter Tommy John outdueling Burt Hooton, his former teammate and good friend. John tossed seven shutout innings before giving way to Gossage, who saved a 3–0 victory. Brown got into the game as a pinch runner in the eighth, scored New York's second run, and played right field in the ninth.

Even without Jackson, who sat out the first two games with a sore left calf, the Yankees were up 2-0 and eyeing a possible sweep. Only seven teams had ever rallied from an 0-2 deficit to win a World Series. As the Fall Classic shifted to Los Angeles, it appeared the Yankees were in good shape.

To make matters worse for the Dodgers, pitcher Alejandro Peña was hospitalized with a bleeding ulcer and out for the rest of the Series. Reporters asked Lasorda who he'd select to fill Peña's spot on the Dodgers' World Series roster.

"Goose Gossage," the Dodger manager quipped.

WHEN PITCHING ROTATIONS FOR the World Series crystallized, one matchup stood out. Game Three in Los Angeles, Dave Righetti versus Fernando Valenzuela. Two red-hot rookie lefthanders, twenty-two and twenty years old, respectively. Righetti had spent the entire season quietly trying to match Valenzuela's exploits. Now, pitching in the World Series, he'd have a chance to beat him head-to-head. Only twice before in Series history had rookies started against each other.

The Yankees and Dodgers were deep into October now. An eighty-degree day turned into a mild, shirt-sleeve night at Chavez Ravine. That morning, two mild earthquakes had rattled Southern California.

Righetti didn't need any help understanding the magnitude of what was about to happen at Dodger Stadium. But Steinbrenner, well . . . he wanted to make sure. The Boss approached the young lefty in the clubhouse and applied his usual tact.

"This is the biggest game of your life," Steinbrenner told Righetti. "Don't fuck it up."

Gossage overheard and considered throwing Steinbrenner out of the clubhouse on his butt. How could anyone, even Steinbrenner, be a big enough jackass to say something like that to a twenty-two-year-old kid about to pitch in his first World Series?

Righetti shared later that Steinbrenner's words didn't have a negative effect on him and actually provided additional motivation. There was more to it than "Don't fuck it up." Steinbrenner was reminding Righetti that this was his chance to show everyone that he was every bit as good as Valenzuela, a point Righetti had been trying to prove all season.

But warming up in the bullpen before the game, Righetti knew something was wrong. He didn't feel nervous. Perhaps Steinbrenner's pregame chatter had rattled him more than he'd figured. Maybe a pregame ticket snafu that briefly left his father, Leo, stranded outside the stadium, had thrown him off. He hadn't pitched in over a week. Maybe that was it?

Whatever the reason, Righetti realized he didn't have good pop on his fastball. He hoped that when he took the mound, adrenaline would make up the difference.

Valenzuela, perhaps finally showing some nerves of his own, struggled through the top of the first inning. Two walks. Twenty-five pitches. But no runs. The Dodger star had survived. Now it was Righetti's turn.

Lopes led off the bottom of the first and lined a 3-2 fastball down the right-field line for a double. Bill Russell bunted past Righetti for an infield hit. The rookie lefty battled back, getting Dusty Baker to pop up, and striking out Garvey on a wicked 2-2 curve. But Righetti's pitches were up, and that pop on his fastball was nowhere to be found.

The next batter, Ron Cey, worked the count full. Righetti and Cerone opted to challenge Cey with a fastball, down and away. Righetti missed his spot and left the 92-mph pitch over the plate. Cey clubbed the ball into the pink twilight, over the wall and into the left-field bleachers.

The crowd roared. Just like that, it was 3–0 Dodgers and the Series felt contested once more.

Cey's blast was only the second home run Righetti had given up all season, and only the fourth home run he'd given up as a Major Leaguer.

He hit the next batter, Pedro Guerrero. Rick Monday reached on an infield hit. Righetti finally escaped the nightmarish inning by getting Steve Yeager to pop out to first.

His second frame was relatively quiet, but Righetti didn't survive the third. Following a lead-off single by Garvey and a walk to Cey, Lemon pulled Righetti after just sixty-two pitches.

"Why did my second bad start of the season have to come in the World Series?" Righetti wondered to himself.

Frazier came on in relief and retired the next three Dodgers to escape the third, then threw a scoreless fourth. In the fifth, though, Frazier began carving himself a unique place in World Series history. The Yankees had fought back for a 4–3 lead, but it didn't last long.

Garvey led off with a high chopper to third for an infield single. It was a tough play for New York's Aurelio Rodriguez, filling in at third for an injured Nettles. Cey walked. Then Guerrero hit another high chopper to third, this one bouncing over Rodriguez's head and down the line for a game-tying double. Cey would eventually score on a double play, giving the Dodgers a lead they wouldn't relinquish. Frazier hadn't pitched badly, but he'd given up two runs and was on the hook for the loss. It was a sign of bad things to come for the young pitcher, and for the Yankees.

In the eighth, Lemon made one of several questionable—okay, weird and inexplicable—calls that cost the Yankees dearly that Series. Still trailing 5–4, the Yankees had runners at first and second with no outs, and pitcher Rudy May due up. Rather than let May bunt, Lemon pinch-hit power-hitting Bobby Murcer, who had a grand total of zero sacrifice bunts all season.

Murcer popped his bunt attempt toward third. Cey made a diving catch, then rifled the ball to first to double up Larry Milbourne, who had sprinted for second when Murcer made contact. A promising rally and a chance to grab a commanding 3–0 lead in the Series vanished.

The Yankees went down in order in the ninth. The Dodgers had a 5–4 win and were back in it, trailing two games to one.

As for Valenzuela, he ended up gutting out a complete-game win. He threw a whopping 145 pitches. He gave up nine hits. He walked seven. But on the many occasions he'd needed to wriggle out of trouble, he was able to do so.

In the battle of the good young lefties, he was the winner.

IN GAME FOUR, IT was Bobby Brown's turn for an infamous moment. Steinbrenner set it up by ordering Lemon to bench Mumphrey for reasons unclear, and to start Winfield in center. When Lemon made a sixth-inning change for defensive purposes, he opted to put Brown in center, rather than the more experienced Mumphrey.

With Frazier pitching in the bottom of the seventh of a 6–all tie, Baker led off with yet another infield chopper that went for a base hit. The next batter, Rick Monday, golfed a sinking liner off the end of his bat toward center. Brown misjudged the ball, took a step back, then couldn't recover. He attempted a shoestring catch, but the ball bounced just in front of his glove and went for a double. Brown thought he'd made a good effort. His teammates, at least some of them, disagreed. As did Howard Cosell.

"Why isn't Jerry Mumphrey in center field?" the broadcaster asked his TV audience with an air of disbelief.

Both runners eventually scored, and once again the Dodgers were ahead for good. They'd go on to win it, 8–7, and square the Series. George Frazier had taken both losses.

Despite all that talent, athletic ability, and sometimes mega-confidence, Brown never blossomed into the Major League star so many foresaw during his dominant years in Columbus. At the outset of the '82 season, Steinbrenner abandoned Yankee tradition and went on a speed kick. Having let Reggie Jackson escape via free agency, the Boss brought in players like Dave Collins and

Ken Griffey Sr., hired a former Olympic track star as a coach, and ordered his players to participate in sprint-based workouts. It was not well-received. Brown clocked in fastest on the team, but like the rest of the players, he thought the approach was misguided and ridiculous.

Steinbrenner lectured his team about needing the sprinting to get ready for the season.

"How about getting me ready to play somewhere else?" Brown responded one day.

It didn't take long. Brown was dealt to the Seattle Mariners before spring training was over. The Mariners released him a year later. He showed flashes of the old B.B. with the San Diego Padres in '83, but his stats declined, punctuated by a 1-for-19 performance in the '84 National League Championship Series and World Series. After a handful of at bats the following season, he was out of baseball.

In Game Five of the '81 World Series, Reuss outdueled Guidry on a Sunday night. The Dodgers, left for dead less than a week before, won 2–1 to move within one victory of a world championship. But the evening is more memorable for what happened well after the game, at the Los Angeles Wilshire Hyatt. Or at least, what George Steinbrenner said happened.

Several Yankee beat writers and columnists were staying at the Wilshire, along with the team. Some had already gone to bed. Around 11:00 p.m., their phones started ringing. There would be a press conference in Steinbrenner's hotel suite in thirty minutes, and they were advised not to miss it.

When the reporters arrived, Steinbrenner answered the door. They were stunned. The Boss had a fat lip, a bump on his head, and scraped knuckles on his right hand. His left hand appeared to be wrapped in some sort of cast. His usual turtleneck and blue blazer had been replaced by a plaid shirt. He looked like he'd just wandered out of a fight at a lumberjack bar.

Steinbrenner sat the reporters down and told his story: On his way to a late dinner, he'd been accosted in the elevator by two twentysomething Dodger fans, one of whom was holding a beer bottle. Harsh words were exchanged, including these: "You're going back to the animals in New York, and you're taking your choke-ass players with you." One of the men threw a punch. Steinbrenner, defending New York's honor and himself, fought the two men, needing three punches to drop them both. Or so he said.

Steinbrenner stressed to the reporters that he was only giving a briefing and that the story wasn't meant for print, despite his summoning six of them to his hotel suite in the middle of the night.

"I clocked them," Steinbrenner said. "There are two guys in this town looking for their teeth."

The two men had allegedly run off. Neither they nor the teeth nor any blood could be found.

There are differing accounts of what happened next, but here's an amalgam.

As Steinbrenner continued, a bleary-eyed Dick Young of the *New York Daily News*, wearing his pajamas and a bathrobe, got up, walked across the room, picked up a phone on the table and dialed the paper's city desk. It was approaching 3:00 a.m. in New York.

"This is Young!" he said. "Get me a rewrite, now!"

Steinbrenner reiterated that he didn't want the story in the papers and was only providing a briefing.

"Briefing, hell," Young responded. "This is news."

Young began to dictate his story over the phone.

"George Steinbrenner, the president of the New York—"

"I'm not the president!" Steinbrenner corrected. "I'm the principal owner!"

Already grouchy and increasingly annoyed, Young started over.

"George Steinbrenner, the principal owner of the Los Angeles Dodg—"

"Yankees!" Steinbrenner bellowed. "Principal owner of the Yankees, not the Dodgers!"

Young tried again. "George Steinbrenner, owner of the Yankees, was involved in an altercation early this morning in a hotel where the Dodgers are staying—"

"The Dodgers?" Steinbrenner yelled. "The *Yankees* are staying here. What the hell's wrong with you?"

Young and his fellow reporters eventually got their stories out. The news dominated papers in New York and across the country until the Series resumed in the Bronx, three nights later.

Many doubted there had been an actual fight, or figured that if there had been, it was unlikely it went down the way Steinbrenner told it. The two men never turned up, though someone claiming to be one of them once dialed into an LA radio station. No lawsuits were filed. To this day, there are numerous theories. But that's it.

BY THE MIDDLE OF Game Six, a Yankee loss was starting to feel inevitable.

Lemon struck again, lifting star pitcher Tommy John for a pinch hitter, in the fourth inning of a 1–1 game. John had pitched brilliantly in Game Two and had been effective in Game Six. Pulling him this early was unorthodox, to say the least. The crowd grumbled. A national TV audience watched John, stunned and angry, pace back and forth in the dugout, waving his arms. It was yet another move that reeked of Steinbrenner meddling. And it didn't work. The pinch hitter, Murcer, hit the ball well but lined out to deep right, ending the inning and stranding two more Yankees on base.

Lemon brought Frazier out of the bullpen in the fifth for what turned out to be another round of hard luck. This time, Lopes started the rally with a seeing-eye single to left, just past the glove of a diving Nettles. A chopper to second by Cey might have gotten Frazier out of the inning. But the ball hit the edge of the infield grass, took a bad hop, and squirted past Randolph, allowing Lopes to score the go-ahead run.

In the broadcast booth, TV analyst Jim Palmer, a pitcher, sympathized with Frazier's plight. "It seems like most of the bad things that happen to the Yankees happen when George Frazier is on the mound," he said.

Dusty Baker followed with a looper just over the head of Randolph. Frazier then made a full-on mistake, serving up a fastball to Guerrero, who tripled over Mumphrey's head in left-center and knocked in two more runs.

The Dodgers pulled away, won 9–2, and claimed the World Series title. A woman sitting near the Yankee wives—including Mary Frazier—stood up and half-yelled, "My God. I can't believe he lost again." Frazier's wife had kept it stoic to that point, but the dam broke, and she burst into tears.

The Dodgers emphasized in postgame interviews that they'd won the Series, as opposed to New York losing it. For the Yankees, there were many people not named George Frazier to blame. Winfield had managed just one hit in twenty-two at bats. Cerone hit just .190. The Yankees left a six-game Series record fifty-five runners on base, one of them when Brown struck out swinging in his lone plate appearance. Usually reliable reliever Ron Davis had struggled. There were base-running mistakes and those questionable managerial (Steinbrenner) calls. As the final game wound down, Murcer was asked who he thought would be named Series MVP for the Dodgers. "It will be either George or Lemon," Murcer responded. "Whichever one of them was making those moves."

Nettles sitting out Games Three through Five with a hairline-fractured thumb hadn't helped. Jackson was healed up and ready to play in Game Three, but Steinbrenner had ordered him benched. There was also the bad luck.

The Boss would cap it all off by congratulating the Dodgers, but also issuing a strange, unprecedented apology to the fans of New York for the play of his team.

The snakebit Frazier became the second pitcher to lose three games in a single World Series. The other, Lefty Williams, wasn't exactly trying his hardest when he lost three for the infamous, Series-throwing 1919 Black Sox, the team that broke my grandfather's heart. Even worse for Frazier, Williams needed eight games to lose his three. The Series was a best of nine back then.

IN THE SOMBER YANKEE clubhouse, a subdued Steinbrenner approached Robertson. "Remember how it feels, Andre," the Boss said. "Remember how it feels."

As for Righetti, Steinbrenner wouldn't forget Game Three, and he'd be hard on his young pitcher in the years to come. Had the Yankees forced Game Seven, the likely pitching matchup would have been Righetti vs. Valenzuela, a rematch of Game Three, two rookies tangling in one of the great Game Seven pitching match-ups of all time. A shot at redemption for Righetti, against the fellow rookie he'd been trying all season to match. Now he was left with only his one bad outing, part of his team's collapse.

Righetti went on to a lengthy career as a Major League pitcher. In 1983 he threw a no-hitter against the Boston Red Sox on the Fourth of July, in Yankee Stadium. In 1986 he set a single-season record with forty-six saves. As a pitching coach, he helped the San Francisco Giants to four World Series appearances, including victories in 2010, 2012, and 2014. That amazing run of success has caused some to wonder: Why is it that only players, managers, executives, and umpires are eligible for the Hall of Fame? Why not coaches?

Despite all that, the Series against the Dodgers continues to haunt Righetti.

"You never get over it," he shared, decades later. "It's a lifetime thing. We lost here (San Francisco) in 2002, then we won and won and won.

"I still think about '81 every day."

There were brighter days ahead for Frazier, too. He'd pitch in the Majors until 1987 and return to the World Series that season with the Minnesota Twins. After baseball, he'd find a new niche as a broadcaster.

But on this night in the Bronx, there was only pain and disappointment for a man who grew up adoring the New York Yankees, dreaming of one day playing in pinstripes.

Classy and patient, Frazier stuck around until 4:00 a.m., answering reporters' questions before driving home to Oklahoma. Before the marathon interview session began, Frazier sat at his locker, dejected. Then he received condolences from a somewhat unlikely source.

"It wasn't your fault, kid," said George Steinbrenner, putting his right arm around Frazier's shoulder, his left arm still in a cast. "You did a good job.

"See you in the spring."

• • •

It's July 15, 1999, and I'm walking up First Avenue toward Seattle's Safeco Field, settled in my new hometown and feeling more confident. The San Diego Padres are in town for the Mariners' historic first game in their brand-new home. A friend has tickets, and I'm in like Gwynn.

There's Mariner broadcaster Rick Rizzs, seventeen years removed from Columbus, giving a speech amid falling confetti to a crowd gathered outside the home-plate entrance. There's Dave Niehaus, the iconic Seattle broadcaster and soundtrack of summer in the Northwest, throwing out the first pitch. It's novel, watching Major League Baseball in Seattle and sitting outside to do so. Free at last from the memory-laden but cryptlike Kingdome.

The Mariner-loving friend who provided our tickets leaves in the second inning to grab us some hot dogs, hoping she won't miss too much of the game. But the brand-new stadium's concessionaires are scuffling. An inning passes. Then another. And another.

I'm feeling terrible. If I knew where she was, I'd tell her to just forget it and come back before she misses the whole game. She almost does miss the whole game, returning in the seventh inning, hot dogs in hand. She's not happy.

Thankfully I decide against taking a nearby fan's suggestion to greet my friend upon her return with, "What? No mustard?"

The Mariners score twice in the bottom of the eighth for a 2–1 lead, lifting her spirits, and we're poised for an idyllic ending. But the task of saving the historic game for starter Jamie Moyer falls, curiously, to struggling reliever Jose Mesa. Talk about scuffling. He's been crummy all season and today he's at his worst, walking four of the five batters he faces to force in the tying run. The Mariners go on to lose, 3–2. Tfffphht.

I call my baseball-loving mom that night to commiserate. Mesa had tormented both of us the previous season, as a member of the San Francisco Giants.

"Someone," my mom says, "should ship that guy to the moon."

MOM DIED IN OCTOBER of 2007. Cancer. We brought her home from the hospital at the end, setting up a bed for her in the family room at the center of the house, with every comfort we could provide. The night before she passed, I spent some time keeping watch by her side. At that point, I wasn't sure she could hear me anymore. But I prayed, and I let her know the World Series was on softly in the background, and that there was a nice fire going in the fireplace nearby. She would have liked that.

Mom was a Cubs fan her whole life. Growing up in rural Indiana, she listened to their games on the radio in the barn. She also came to enjoy the Giants a great deal after relocating to the Bay Area with our family. Later in life, when the kids were grown and the demands on her had lessened somewhat, she watched those Giants almost every night, wishing they'd break their long championship drought. I loved to talk baseball with her.

When San Francisco *finally* broke through and won the World Series in 2010, with black-bearded reliever Brian Wilson striking out Texas Ranger Nelson Cruz on a 3-2 pitch to end it, I cried. Not just for all those ninety-loss seasons and postseason disappointments over my twenty-eight years as a Giants fan, but because I knew how happy my mom would have been, or maybe how happy I believed she was, at that moment. Then I teared up again in 2016, when the Cubs finally had their turn, after 108 years of no titles. Mom's whole life, and then a lot.

IT'S LATE WINTER IN 2013. My dad's health had been declining for a long time, but after my mom died, things got worse. More than five years later, he's markedly not the same, and he never will be. We've moved him into a nursing home in Sunnyvale. I visit him from Seattle, not as often as I'd like or as I should. I start the grieving process early.

I dig out the cassette tape with Rick Rizzs's call of Andre Robertson's home run. I'm not sure it will still play, but I pop it into an old tape deck to find out. It does. The sounds are faint, though, and some are distorted. The familiar musical flourish that started the pregame show. "Near the wall, going, GOING . . ."

The call has been rattling around in my head for years. I wonder whatever happened to all those guys. I know some details about the ones who made it to the Majors and stuck for a while. I know the basics on how the season ended, having looked it up some years after we left Columbus, but I find myself needing more details. I realize it's something I want to write about. A book. There might be enough for a book. I'm married with two young children and a third on the way, and I have a demanding full-time job. Writing a book doesn't make a whole lot of sense. My own old tapes start playing, the internal ones. You couldn't pull something like that off. You don't have the time or the talent. You're not good enough.

Still, I look up the roster online and create a Word document listing every player and coach alphabetically, with some space under each to start gathering notes. I include "Herman, Jim." I get started.

THE NEXT TIME I visit my dad, I tell him about the project and ask him if he remembers anything about the team. His short-term memory is mostly gone, and his long-term memory isn't what it once was. He's short on details. Still, he closes his eyes and recalls the feeling of the ballpark and of spending time there with his son. He smiles. Good project, he says. He can't wait to read it. I still hope I'll be finished in time for that to happen. I won't. But I'm grateful for this connection over baseball, in this moment, and all those years ago, and over all the years in between.

Our visit winds down. We say good-bye. For reasons I can't remember, a nursing home employee is rolling him away in his wheelchair.

"Col-um-bus Clippers," he sings softly, nailing the song perfectly before stumbling on the next words. "Watch the way they bat." He gently waves a finger in the air, as if he were conducting a small orchestra. His voice trails off.

Those words are the last he ever says to me in person.

13

"There's Something I've Got to Tell You"

IN OCTOBER OF 1982, following the conclusion of the International League season, the Yankees organization abruptly fired Frank Verdi from his job as the Columbus Clippers' manager.

At the time, very few people knew why. Verdi certainly didn't. All he was told, by phone, was that the Yankees had to "cut back on some things." It didn't make a lot of sense.

It wasn't the team's performance. Yes, Columbus had failed to win a record fourth straight IL title, but the Clippers had finished a strong second—despite some inexplicable roster moves handed down from New York—before losing to Tidewater in the Governors' Cup playoffs. It wasn't Verdi's occasional running afoul of the Yankees front office, at least not directly. And it wasn't that Verdi was getting rich off Steinbrenner's payroll. Closer to getting by, on $26,000 a year, including $1,000 of Sisler's own money.

Whatever the reasons, Verdi was fifty-six and out of a job. His family wondered if he would head back to the race track to work as a security guard. He began searching for other baseball work, starting with a manager's job in Puerto Rico. It was there, that winter, that he learned the truth about what happened.

After a game one night, Yankees scout Birdie Tebbetts knocked on Verdi's office door. "There's something I've got to tell you," Tebbetts said, "because it's been eating my stomach away."

The old Yankees scout told Verdi about a postseason meeting that included Steinbrenner and others from the Yankees front office, along with the team's Major League coaches and scouts. The group took stock, planned for the future, and discussed who would coach, and where, in 1983.

According to Tebbetts, Steinbrenner brought up Frank Verdi, said he'd had a good year and suggested he be brought up to the

Majors, as a Yankees coach. There were head nods around the room, a consensus that Verdi deserved the promotion, that "he'd forgotten more baseball than most people ever knew," that sort of thing. Verdi's dream of returning to the Majors was about to come true. It was all but a done deal.

Then a snake-in-the-outfield grass named Clyde King spoke up.

To his proponents, of whom Steinbrenner was one of the biggest, King was a brilliant baseball man, a doctor on call for fixing whatever ailed a team, and a steadfast Christian. To his detractors, King was an overrated yes-man and an in-house spy. Billy Martin once referred to King as a "Bible-toting hypocrite." Stan Williams would later call King a "conman and an asshole" and the "worst backstabber in baseball." King and Verdi had some history, dating back to the 1950s, and never really cared for one another.

Per Tebbetts, King told the room he hadn't liked Verdi pitching Jay Howell on three days' rest. That coaching decision never happened. Even if it had, it wasn't germane, nor a particularly serious offense. But the impetuous Steinbrenner did a sudden one-eighty on Frank Verdi.

"What?" Steinbrenner roared.

"FIRE HIM!"

The words hung there in the air for a while. Tebbetts told the Boss his reaction seemed overly harsh. But Steinbrenner wasn't going back. Verdi wasn't coming to New York. He wasn't even returning to Columbus. His last, best chance to return to the Major Leagues was shredded.

The following spring, Verdi found himself on the other side of the country, managing the rag-tag, Single-A, independent San Jose Bees, a million miles from Yankee Stadium. He never really blamed Steinbrenner, whom he generally liked and appreciated.

As for Clyde King, Verdi would hold onto that resentment until the day he died.

• • •

Life as a rising star in the Major Leagues wasn't always glamorous for Andre Robertson. Early on, he tried to access Yankee Stadium, only to have a policeman slam a garage door in—and onto—his face. The policeman thought Andre was some skinny kid trying to sneak in to watch the game. The shortstop came out of the exchange needing fourteen stitches.

He also learned about the fans at the stadium, whose love and appreciation for him had limits. He recalls staying too long to sign autographs one day with a large group still waiting, patiently for the most part. Eventually he needed to stop. It was time to take infield. He tried to politely explain and slip away. "When that happened," he recounted, switching to a faux Bronx accent, "it was like, 'You motherfucker!'"

At least one fan's love lacked those limits. Rhonda Rawlings was just a girl when she first met Andre. Her father brought her to numerous games at Yankee Stadium from their home in nearby Mount Vernon. They'd arrive early and watch batting practice, and starstuck Rhonda developed a crush on Andre. "My God," she'd pine. "He's so cute." His quiet charm fueled her devotion even more.

Rhonda always tried to say hello and speak to the young shortstop, and soon, he began to recognize her. Rhonda's pregame fawning might have gotten on his nerves. Instead, he usually made time to talk with her. Over time, he evolved into a big brother of sorts, asking her how her schooling and life in general were going. He'd tell her how proud he was of her.

Years later, from a hospital bed, Andre would look up at Rhonda and introduce her to his father as "my biggest fan."

On the field, Robertson covered enough ground at short to allow his third baseman, Nettles, to cheat toward the line. Second baseman Willie Randolph was delighted with his new double play partner and figured the Yankees had found their shortstop for the next decade, maybe longer. Al LaMacchia, the scout who landed Robertson for Toronto, likened him to Phil Rizzuto and never forgave the Blue Jays for letting him go.

There were holes in Robertson's offense, but they were closing, one way or another. In a spring training B game in '82, he fouled out attempting to bunt. Steinbrenner ordered him to lay down one hundred bunts in the batting cage after the game, under the tutelage of Rizzuto himself. Robertson took on the assignment agreeably, noting that he needed to develop more discipline at the plate.

Massie, who covered Robertson in Columbus and later in the Major Leagues, was also impressed and sometimes in awe. Looking back, Massie wonders what might have been, even suggesting that Robertson could have been "the bridge to Jeter."

BY 1983, AFTER SOME shuttling between Columbus and the Bronx, Andre Robertson was the New York Yankees' starting shortstop, having overtaken Roy Smalley. Robertson wowed national TV audiences with his defense. He increasingly drew comparisons to Rizzuto, a Yankee legend. The "Will he hit?" question continued to come up, but less frequently. By August, Robertson hovered around a not-spectacular-but-respectable .250, and the Yankees were in the mix for the American League pennant.

Five years earlier, before Yankees or Clippers or national spotlights, he'd met a young woman named Shenikwa Nowlin at the University of Texas. He was a star on the Longhorn baseball team. She was a UT cheerleader, a former Miss North Texas, and a ballet supertalent. When she was just fourteen, she'd become the youngest ballerina to dance with Arthur Miller's renowned Harlem troupe. She performed before Queen Elizabeth and Norway's King Olav. But homesick for Texas and ready to regain a more normal life, she'd placed her dancing on hold and enrolled at UT.

Andre thought Shenikwa was cute. She thought he was different from the other guys she knew, quiet, gentler. "If it happens, it happens," he thought. When it came to UT, he was there to get out of there, more interested in "chasing the little white ball with the red threads." They'd dance, and talk, drifting between "acquaintances" and "friends."

When Shenikwa returned to New York late in the summer of '83, Andre was happy to pick her up at the airport with plans to show her his New York. Their relationship was still platonic, which was a particularly good thing for Andre, as Shenikwa was now dating a six-foot-five, 240-pound tight end for the Philadelphia Eagles. Shenikwa hadn't been back to New York in seven years.

She visited with another friend from Texas. She spoke to Miller about resuming her dancing career. She made plans to spend that time with Andre.

The Yankees game against the Chicago White Sox on the night of August 17 went late, past midnight. Smalley had started this one, but Andre came in late as a defensive replacement. He'd ended the ninth inning by grounding into a double play, and singled in the bottom of the twelfth of a 7–5 loss. He was tired. But not tired enough to give up his plans with Shenikwa. They danced at Studio 54. No alcohol. No drugs. Platonic.

The sun would be up soon. Shenikwa wanted to see the Statue of Liberty. "I should get my camera," Andre thought, and they made the half-hour drive from Shenikwa's hotel in Midtown, across the George Washington Bridge, to his apartment in Fort Lee, New Jersey. Then back across the bridge, south on the Henry Hudson Parkway. Past 125th Street. Past 96th. Past a sign warning of a dangerous curve, which should have been posted well before the Henry Hudson turned into the West Side Highway, instead of right on top of it. It was about 5:30 a.m., still dark.

They were traveling at about seventy mph in a fifty-mph zone. Neither was wearing a seatbelt.

Andre's jade-green, 1982 Buick Riviera smashed into a concrete divider. Then into a metal retaining wall. The car then flipped over, ejecting both passengers into the roadway where they were found unconscious, both badly hurt, the highway littered with wreckage.

FOR ABOUT THREE DAYS, Andre was heavily sedated at Roosevelt Hospital. That first night, the Yankees had completed the famed "Pine Tar Game" against the Kansas City Royals, without him. He'd suffered a broken neck, a deep contusion on his throwing shoulder, a broken rib, and severe lacerations. Doctors would tell him that he was three millimeters away from being a paraplegic, lucky to be alive. They gave no assurances about his playing career. His team would fade from pennant contention and finish well back in the standings.

Andre woke up surrounded by loved ones and doctors. "It was

like the old movies," he'd recall, "where you're looking up, and people are looking down at you."

His thoughts soon turned to his friend. "How's Shenikwa?" he asked. "Where's Shenikwa?"

She lay in the same hospital in a coma. When she awoke a month after the accident, she learned that her spine had been severed, and that she'd never dance or walk again.

ANDRE ROBERTSON WENT FROM the New York Yankees back to being "Boe's boy." That's how he was regarded, at least initially, back in Orange at the DuPont factory, where his father had worked for so many years, and where Andre would start a new career after his time playing baseball was over.

The accident on the West Side Highway hadn't ended his baseball career, but it would never be the same.

As the rest of his body recovered in the months following the accident, his shoulder did not, at least not fully. At one point he went to the refrigerator at his parents' house for some milk. He pulled the jug toward him, but as it cleared the refrigerator shelf, it crashed to floor. The milk was too heavy, the shoulder too weak.

When he reported to spring training in 1984, the Yankees were optimistic. Their hopes for their one-time hottest prospect dimmed, though, as he struggled with the shoulder injury and lingering neck problems. Less than five years earlier, Robertson's arm had impressed Gene Michael enough to earn the young shortstop a trade to the Yankees. Now Robertson was having a tough time zipping the ball to first base, and even getting it there at times. His fluidity in the field had been replaced by something more average looking. By early April, he was back with Columbus. He was recalled just three weeks later as his replacements in New York booted ball after ball. Then sent back down again. A different sort of long baseball journey had begun.

He spoke to Shenikwa on two occasions, a few months after the accident. He told her he was sorry. There were no warning signs. He didn't know the road.

She would sue him—and the city of New York. He might also

have filed suit against the city, but he missed a deadline to do so, and his claims that memory loss caused the delay were rejected.

ROBERTSON COLLECTED ANOTHER 288 at bats for the Yankees from 1984 to 1985, playing shortstop, second, and third. He tore up his knee during spring training of '85, and doctors determined at the time that he'd also never recovered from the knee injury he suffered back in '81, in the home-plate collision with Steve Herz. Doctors also diagnosed Robertson with astigmatism.

With new contact lenses and his most recent knee injury healed, Robertson returned to the Yankees later that season, hit .328, and wondered more than ever what might have been. He slowly recovered more of the form he had before the car accident. Bobby Meacham had replaced Robertson as New York's regular shortstop, but Billy Martin, back for another round of abuse as New York's manager in '85, loved Robertson at third. "Sensational," Martin said. "He's making plays that only the best third basemen make."

Still, the following season, the Yankees shipped Robertson to the Atlanta Braves, who assigned him to Triple-A Richmond. With those Braves, Robertson was part of an infield of all former Major Leaguers that earned more money than the young San Francisco Giants infield that season. Richmond won the IL pennant and Governors' Cup. Robertson remained stuck in the Minors. He bounced around the Mariners and A's organizations before trying to catch on with the Texas Rangers in 1989.

He nearly, *nearly* made it all the way back to the Majors. On June 24, the Rangers called him up to fill the roster spot vacated by a retiring Buddy Bell. Four days later, against the White Sox in Chicago, Robertson grabbed a bat to pinch-hit in the top of the ninth inning.

The Rangers were comfortably ahead, leading 10–5. As Robertson stood in the on-deck circle, ready to hit in the Majors for the first time in four years, Rick Leach took his lead off first base, with Steve Buechele batting against Tom McCarthy.

Buechele sent a ground ball to Ozzie Guillen at short. Guillen threw to second for the force on Leach. Inning over. Robertson was left in the on-deck circle, and he'd soon find himself back in Oklahoma City with no at bats as a Ranger. There were shades of Frank Verdi, but unlike his old Clippers manager, Robertson had made it at one point. He'd been a star in the Major Leagues.

Later that season in Oklahoma City, Robertson took a ball hard off his kneecap while warming up pitchers. He decided at that moment that he'd had enough pain. After the 89ers' last game that season, he didn't even take a shower. He took off his uniform, got into his car, and drove home to Texas. That was the last day Andre Robertson played.

SHENIKWA NOWLIN'S AFTERMATH WAS far more difficult. The one-time ballet prodigy faced life in a wheelchair as a paraplegic. Her boyfriend left her. Depression smothered her. She cried every day, and much of the time, for the first three years. Then she decided it was time to get on with her life. She went back to school and finished the law school classes she'd been taking at the time of the crash. She married an attorney named James Cox, who gently carried her up the stairs on the night of their first date and would talk of how her wheelchair was nothing more than a sometimes inconvenience.

The first time Shenikwa took the bar exam, there were no facilities for someone in a wheelchair, and her only option was to find a corner and take the test on her lap. She failed the exam. She tried again and failed. She tried a third time and failed. Then on the fourth try, she passed. She was on her way to a new career as a personal injury lawyer, back in her home state of Texas.

She first filed suit against the city of New York—and Andre Robertson—in 1984. The court case and appeals would take many years to resolve. In December of 1990, she returned to New York to testify before the state's Supreme Court. "I was a dancing girl who was finishing her law school classes and was here on vacation to have a good time," she said. "And that was the last fun time I had."

The court ruled that the city was two-thirds responsible for the accident due to the improper placement of the warning sign.

It found Andre to be responsible for the rest. But he was more or less broke at the time, so the city was obliged to pay all of the damages–$14.3 million. The amount was reduced to $7.5 million after two appeals.

When Andre saw Shenikwa in court in 1990, he told her she was pretty as ever, and that he wished he were in the wheelchair instead of her. Over time, she came to see her old friend more as another victim of the accident, and less as the man responsible for the shattering of her life. Many years later they even discussed making a return trip to New York, to drive the West Side Highway together, for catharsis. She was still thinking about the accident every single day.

As of 2018, they'd drifted apart again, and that trip back to New York together hadn't happened.

• • •

Despite his heroics down the stretch in 1981, John Pacella figured he'd be starting the '82 season back with Columbus. He hadn't thrown particularly well that spring. The big league roster was loaded as usual. The pressure seemed to be off, and Pacella felt relaxed, so much so that in a Grapefruit League game against the Reds on April 1, at Lopez Field in Tampa, he sat by himself in a sunny corner of the dugout with his sleeves rolled up, covered in tanning lotion, and neither paying attention to the game nor thinking about pitching. The Yankees had no plans to use him that day and he wasn't going anywhere, so he might as well enjoy himself, right?

Manager Bob Lemon looked to Goose Gossage to save a 3–2 game in the eleventh, until the Goose's forearm suddenly tightened during warm-ups. Pacella was jerked from his brief vacation and told to warm up himself. He's not sure he didn't still have some hot dog in his mouth. He finished adjusting his jersey as he walked out to the mound.

"Go get 'em, Johnny!" Gossage yelled with a laugh.

Upon entering the game, Pacella learned the Reds had the bases loaded with nobody out and that he'd better get to work. He proceeded to retire all three batters he faced, two via strikeout, to preserve the win. He was throwing fastballs the Yankee coaching staff had been hoping to see all spring. And it just so happened that Steinbrenner was there that day with an entourage of about thirty people, celebrating somebody's birthday. The Boss must have appreciated the thrill Pacella provided. After the game, pitching coaches Jeff Torborg and Ellis approached Pacella. "You big freakin' guinea," he recalls one of them saying. "George just sent word. You're coming with us to New York."

A year after being told he shouldn't ship anything to New York just yet, Pacella was back in the Majors with the Yankees. Unfortunately, he'd barely have time to unpack.

Stan Williams would note that "George changed pitching coaches like other people change socks." That was never truer than in 1982, when no less than five different men found themselves in the role. They included Williams, Torborg, Ellis, Jerry Walker, and Clyde King. As the season began, Torborg and Walker were co-pitching coaches. Pacella missed Ellis, and the lack of coaching stability didn't help, either. Pacella struggled. And when he did, he had multiple people around the team trying to tweak his mechanics. Plus, he arguably still wasn't ready to make the jump. In late April he was sent back to Columbus after allowing eight earned runs on thirteen hits and nine walks, in just ten miserable innings. He considered not reporting back to the Clippers, then changed his mind. A trade to the Minnesota Twins soon followed.

It was bounce-around time for the rest of Pacella's career, though he'd learn to throw a splitter and show flashes of his old brilliance. He appeared in twenty-one games for the Twins in '82, but he struggled. He sipped the proverbial cups of coffee with the Orioles in '84 and the Tigers in '86. He dealt with arm injuries and cracked his ankle in the spring of '83, hit by a line drive.

He made a last kick in '87, dominating in an appearance with the Toledo Mud Hens, before representatives from the Yomiuri Giants. The Japan Central League team inked Pacella to a guaranteed two-year contract, and before long he found himself in the Tokyo airport, unshowered after a seventeen-hour journey, mobbed by fans telling him he would "save Giants."

"I've got about a gallon of cortisone in my shoulder that you don't know about," Pacella thought to himself, "which if I didn't have it, I wouldn't be able to throw. Nobody's savin' anybody. Who do they think I am, Jack Morris?"

He started to get nervous when he saw four limousines waiting for him outside the airport. What did these people actually expect of him?

Pacella spent two years with Yomiuri. He never threw a single inning for them. He'd been signed to replace an injured ace reliever, Luis Sanchez. Except that when Pacella arrived, Sanchez was not only uninjured but in fine form. Pacella showed up at every workout and did everything the Giants asked of him. He played in some Minor League games. He lived in a fancy apartment with his by-then wife Caryn and their two young children, collecting his salary. The team flew his mother and sister to Tokyo, first class. At the end of two years, the Giants thanked him for his service and bid him a respectful good-bye.

When he returned to the states, friends referred to him as Jesse James, the infamous bank robber.

Pacella did some coaching and managing in the Minors. Since then, he and another former Clipper and Major Leaguer, Dan Briggs, have operated the well-regarded Big League Baseball School in Worthington, a Columbus suburb. Here's the pitch from Pacella:

"It's two knuckleheads who don't know how to do anything else."

• • •

Wayne Harer played one more season with the Clippers before retiring. The conclusion of his baseball career didn't go quite as he expected.

Columbus was in Richmond for the final regular-season game of 1982. The Clippers' string of pennants was ending. Richmond had clinched it this time, and the two teams were tuning for the Governors' Cup playoffs, at most. The game was essentially meaningless, at least in itself. Beforehand, a sportswriter approached

Harer—about to play his final regular-season game—with a question. Are you aware, the writer asked, that you only need one more hit to reach 1,000 for your career?

"Why the fuck is he telling me this?" Harer wondered.

Matt Sinatro was catching for the Braves that day. Harer briefed him on the situation, and Sinatro tipped Harer off on pitches for the entire game. In his first three at bats, Harer laced three bullets, two to short and one to center. All were caught. He came to the plate in the ninth inning for one last chance.

"Matt," Harer said to Sinatro, "I'm gonna bunt."

Harer got his pitch, a little up and away. But he left a millisecond early and popped it up toward third. Would it fall? Would he beat it out for hit number 1,000?

Richmond's Steve Curry, a third baseman just up from Double-A and playing like it was Game Seven of the World Series, came charging. The entire Clipper dugout jumped up and yelled in unison.

"DROP IT!"

Curry didn't. Postseason stats aren't included in career stats. Wayne Harer is stuck forever on 999.

Harer stuck around Columbus after his baseball career ended, raising a family with wife Paula. In his next career, commercial real estate, he *did* make it to the Majors. After former teammate Greg Cochran helped him get started in the industry, Harer rose quickly through the ranks, all the way to vice president at heavyweight Continental Realty. He's sold or leased properties with a combined value topping half a billion dollars, and counting, including many of the buildings in the city's relatively new and bustling Arena District.

He's also maintained ties to the Clippers, handling color announcing for TV broadcasts, and serving as chairman for the team's board of directors.

• • •

On a late spring night in 1995, the Sioux Falls Canaries worried that Frank Verdi was going to die right there on the team bus.

"THERE'S SOMETHING I'VE GOT TO TELL YOU"

Verdi, age sixty-nine and long past worn down, had returned for his third season as manager of the Canaries, a small outfit in the independent Northern League that played in a stadium nicknamed "The Birdcage." Verdi never had figured out how to say no to baseball, and he needed the money. His previous season had been interrupted by quadruple-bypass surgery. He'd tried to come back too soon. Now Verdi—the oldest manager in professional baseball that season—and his team were enduring a bus ride back to Sioux Falls from Duluth, a trip of about nine hours. The old man was coughing and hacking loudly for much of the journey. By all accounts other than his own, he looked terrible.

Harry Stavrenos, the team's general manager, had been worried about Verdi since before the season began. The Northern League covered a vast chunk of Canada and the northern U.S., with its furthest outposts more than six hundred miles apart. Bus rides could be crazy long, services few and far between. "If something were to happen to him two hours out of Thunder Bay," the GM wondered, "What would we do?"

Verdi insisted he was fine, but his struggles on the road trip intensified Stavrenos's worries. On the night of June 13, with the Canaries mired in a losing streak, the GM telephoned Verdi and broke the news to him as gently as he could. Verdi was out as the Sioux Falls manager, replaced by coach Dick Dietz.

Stavrenos offered Verdi the hitting coach's job. No more traveling, though. When the team bus left for Winnipeg at 6:00 a.m. that Friday, it would leave Frank Verdi behind.

You can imagine how well this went over with Verdi. The Sioux Falls gig was supposed to be his chance to finally manage without "some SOB" looking over his shoulder. He took the coach's job and held himself together. But he was furious, so much so that he wouldn't talk to Stavrenos for the rest of the season and later filed suit against him for age discrimination. The suit was eventually tossed out.

Verdi and Stavrenos had been friendly, with the GM even staying with Verdi in Sioux Falls. Verdi would cook delicious Italian fare for his guest, and the two men would talk baseball. The old man kept his own room ice-cold.

"If I die in the night," Verdi would quip, "It won't smell too bad."

Canary players who might have been great-grandsons weren't sure what to make of Verdi. He had his rules, including no flip-flops on the bus, and no music on the bus unless you had what he referred to as an "earplug." The players would mess with Verdi, pulling the jack of their headphones out and allowing music to blare, only to plug the headphones back in just as Verdi turned around.

"Alright," he'd say, "who's the smart guy?"

There were also practical jokes, which included leaning buckets of water against Verdi's motel room door, knocking, then running off.

Before the '95 season, Verdi—recovering from his surgery and touched by an outpouring of support from the Sioux Falls community—wrote an old-school fight song for the team. He sang it for his wife, Pauline, who put the words and notes on paper, and the team made plans to record it. Lyrically, it resembles the Columbus Clippers fight songs that Verdi had heard so many times.

> Hey Canaries, we've come to see you win,
> Hey Canaries, so let the game begin,
> You've got the big bird on the speed
> And the little birds on the need
> To win for old Sioux Falls.
> Hey Canaries, go out and do your best,
> Hey Canaries, we'll help you do the rest,
> Just give us your best show,
> That's all we need to know,
> Hey Canaries, go, go, go!
> Hey Canaries, go, go, go!

The Canaries were 3-6 when Verdi was replaced, leaving him with a lifetime Minor League managerial record of 1,436 wins against 1,408 losses, and with 2,844 games as a manager. And that doesn't include any of the many playoff games Verdi managed in, nor his multiple seasons coaching winter ball.

After Sioux Falls, Frank Verdi's long managerial career was over. He still had some baseball life left in him, though. Just a year after he was kicked to the curb in South Dakota, Verdi was back in Florida, working as an assistant coach for Springstead High School in Spring Hill. Head coach Tony Zefiretto brought him on board and became one of Verdi's closest friends. The Springstead Eagles won the district title that season, the first in the school's twenty-one-year history.

Zefiretto worked his way into professional baseball. In April of 2002 he joined the Newark Bears of the Independent Atlantic League as a GM. When he fired his pitching coach and needed a replacement, he dialed Verdi, who was now seventy-seven years old, and told him about the job.

"Well," Verdi said, after considering Zefiretto's offer, "are you flying me there, or am I paying for this myself?"

Zefiretto would handle the airfare. After Verdi hung up, his son Mike asked him if he realized who the owner of the team was.

"It's Cerone," Mike said.

"What?" his dad responded.

Frank Verdi and Rick Cerone had some unpleasant history. Many years earlier, Verdi had pulled Cerone from a game after the hot young prospect jogged into an out at first. A heated exchange followed. So it's not surprising that Cerone didn't react all that positively in 2002 when he learned of Zefiretto's plan.

"Frank Verdi?" Cerone said to his GM. "Frank Verdi is dead."

"He's not dead," Zefiretto explained. "He's coming here."

"He was a miserable old man and he must have died years ago," Cerone maintained. "He'd have to be at least one hundred years old."

Zefiretto convinced Cerone that Verdi was, in fact, still alive. Reluctantly, Cerone went along with the hiring. And thus, Frank Verdi was lured out of retirement and back to the diamond once again.

It worked out well for the Newark Bears. With the old man stabilizing the pitching staff, Newark went 68-56 and earned a spot in the league championship series against the Bridgeport Bluefish. In game two of that series, Newark manager Marv Foley and

Bridgeport catcher Cesar Devares brawled on the field and earned suspensions.

You can probably guess who stepped up and managed Newark in game three. The Bears won 10–3 behind Frank Verdi, completed a three-game sweep, and earned the Atlantic League title. It was the last time Frank Verdi put on a baseball uniform. He went out a winner.

• • •

Marshall Brant is stuck in another bad dream. This time, he's due up at the plate, but he's not there. He's back in the clubhouse, trying frantically to dress for the game. Parts of his uniform are nowhere to be found. He's trying to put on his sanitary socks. They keep ripping. There's a radio somewhere nearby, and the game is on. The announcers can't figure out where Brant is. A young prospect named Don Mattingly is about to take his place in the batter's box.

IN 1983 BRANT WAS coming off his best season yet and having a terrific spring. He'd spent the last nine seasons in the Minors, save for those six fruitless at bats with the Yankees at the end of 1980. But he was hitting the ball exceptionally well. This would finally be the year. It had to be.

Then one day, Yankees coach Johnny Oates pulled Brant aside. "Here are the orders I have," Oates said. "They don't want Donny in left field anymore. They want him to play first."

"Are you serious?" Brant asked.

Any last hopes Brant had of making the Yankees were snuffed out. By June he was gone from the organization, traded to the Oakland A's.

Could Brant have beaten Mattingly to the Major Leagues? Been promoted concurrently, with another team? Brant's numbers at the Triple-A level, at least his power numbers, were better than Mattingly's.

There were key differences between them, though. Brant's work ethic was outstanding, but Mattingly's was even better. In fairness to Brant, *no one* matched Mattingly on work ethic.

"THERE'S SOMETHING I'VE GOT TO TELL YOU"

FIG 30. Beloved by fans, Marshall Brant played for Columbus from 1980 to 1983. *Columbus Citizen-Journal*, Scripps Howard Newspapers/Grandview Heights Public Library/Photohio.org.

At the plate, Brant needed everything to be perfect. His gloves had to feel just right. The pine tar couldn't be too slick.

Mattingly was less likely to let stuff like that bother him. He just went out and hit.

Mattingly rarely struck out. For Brant, strikeouts were an issue he'd been branded with.

Brant needed a good dose of at bats to feel comfortable in the plate, to get into a grove. Mattingly was usually already in one, and if he wasn't, a groove wouldn't take long to establish.

If Brant had a bad at bat, it would stay with him. Mattingly would "flush" his bad at bats, though strikeouts did bother him sorely, at least early in his career. Brant recalls seeing Mattingly by his locker after a game with the Clippers, his head buried in a towel. Was he crying?

Brant asked Balboni what was going on. Was Mattingly okay? Was his family okay?

"He struck out tonight," Balboni whispered.

"So what?" Brant whispered back. "I struck out twice."

"It was his first time all season," Balboni explained.

Brant was filled with self-doubt. Mattingly was confident he was on his way up, often wondering what he was still doing in the Minors.

Mattingly, of course, went on to stardom with the Yankees. There's a strong argument that he should be in the Hall of Fame, despite his career being cut short by injury. Over fourteen Major League seasons, he collected nine Gold Glove awards. He hit .307 with 222 home runs, 1,099 RBIS, and an OPS of .830. He tied a Major League record by homering in eight straight games, with Rizzuto calling the record-tying shot. "Holy cow, he did it!" the Scooter intoned. "Holy cow, Mattingly is unbe-LIEVE-able!"

Brant would end his Major League career with just twenty at bats.

He did get another taste of the Majors with Oakland. On June 28, playing near his hometown, Brant started at first base against the Kansas City Royals. I watched on TV, now thirteen years old and fifty miles south of the Oakland Coliseum, glad for another chance to see my hero.

In the bottom of the second inning, Brant stepped up to face veteran lefty Bud Black. The rookie might have benefitted from a kind word or scrap of advice from one of his new teammates or coaches. "Have you faced Black before?" or "You might look for this," something like that. But no one said a word.

Brant felt the bat in his hands. Man, it feels heavier than it should, he thought.

He glanced down at the plate. Man, it seems wide.

He glanced up at Black. Man, he seems close.

Brant worked the count full. Shorten up, he thought. Protect the plate. He'd tried too hard to crank during his brief time with the Yankees at the end of '80, striking out three times in the six hitless at bats, and further cementing his reputation as a power hitter who whiffed too much. Don't give the A's any reason to think that's the case.

Black threw a curve with some hang to it. Brant lined a ball into the gap in left-center. Base hit. Jeff Burroughs came around to score. The ball got by Royals leftfielder Leon Roberts, and Brant took second on the error, sliding in. It had taken nine years of professional baseball, but he finally had his first Major League hit and RBI.

"How old are you, anyway?" asked U.L. Washington, the Royals' veteran shortstop, a toothpick dangling from his mouth.

"Twenty-seven," Brant answered.

"Oh. No wonder that full-count curveball didn't fool you."

For Brant, there was no sense of relief, no enjoyment of that first Major League hit. In his mind, he'd already moved on to the next at bat, and the fear of failure around it.

The following night, Brant got another start at first and learned a secret to success that had been eluding him. The lesson came from a future Hall of Famer, Kansas City's George Brett.

In the top of the first, Brett stepped to the plate against Curt Young. The Oakland pitcher served up a Dave LaRoche–style floater. Brett hacked at the pitch, looked foolish and meekly tapped a grounder to short.

The moment remains vivid in Brant's memory: George Brett, a superstar who'd just swung like a Little Leaguer, running to first base laughing hysterically about how bad he just looked.

"The next time he was up," Brant recalled, "he just undressed me at first base with a line drive right by me. It's one of the hardest balls I've ever seen hit. I remember going, 'There, there . . . that's the secret. He laughed it off."

Marshall Brant never would learn how to do that.

In the fifth inning, Brant picked up another hit, an RBI single off Steve Renko. That would be it. Twelve days later, with two hits in fourteen at bats and an uncharacteristic error at first base, Brant was sent back to Triple-A, this time with the Tacoma Tigers in the Pacific Coast League.

Even for the "Man Who Would Not Quit," as sportswriter Dick Schapp would describe Brant in a feature story later that season, falling just short was becoming too painful to bear. He was still hitting home runs. But his misery increased. Another season in the Minors dragged on. Brant had only enjoyed playing baseball so much, but the enjoyment he did have was gone. He started keeping a diary of everything he hated about the sport.

He'd finish the season with Tacoma, then play for two seasons in Japan with the Nippon-Ham Fighters. As the Ham Fighters' "gaijin"—a term used to describe American players—he played respectably but was frequently blamed for the team's struggles.

After that, Marshall Brant's long baseball journey was over, save for in his own mind, and those dreams he'd keeping having.

AFTER HIS BASEBALL CAREER ended, Brant kept his distance from the game. He returned to Santa Rosa and got his real estate license. He later landed a job at a car dealership through one of Diana's relatives. He sold for a few years, then worked as a sales manager and a general manager. Diana settled in as a receptionist at a brokerage. Their daughter and son grew into adulthood, and grandchildren came along. Which brings us to recent years.

In many ways, Brant feels blessed. Beautiful family, nice home, success in another career. He's still charming and polite, and widely considered to be a great guy, as he pretty much always has been. But his inability to stick in the Major Leagues continues to haunt him. When he talks about it, he uses the word "failure," despite all the joy he brought to me and other fans over the years, all those kind words to kids, all of the heroics and inspiration he provided.

A few years after he left baseball, Brant found himself back at a Major League game for the first time in a while. He drove south to San Francisco's Candlestick Park. The Houston Astros were in town to play the Giants, and Brant wanted to see his old buddy, Mike Scott, pitch.

Brant sat in the stands, his stomach churning. There was something he missed about playing the game. What was it? He couldn't place it, and his anxiousness increased.

In the bottom of the first, Giants star first baseman Will "the Thrill" Clark stepped to the plate against Scott with two men on.

"Do I want to hit?" Brant asked himself. In his mind, he smelled the pine tar again. No, that wasn't it.

"Do I want to play first?" No, that wasn't it either.

On the next pitch, Clark launched a long home run. The crowd erupted. That was it. That was what Brant missed.

"You don't hear forty thousand people stand up and roar after you sell a car," Brant would say, years later. "Or whatever it is we do."

It's November 20, 2014, and I'm meeting Marshall Brant for the first time, at his home in Santa Rosa. He's graciously agreed to an interview, and I'm hoping to talk to him for a couple of hours. We end up speaking for ten hours. The next day, I come back and we talk for several hours more. And as I listen to him share about growing up, and playing the trombone as a kid, and struggling for a father's attention, and the shyness and the fear of not being good enough, and putting on a brave face while tearing yourself up inside, it occurs to me: My childhood hero is a lot like me.

The following summer, a silver-haired Brant returned to Columbus for a pregame celebration at Huntington Park, the Clippers' new home, marking his induction into the International League Hall of Fame. During batting practice, he walked across a patio beyond the left-center-field wall. He heard the crack of the bat from behind him and instantly knew a ball was headed his way. Brant straightened up, whipped around, spotted the ball in the air, fielded it cleanly on one hop and flipped it to his adult son, Matti.

Balboni was at the park that day, too. He'd been inducted a couple of years before. He just hadn't been able to break away from his job as an advance scout for the San Francisco Giants, at least not long enough to make a trip to Columbus, until now. Harer and Pacella also attended, and the four had a minireunion. It was the first time the four of them had been together in more than thirty years.

The team honored Brant and Balboni in a pregame ceremony, their careers boiled down to brief-but-heartfelt speeches by Schnacke. The fans, many of whom were too young to remember the two sluggers' heroics, applauded politely. As Brant and Balboni walked off the field, perhaps for the final time in Columbus, a familiar song mostly stashed away in recent years came to life over the sound system.

"The Clippers, Columbus Clippers . . . The Clippers are, our hometown heroes . . ."

• • •

Following their loss in the '81 World Series, the New York Yankees didn't make the postseason for another fourteen years. With Mattingly leading the way, they came close a few times. But Steinbrenner's tendency to trade away youth for aging veterans caught up with him, especially in the late '80s and early '90s. In 1990 the Yankees lost ninety-five games, a franchise worst since 1912, when they played as the New York Highlanders. New York fans were patient and gentle during these difficult years. I'm joking. They were furious, and they let the Boss have it. The "Steinbrenner sucks!" chant—previously best known from when Steinbrenner let Reggie Jackson leave for the California Angels after the '81 season—was heard at Yankee Stadium. The Boss took it with a mix of frustration and sadness.

In the middle of that miserable 1990 season, baseball commissioner Fay Vincent banned Steinbrenner from day-to-day running of the team—for life. The Boss had been feuding with Dave Winfield, his superstar free agent signee of 1981. It reached a low point when Steinbrenner paid a man named Howard Spira to dig up dirt on Winfield, and when the plot was exposed, Vincent stepped in.

The Boss maintained his ownership, but the tactics now fell to baseball men like Gene Michael. With Steinbrenner sidelined—and less of a meddler after his reinstatement in 1993—the Yankees rebuilt their farm system. It was soon producing in a big way, turning out players like Derek Jeter, Mariano Rivera, Jorge Posada, and Andy Pettitte. Baseball fans know the rest. The Yankees returned to a dominance they hadn't known for decades, winning World Series titles in '96, '98, '99, '01, and '09. They made the postseason all but four years from 1995 through 2018.

The '09 title was the last George Steinbrenner would enjoy. He died in 2010 at age eighty, having been largely forgiven and again thought of fondly by many Yankees fans. When the All-Star Game came to Yankee Stadium in 2008, Steinbrenner, his health declining, rode to the mound in a cart to deliver baseballs for the ceremonial first pitch, and he received a warm welcome.

• • •

The pool system agreed to at the end of the 1981 baseball strike proved to be clumsy, confusing to all, and not as advantageous to the owners as they'd hoped. As part of the '81 settlement, the Basic Agreement between players and owners would last until 1984. At that point, owners in particular were anxious to scrap the compensation draft, and it was abandoned.

With that system gone, owners retrenched. A series of efforts to reestablish their upper hand followed, with the arbitration system among their targets, collusion among their practices, and a salary cap among their goals. There was a brief player strike in August of 1985 and a lockout during spring training of 1990. In 1994, a strike that began on August 12 wiped out the rest of the season. For the first time since 1904, there was no World Series. Players didn't return to work until the following spring.

New agreements and a long period of relative labor peace have followed. Salaries have continued to soar, and owners—to this day—are trying to figure out how to rein them in. As of 2018, the minimum annual salary for Major League Baseball players is $555,000. The average annual salary is about $4 million.

Jim Lewis did the math. After ace pitcher Clayton Kershaw

signed a seven-year, $215 million deal with the Dodgers in 2014, Lewis calculated that Kershaw was making more for pitching a single inning than Lewis made in his entire baseball career.

• • •

Since his baseball career ended, Andre Robertson has spent most of his time back home in Orange. After working as a substitute teacher and as a contractor at a paper mill for a short time, he got his feet under him and took a job at the same plant where his father worked. They actually spent about two and a half years as coworkers. Harvest "Boe" Robertson kept right on being a great role model as grandchildren came along. He always seemed to have a smile on his face. But those grandkids knew better than to get into any trouble with their grandpa around. Boe died in 2010, his wife, Julia, in 2015.

Andre and Lanier raised three children. Andre is prouder of them than he is of anything he accomplished on the baseball field. Among the many accomplishments of the Robertson kids, son Ryan was valedictorian at his dad's old school, now known as West Orange–Stark. Ryan was the first African American student to accomplish that at the school.

Lanier is a few years younger than Andre, but the two of them grew up together. At the time of this writing, they've been married for thirty-two years. They haven't grown rich, at least not financially, nor as well-heeled as they might have been had Andre's Major League career lasted into the era of megacontracts. But there don't appear to be any regrets. Quite the opposite, actually.

"Emotionally, he was very strong," Lanier said about her husband's big league career cut short. "He never whined or lamented about what could have been."

"You choose to be happy. I think that's probably our mantra."

• • •

After fifty-some years in professional baseball, Frank Verdi earned a monthly pension of just $142.60. He regretted that his life's work had amounted to zero financial stability for himself and Pauline, his ever-patient wife. Thankfully, their children stepped up and helped out when needed.

The Verdis had a treasure trove of home-movie clips, originally shot on an old 8mm Bell and Howell camera. Many of them melted in an attic, but the surviving film was salvaged enough to create a VHS tape. It began with a shot of Manhattan coming into view during a car ride from Brooklyn. It included footage from Frank's playing days, including the home run he hit off Satchel Paige. There were also numerous clips of Frank, Pauline, their young family, and numerous relatives.

Their son, Frank P. "Flashing the *H*" Verdi, and his wife, Linda, threw a big party to celebrate his parents' fiftieth wedding anniversary in 2001. The younger Frank figured he would play the VHS tape during the party. It hadn't been watched in a while, so before the guests arrived, he popped the tape into a VCR, just to make sure it still played okay. The opening shots of Manhattan flickered to life. Then they turned to garble and morphed into the broadcast of a recent Super Bowl. The technologically challenged, elder Verdi had accidentally taped over the family footage. All of it. His son had to fight back tears before the party got underway, and he never did tell his dad what had happened.

"It was gone," the younger Verdi recalled. "Our childhood. Up in smoke."

"Pops"—as his sons knew him—was added to the Syracuse Baseball Wall of Fame in 1999. He was inducted into the Binghamton Baseball Shrine in 2004 and into the International League Hall of Fame in 2008. He received an honor even greater, he felt, when Frank P. and Linda named their son after him. Well into his eighties, the old manager still received autograph requests from Yankees fans, sent to his home in New Port Richey, Florida. He was proud of that.

God went to the mound to get Frank Verdi on July 9, 2010. He was eighty-four.

14

Heroes

THE TRANSITION FROM PROFESSIONAL baseball player to truck driver took a while for Dave Coleman. With each passing summer during his playing career, his chances of returning to the Majors diminished. He hadn't wanted to hang on too long. He hadn't wanted to quit too soon and wonder a few years later whether he should have given it one more try.

Following the 1981 season, his twelfth in the Minors, it was time for something else. A few months removed from his late-season heroics and taste of Major League life as Steinbrenner's guest, with his baseball dreams exhausted, and a growing young family to consider, Coleman was delivering potato chips for a Dayton company called Mikesell's. It was good, steady work. He'd do it for thirty-two years, before retiring.

These days, he wonders: Why would anyone care about his baseball career?

He still occasionally receives cards in the mail, requesting autographs. A blogger, writing about Red Sox games he shared with his father, wonders if Coleman would be willing to sign a bat for him. Some guy from Seattle is writing a book about one of his old teams and keeps trying to get in touch.

Why? It was so long ago, more than thirty-five years now. His time in the Major Leagues was vanishingly brief. Getting inducted into Dayton-area athletic halls of fame is nice. But how many people in attendance at those inductions really remember his playing days, or what he accomplished? Those requests for autographs and interviews usually wind up in the trash, both literally and in Dave Coleman's mind. Old teammates, even his closest friends from those days, would like to get back in touch, but aren't sure where to find him. After retiring he played some semipro ball and did some coaching, but that, too, seems far in the past. For a while now, he has let baseball fade, unchecked.

For whom is Dave Coleman a hero anymore? Was it a status he ever deserved? How deserving is anyone of being called a hero for playing baseball? Brant, Coleman's old friend and teammate, insists that the real heroes are firefighters, police officers, members of the military, men and women who truly dedicate their life to the service of others. Generally speaking, he's correct. I'd also submit those who speak truth to power, especially these days.

There is something to be said, though, for coming off the bench in the tenth inning of a playoff game, in the last moments of a long season and a long career, and staring down an opposing pitcher, and delivering a series-winning hit.

For going all in, for yourself and your teammates, even after your Major League dreams have been dashed, and the ESPN cameras and big-city newspaper reporters have gone home.

For even just sometimes facing your fears, of losing, of not being good enough, of falling on your face in front of others, or at least short of their expectations, of getting booed, literally and figuratively.

For not quitting when most people would.

For being part of a team, and of a sport, which showed up just in time and gave a shy kid something to cheer for during an uncertain summer, and a way to connect with his dad, so many years ago.

I figure you don't have to make it in the Major Leagues for very long, or at all even. You can still be a hero.

• • •

I'm still a baseball fan. Remember, after that Robertson walk-off, there wasn't much of a choice. Since I got married and we had three kids, though, time for truly following baseball is short. I don't pour through box scores these days. The Mariners play just down the freeway, but I'm lucky to get to a couple of games a season. I can't remember the last time I sat down and watched a whole game on TV, or even listened to a whole game on the radio. When

I do tune in to hear Rick Rizzs call a Mariners game, his familiar voice is usually on in the background, while I'm doing dishes or completing some other grown-up task. Maybe that will change someday, as it did for my mom after her kids were grown.

That's where I find life these days.

I shouldn't complain too much, though. Less time for losing myself in baseball means more time for being present for other things. Family, mainly.

It's a good trade. Way better than Bob Sykes for Willie McGee.

It's June 12, 2017, thirty-six years to the day after Andre Robertson's walk-off grand slam. My son, Nate, has taken up baseball at age eight, joining a team called the Pirates with many players who already have at least a year of the game under their yellow belts. He's raw, and I've never been much of a coach, so I haven't been much help despite my best efforts. His real coaches are bringing him along, keeping it fun. But for a while, it's rough on the field, and hard on him. Like me, he wants so much to succeed, to be good enough.

"What are the first three rules of baseball?" I ask him from time to time. "Try your hardest," he answers. "Listen to your coaches. Have fun." He keeps at it.

Today, the Pirates have a playoff game against the Angels. For the losers, the season will end. Heading into the sixth and final inning, the game is tied at thirteen. In the coach-pitch North Seattle Baseball League, there's no five-run mercy rule in the sixth. You can just keep scoring until the other team records three outs, which can take a while. If you're batting in the top of the sixth in a close game, you'd better score a lot of runs, because even big leads can slip away in the bottom of the inning.

My son comes to bat with two runners on base. He already seems so grown-up.

We've got a couple of runs in, but more are needed. Nate stands at the plate in the batting stance he's been working on. He cocks his bat. His coach delivers a pitch. Nate swings and lines a ball past third base. Two runs score. He winds up at second with his first extra-base hit of the season.

After the game, a Pirate victory, he runs up to me with a big smile on his face.

I've found a baseball moment that tops that magic home run my dad and I watched together, way back on June 12, 1981. The one I thought would never be topped. And there will be more. Much more to cheer for as Nate and his sisters—Ella and Thea— take the field.

ACKNOWLEDGMENTS

I BEGAN THIS PROJECT in 2013 with a dream and a ton of uncertainty around how and if I could achieve it. I'm grateful for all the help and encouragement I've received since.

I first spoke with Glenn Stout after reading his blog post recounting Dave Coleman's series-winning hit against Rochester. I learned that in addition to being an award-winning author and editor, Glenn is at least as big a fan of the 1981 Columbus Clippers as I am. He was there that year, taking in dozens of games when he wasn't selling ticket packages for the team. As luck would have it, Glenn is also a publishing-industry expert who teaches seminars on crafting book proposals. We ended up working together on the proposal for *Almost Yankees*. Glenn is a terrific editor and coach, and I'll always be grateful for his help and advice.

Dan Raley covered the Seattle Mariners for many years with the *Seattle Post-Intelligencer* and has written several excellent books, including a fun history of the Seattle Rainiers entitled *Pitchers of Beer*. I had the good fortune to work with Dan at MSN.com for a few years. He was there from the start on this project, convincing me that it was worth starting, then that it was worth continuing, and that I could do it. In later stages he read my first draft and offered many spot-on edits and suggestions.

My early research included an email to Ken Schnacke, the Clippers' president and general manager. He responded to my first inquiry almost immediately, with one line: "We'll help you any way we can!" Indeed, Ken and his staff were extremely helpful these past few years, helping me track down former players, old photographs, answers to obscure questions, and much more. The Clippers are a classy organization. I've visited Huntington Park several times for research, baseball, and connections with great people. It has become one of my favorite places to be.

One of the best things about Huntington Park is team historian Joe Santry, who—as I mention in the book—is there most of the time. He fielded numerous questions from me about the '81 Clippers and baseball in general. I could listen to him tell baseball stories all day, and a couple of times, I've come close. Joe loves the game, and he's a tireless treasure for baseball history buffs.

I'd never figured on having an agent for anything, except maybe for car insurance, but I ended up with a good literary one in Jim Hornfischer. His enthusiasm for the project provided a well-timed boost, and I'm thankful to be working with him.

I'm grateful to the many former players, coaches, and others connected to the '81 Clippers who've trusted me with their stories. Extra thanks to Marshall Brant, Paul Boris, Wayne Harer, Jim Lewis, Frank Ray, and Andre Robertson for going extra innings on interviews, behind-the-scenes help, and enthusiasm for the project.

Frank P. Verdi and his wife, Linda Verdi, welcomed me into their Florida home and treated me like family, just as I suspect Frank's dad and mom would have done. I've continued to feel like part of the family as Frank P. has answered numerous queries from me since then, via phone calls, texts, and emails. I'm grateful for the connection as well as for his help with telling the story.

Thanks also to Shawn O'Reilly, his wife, Paula O'Reilly, and their two daughters. Shawn and I went to grade school together in Columbus. Before my first research trip there in 2013, I messaged him on Facebook and asked if he'd like to meet up for lunch. I hadn't seen Shawn for thirty-one years, but he quickly invited me to stay at his home during my visits. Getting to reconnect with my old friend and meet his wonderful family is one of the reasons this project would have been worth it regardless of whether an actual book came out of it. I'm also indebted to my friend and coworker Jeri Condit and her family, who treated me like gold during a visit to the Houston area. And to Diana Brant, Lanier Robertson, and Harold and Kathy Fuqua for welcoming me into their homes for interviews.

Thank you to the following for assisting during my research: Carl Kaproth, Martin Burgess, and the rest of the staff at the Seattle Central Library; Rebecca Felkner, Wendy Greenwood, and the staff at the Grandview Heights Public Library in Columbus; Scott Caputo at the Columbus Metropolitan Library; and Matt Rothenberg with the Giamatti Research Center at the National Baseball Hall of Fame and Museum. Charlie Danrick, Paul Hiatt, Joel Santisteban, and Allen Sniffen helped me track down audio recordings of '81 Clippers broadcasts. Jim Moorehead with the San Francisco Giants, Tim Hevly with the Seattle Mariners, Monica Barlow with the Baltimore Orioles, Nate Rowan with the Rochester Red Wings, and Rachel Levitsky with the Major League Baseball Players Alumni Association helped me get in touch with former players, coaches, and broadcasters. Evelyn Long shared her own stories and connected me with others who lived through the Cardington tornado and its aftermath. I'm also grateful to the Society for American Baseball Research for my membership and the fellowship it provides, as well as the many research resources it offers. Rick Huhn, Mark Knowlton, Mary Lloyd, Greg Prato, Meghan Stevenson, and Jim Vankowski have also provided advice and encouragement.

I'm thankful for many friends who've supported me in this project, but I want to call out a few who have provided extra encouragement, enthusiasm, and expertise: Billie Grable, Mike Harms, Mike Hipple, Ozo Jaculewicz, Devin Liddell, Ryan Liddell, George Malone, Doug Miller, Emeri Montgomery, Chris O'Claire, Dave Piechowski, Phil Ryan, Don Sena, Ken Smith (my coworker and friend, not either of the Ken Smiths mentioned in the book), Sandy Swift, Mark Talkington, Scott Trimble, and Brian White.

Thank you, Rick Rizzs, for providing so much inspiration around baseball and sports journalism. And for being so generous with your time during this project.

Thanks also to Jim Massie and Jack Torry, for granting multiple interviews as well for the great work both did covering the Clippers in 1981 and beyond.

Thank you, everyone at University of Nebraska Press, for giving this book a chance. I'm especially grateful to the UNP's Rob Taylor, Courtney Ochsner, Anna Weir, Joeth Zucco, and Ann Baker. And to Karen Brown for the copy edits.

Thank you to my four wonderful sisters: Karen, Mary, Jayne, and Julie, and their families, for all their love and support. And to my parents—I hope that someday, we'll get to watch a baseball game together again.

And finally, thanks to my wonderful wife, Karin, and our three awesome children—Nate, Ella, and Thea—for your support, love, and patience. I am a lucky husband and father. I love you.

ACKNOWLEDGMENTS

NOTES ON SOURCES

Two terrific beat writers, Jim Massie of the *Columbus Dispatch* and Jack Torry of the *Columbus Citizen-Journal*, covered the 1981 Columbus Clippers. Their accounts have been invaluable. I've listed many of their articles below but haven't attempted to include all of them (there are hundreds).

I set out to interview every player from the '81 Clippers roster and managed to track down and speak with twenty-eight of the thirty-six. Some chose not to participate, and there were others I couldn't find, despite my best efforts. I also spoke with players' family members, former coaches and team executives, writers, broadcasters, and former members of the Yankees organization, among others. Many of the interviews were conducted during multiple research trips to Ohio, as well as visits to California, Florida, and Texas.

Frank Verdi died about three years before I began this project. In telling his story, I relied heavily on accounts from his son, Frank P. Verdi, and from former Syracuse sportswriter Bob Snyder, as well as feature stories from newspapers across the country. Tony Zefiretto and Harry Stavrenos shared several stories from later in Frank Verdi's life. Zefiretto interviewed Verdi in the mid-2000s and gathered the old manager's recollections in a manuscript which I hope will be published someday.

I reached out to members of the Steinbrenner family but was not granted any interviews. Former Clippers players, along with ex-Yankee coaches and executives, shared their memories of "the Boss." Additional background came from Steinbrenner biographies, including Bill Madden's *Steinbrenner*; Madden's joint effort with Moss Klein, *Damned Yankees*; Peter Golenbock's *George*; Ed Linn's *Steinbrenner's Yankees*; and Dick Schapp's *Steinbrenner!*.

Information on baseball's complicated labor history came from numerous newspaper accounts, as well as John Helyar's *Lords of the Realm* and Jeff Katz's *Split Season*.

BaseballReference.com was a primary source for statistics, Major League box scores and game recaps, as well as details on transactions. Clippers box scores and statistics were referenced via the *Dispatch*.

Audio and video from the '81 Clippers season helped tremendously. In addition to my own worn-out tapes of WBNS broadcasts, I was able to obtain copies of ESPN, USA Network, and WABC radio broadcasts of Clippers games played during the '81 labor strike. I remain on the hunt for more.

Prologue

Scenes from the first day and night of the Major League strike were re-created via newspaper accounts from June 13, 1981, including Chaz Scoggins, "Weathering the Strike," *Lowell Sun*; Jim O'Donnell, "Baseball Strike Silences Announcers," *Chicago Daily Herald*; George Vecsey, "Bleakly Looms the Summer," *New York Times*; and Michael Wilbon, "Dirge for a Dream at Wrigley Field," *Washington Post*. Author Glenn Stout contributed to these accounts and shared his own memories of Franklin County Stadium and Columbus in the early 1980s. Details from the Tidewater-Columbus doubleheader came via interviews with Stout, Robertson, John Pacella, Frank Ray, and Marshall Brant. See also Jim Massie, "Late Strikes Lift Clippers to Two Wins," *Columbus Dispatch*, June 13, 1981; Jack Torry, "Clippers Rally to Beat Tides," *Columbus Citizen-Journal*, June 13, 1981; Ira Berkow, "Business As Usual in the Minors," *New York Times*, June 14, 1981; Steve Jacobson, "Only This Far from the Big Leagues," *Newsday*, June 13, 1981; Jack Lang, "Beating the Bushes Finds Tides and Clippers at Bat," *New York Daily News*, June 13, 1981; Jack Lang, "And Down on the Farm . . . ," *New York Daily News*, June 14, 1981; and George McClelland, "Tides Go Down Hard Twice to Clippers," *Virginian-Pilot*, June 13, 1981. Pat Tabler and Dan Schmitz shared the story of Tabler's trade to the Cubs organization in interviews.

"I think I've hit a few": "Steve Balboni profile Nashville Sounds 1980," YouTube video, 3:56, posted by "Bob Parker" on September 9, 2008.

"After you hit one like that": Andre Robertson interview, 2013.

"Heeere's the 1-2 on the way": Audio tape of WBNS radio broadcast, Tidewater Tides at Columbus Clippers, June 12, 1981.

"George, it doesn't get any better than this" and "That home run is the beauty of the game": Frank Ray interview, 2013.

1. "I Wouldn't Ship Anything to New York Just Yet"

Details on John Pacella's final days with the Padres organization came from interviews with Pacella, articles by Phil Collier for the *San Diego Union*, and game stories and Cactus League box scores and schedules in the *San Diego Union*. Information on Pacella trades came from Tim May's coverage in the *Columbus Dispatch*. Information on the Clippers' 1980 season and the Yankees' 1981 spring training moves came from the *Columbus Dispatch* and the *Columbus Citizen-Journal*. Details on Dave Coleman are from a 2017 interview with Coleman and newspaper accounts. Frank Verdi's experience in Cuba is described from numerous accounts, including Verdi's own, penned the day after for United Press International. Other sources include AP, "Gun-Shy Team Won't Play," July 26, 1959; Pat Doyle's "Gunfire in the Ballpark," *Baseball Almanac*, February 2003; Dick Hudson's "Warming Up," *Charleston (WV) Daily Mail*, July 26, 1960; Tyler Maun's "The Minor League's Last Nights in Havana," MiLB.com, March 16, 2017; and Gabriel Schechter's "A Life Saved by a Beaning," *Never Too Much*

Baseball (blog), April 21, 2013. Information on Verdi saving Whitey Ford's life, and Verdi's time managing the Rochester Red Wings and scouting for the Yankees is from multiple interviews with his son, Frank P. Verdi, and Ford with Pepe, *Slick*. "Jack" Jackson's meeting with Reggie Jackson is described in Jim Baumbach, "Long Islanders Have the Same Name, but Play a Different Game," *Newsday*, October 22, 2011; Kaye Kessler, "Young Clippers' Hopeful Really Is Another Reggie," *Columbus Citizen-Journal*, March 18, 1981; and "Sports People: Reggie Who?" in the *New York Times*, June 14, 1982. Information on Mark Letendre was obtained via interviews with Letendre, Marshall Brant, and Rick Stenholm, and also from "Major League Baseball's Mark Letendre Honored by the National Athletic Trainers' Association," MLB.com, June 24, 2010; and "MLB's 'Rookie' Letendre Receives Award from University of Maine Alumni," *Scottsdale Independent*, March 9, 2017. John McSherry's death is described from Murray Chass, "Umpire Dies after Collapsing on the Field," *New York Times*, April 2, 1996; and Tim Sullivan, "The Game Couldn't Go On," *Cincinnati Enquirer*, April 2, 1996. Information about Balboni's Minor League hitting exploits came from Steve Wulf, "Hello Balboni, Bye-Bye Ball," *Sports Illustrated*, June 9, 1980; and Steve Hummer, "Balboni's Titanic Home-Run Shots Stirring Wonder," *Sporting News*, June 9, 1979.

"Mumphrey, Pacella!": John Pacella interview, 2013.

"This club . . . is a cinch," "Talentwise, prospectwise," and "If I don't screw this staff up": Kaye Kessler, "Sisler Calls 1981 Clippers 'a Cinch' to Be Better Than '80 Club," *Columbus Citizen-Journal*, March 21, 1981.

"It's the best group of young arms": Jim Massie, "Clipper Stripes Not Appealing to Kammeyer," *Columbus Dispatch*, March 16, 1981.

"I was standing there coaching," "Frank, are you alright?" and "I read in the paper": Frank Verdi, "Two Inches to the Left—and a Flower Fund," UPI, July 26, 1959.

"An atmosphere of peace": AP, "Gun-Shy Team Won't Play," July 26, 1959.

"You see him fielding that ground ball?": Harry Stavrenos interview, 2015.

"Get him off the field!": Frank P. Verdi interview, 2017.

"He was without a job": Ford with Pepe, *Slick*, 42.

"What's this crazy old man doing?": Andy McGaffigan interview, 2015.

"Donahue! Grapes!": Wayne Harer interview, 2013.

"Reggie Jackson, meet my son": Kaye Kessler, "Young Clippers' Hopeful Really Is Another Reggie," *Columbus Citizen-Journal*, March 18, 1981.

"Ah, what a fuckin' rookie": Mark Letendre interview, 2014.

"Psychologist, medic, chef": Kaye Kessler, "Letendre Tends to Clippers," *Columbus Citizen-Journal*, April 14, 1981.

"Hold on": Tim Sullivan, "The Game Couldn't Go On," *Cincinnati Enquirer*, April 2, 1996.

"Only man ever to do it": Kaye Kessler, "George Also Has a Wealth of Words," *Columbus Citizen-Journal*, March 24, 1981.

"You look more like a goddamn truck driver": Stan Williams interview, 2015.

2. Locked Out

In addition to John Helyar's *Lords of the Realm*, this chapter draws from Murray Chass, "Insiders Recall Birth of Free Agency 10 Years Ago," *New York Times*, December 22, 1985; Murray Chass, "Baseball's Transfer of Power," *New York Times*, December 23, 2000; Jon Shelton, "How Free Agency Changed the Course of Baseball's Labor History," In These Times (website), December 23, 2015; AP, "Timeline of Major League Baseball Strike," August 1, 1981; biography of Peter Seitz, BaseballReference.com; Ralph Ray, "Complex Labor Pact Called 'Experimental,'" *Sporting News*, August 7, 1976; and Doug Pappas, "A Contentious History: Baseball's Labor Fights," ESPN.com (undated). The 1976 lockout is described further from multiple articles in *Sporting News* by Ralph Ray, including "Camps Delayed—Players-Owners Gap Still Wide," March 6, 1976; "Appeals Court Key to Baseball Peace?" from March 13, 1976; "Talks Resume after Both Sides Swap Verbal Blasts," March 20, 1976; and "Break Seen in Baseball Labor Impasse," March 27, 1976. Also from Stan Isle, "Kuhn Opens Doors to Spring Training Camps," *Sporting News*, April 3, 1976. Details on Tom Seaver's spring camp are from Jack Lang, "Seaver Camp a Great Idea—While It Lasted," *Sporting News*, March 27, 1976. Curt Flood's story is told with help from the Society for American Baseball Research biography by Terry Sloope; Maury Brown et al., "The Lineup Card: 12 Baseball Players We'd Like to See as President," BaseballProspectus.com, January 25, 2012; and "The Ballplayer Who Opened the Door," *New York Times* (op-ed piece), January 22, 1977. Information on Bobby Brown came from interviews with Brown, George Frazier, Stan Williams, Jeff Torborg, and Mark Warren. Additional details on George Steinbrenner's life are from Nettles with Golenbock, *Balls*; Prato, *Just Out of Reach*; Lyle with Golenbock, *Bronx Zoo*; Kahn, *October Men*; and Fathow, *Steinbrenner*. Tucker Ashford, Mike Griffin, Dan Schmitz, and Juan Espino shared their stories in interviews, with additional information on Espino coming from Rick Stenholm. The story of Greg Cochran, Gene Nelson, and the fight for the final spot in the Majors is described from interviews with Cochran, Stan Williams, Andy McGaffigan, John Pacella, and Dave Righetti. Also from numerous articles by Jack Torry in the *Columbus Citizen-Journal*, including "Clips' McGaffigan Tight Over His Sore Elbow," April 1, 1981; and "Right-hander Cochran Hopes for Sign of Certainty from Yankees," March 25, 1981; numerous articles by Jim Massie in the *Columbus Dispatch*, including "McGaffigan Patiently Awaits Return, Shot at Yanks," April 23, 1981. Other sources include Joseph Durso, "Mets Loath to Rush Leary into Big Time," *New York Times*, March 6, 1981; Durso,

"Leary Earns a Place on Mets' Roster and Will Face Cubs on Sunday," *New York Times*, April 6, 1981; Durso, "Leary Goes 2 Innings, Leaves with Stiff Elbow as Mets Win, 2–1," *New York Times*, April 13, 1981; and Steven Goldman, "The BP Wayback Machine: The Gift of Kuhn," BaseballProspectus.com, November 20, 2012. Opening Day in the Majors was described with help from AP, "Tie Yellow Ribbon around Baseball Debut," April 5, 1981, and Katz, *Split Season*.

"I do not feel that I am a piece of property": Helyar, *Lords of the Realm*, 103–4.

"The grievances of Messersmith": Helyar, *Lords of the Realm*, 169.

"The greatest Minor League player I've ever seen": Mark Warren interview, 2013.

"All these people here to see B.B.": Dennis Werth interview, 2014.

"You're my wife": Bobby Brown interview, 2014.

"I'm going home": Jack Torry, "Bobby Brown Balks at Going to Clippers," *Columbus Citizen-Journal*, March 24, 1981.

"I don't like to hurt people": Fathow, *Steinbrenner*, 16.

"We've seen enough of Tucker Ashford": Madden and Klein, *Damned Yankees*, 136.

"We had to find out about our young pitchers": Murray Chass, "Steinbrenner Puts Griffin out of Yanks' Picture after Loss to Mets," *New York Times*, March 23, 1981.

"I had a bad spring": Mike Griffin interview, 2013.

"Fuck you, you fat motherfucker!": Nettles and Golenbock, *Balls*, 12.

"You're a fucking chicken-shit liar": Madden and Klein, *Damned Yankees*, 62.

"Come out of there, you fat fucking Fauntleroy!": Madden and Klein, *Damned Yankees*, 205.

"Fuck him! He never played a game for this team": Madden and Klein, *Damned Yankees*, 201.

"If you want to fire me, then get your fat ass out here to Chicago and just do it": Katz, *Split Season*, 218.

"Steinbrenner sucks!": Golenbock, *George*, 214.

"He's an overbearing, arrogant, arbitrary": Dick Schapp, *Steinbrenner!*, 85.

"All you motherfuckers with a fuckin' pen": Alex Belth, "The Greatest Yankee Meltdown Ever Captured on Tape," Deadspin.com, August 19, 2013.

"Your husband really fucked this game up": Linn, *Steinbrenner's Yankees*, 233.

"It's the first smart thing he's ever done": Schapp, *Steinbrenner!*, 105.

"Executives who are harsh with their people": Schapp, *Steinbrenner!*, 85.

"George Steinbrenner would give a World Series ring": Schapp, *Steinbrenner!*, 58.

"Which one's Espino?": Madden and Klein, *Damned Yankees*, 105.

"Between the two of us": Dan Schmitz interview, 2013.

"Cochran: Clear Path to Yank Job?": by Phil Pepe, *Sporting News*, February 14, 1981.

"The breaking ball looks pretty good today" and "You looked pretty good today":
Greg Cochran interview, 2013.

"Okay, you guys want youth?" and "went out there and shit on the mound": Stan
Williams interview, 2015.

"Good luck, kid": Mike Lupica, "Rookie Nelson Dons Pinstripes," *New York Daily
News*, April 12, 1981.

3. For Openers

Jack Torry, Jim Massie, Marshall Brant, and others shared their memories of Watt
Powell Park in interviews. Additional information came from Torry's "Charleston Isn't Outstanding in Its Field," July 24, 1981. Opening night of the '81 season
was described via Massie's "Clipper Power Lights Up Charlies," April 11, 1981;
and Torry's "Clippers Win Opener in Charleston," April 11, 1981. Pacella shared
details of his upbringing, early career, and strikeout of Hank Aaron in multiple
interviews. Additional details on the Hall of Fame Game are from Tom Row-
ley, "Hall of Fame Ceremonies Rained On; Mets Bow," *Oneonta (NY) Daily Star*,
August 10, 1976. The first Richmond game is described in three accounts from
April 17, 1981, including Jack Torry, "Verdi Is Ejected as Columbus Loses"; Jim
Massie, "Clippers, Skipper Endure Bad Night" and Bob Hunter, "Richmond's
Runge Relishes Rare Win Over Clippers," *Columbus Dispatch*. Additional details
on Pete Calieri came from his biography on BaseballReference.com and his
obituary in the *Buffalo News*, December 22, 2014. Robertson's injury and the
Clippers' retaliation were described by Robertson, Bill Castro, and Sam Ellis
in interviews. The Clippers' success with Robertson in the lineup was noted
by Peter Gammons in "Robertson's Winning Touch," *Sporting News*, August 23,
1980. The Clippers' early-season losing streak is detailed via numerous *Columbus Dispatch* and *Columbus Citizen-Journal* accounts, including Massie, "Robertson Hopes to Play During Clippers' Road Trip," May 3, 1981, and Jack Torry,
"What's Wrong?" from May 5, 1981. Dave Righetti's early life and career are
described via interviews with Dave Righetti, Sam Ellis, and Ken Schnacke, as
well as Jill Lieber, "The Relief Is Not So Sweet," *Sports Illustrated*, April 16, 1990;
Prato, *Just Out of Reach*, and numerous accounts in the *Columbus Dispatch* and
Columbus Citizen-Journal from 1980–81. Righetti's friendship with Pacella was
described by both in interviews, with additional details provided by Mark Letendre and Ken Schnacke. Information on Mike Patterson came from interviews
with Andre Robertson and Nick Peters, "Giants, A's Phenoms Old Pals," *Sporting News*, April 18, 1981; "Pacific Coast League Notes," *Sporting News*, August 4,
1979; and Jim Massie, "Fans, Chicken Turn Out for Clipper Party," *Columbus
Dispatch*, June 20, 1981. Brant and Balboni recalled their April call-ups during
multiple interviews. Additional details came from Jim Benagh, "Lucky to Be
a Yankee," *New York Times*, May 11, 1981; Jim Massie, "Rule Stops Brant Call to
Yanks," *Columbus Dispatch*, April 21, 1981; Jack Torry, "Balboni, Brant Trade Uniforms," *Columbus Citizen-Journal*, April 21, 1981; and "Balboni, Showalter Victims

of Surprise," *Columbus Citizen-Journal*, April 30, 1981. Also from three stories by Murray Chass in the *New York Times*: "Yanks Beat Tigers, Cerone Out Six Weeks," April 21, 1981; "Yanks and Bird Defeat Tigers 2–0," April 22, 1981; and "Balboni Sparks Yanks," April 23, 1981.

"Fantasy Island in reverse": Jack Torry, "Charleston Isn't Outstanding in Its Field," *Columbus Citizen-Journal*, July 24, 1981.

"D'ya know what kind of ahhm," "It was like I could wave," "Will the owner of the El Dorado," "Did you really have to leave the car," and "The asshole's here": Pacella interview, 2017.

"Hank Aaron. Hank Aaron?": Pacella interview, 2013.

"Where's Tabler going?": Jim Massie, "Clippers, Skipper Endure Bad Night," *Columbus Dispatch*, April 17, 1981.

"This is who we're going to throw at" and "I drilled him pretty good": Bill Castro interview, 2014.

"Balboni couldn't have caught a cold today": Jack Torry, "Clipper Fielding Miscues Give Toledo 6–1 Victory," *Columbus Citizen-Journal*, April 19, 1981.

"Are ya blind, Pete?": Jim Massie, "Clippers' Play Merits Overcast Day," *Columbus Dispatch*, April 20, 1981.

"I wasn't bitter": Greg Cochran interview, 2013.

"skinny kid from California," "the next Ron Guidry," and "Hey, I'm a good young lefty, too": Dave Righetti interview, 2015.

"turned that league on its ear," "I want to put the heat on Righetti," "Can you pitch in the big leagues?" and "folded like a cheap suit": Sam Ellis interview, 2015.

"I've grown up": Jack Torry, "'New' Righetti Relies on More than Sheer Ability," *Columbus Citizen-Journal*, April 9, 1981.

"Well, at least it will never happen": Jim Massie, "Fans, Chicken Turn Out for Clipper Party," *Columbus Dispatch*, June 20, 1981.

"Bonesy, that's my ring": Marshall Brant interview, 2015.

4. "A Ball Never Comes to Me"

Marshall Brant shared his life and career stories via three in-person interviews and numerous phone calls, emails, and texts. I also spoke with his wife, Diana, on numerous occasions. Other sources include interviews with Glenn Stout, Ken Schnacke, Greg Cochran, and Wayne Harer, as well as articles from the *Ukiah Daily Journal*, *San Rafael Daily Independent Journal*, *Columbus Dispatch*, *Columbus Citizen-Journal*, the *New York Times*, *Yankee Magazine*, and the Associated Press. Also see Dick Schapp, "The Man Who Would Not Quit," *Parade Magazine*, August 7, 1983; and Prato, *Just Out of Reach*. The thirty-three-inning Pawtucket-Rochester game is described in Dan Barry's *Bottom of the 33rd*; AP, "32 Innings and Nobody Won," April 20, 1981; Ray Fitzgerald, "32-Inning IL Marathon Still

Must Be Finished," *Boston Globe*, April 20, 1981; Dave Anderson, "Pawtucket's 32-Inning Game," *New York Times*, April 21, 1981; and Scott Pitoniak, "The Game that Went on Forever Will Live Forever," *Rochester Democrat and Chronicle*, April 19, 2001. Paul Boris and Tucker Ashford gave descriptions of the Clipper clubhouse that season. Frank P. Verdi shared many stories of Frank Verdi's early life and career in multiple interviews. Frank Verdi's near at bat with the Yankees and other career details are taken from Ford with Pepe, *Slick*; Mick Garry, "Verdi Back to Continue the Battle," *Sioux Falls Argus Leader*, June 2, 1995; Kaye Kessler, "Verdi Can't Wait to Start at the Top," *Columbus Clippers 1981 Program*; Jack Slattery, "Highlighting Sports" column, *Syracuse Herald-Journal*, May 15, 1953; "Former Binghamton Triplets Manager Verdi Dies at 84," *Binghamton News*, July 11, 2010; Randy Turner, "Baseball Lifers Had Brush with Fame," *Winnipeg Free Press*, August 23, 1995; Richard E. Goldstein, "A Day in the Lives of Big-Leaguers Was a Career," *New York Times*, June 14, 1982; "Moonlight Graham Comes to New York," *Sliding into Home* (blog), 2010; Bob Snyder, "Verdi Joins Local Legends," *Syracuse Herald-Journal*, July 30, 1999, and "Sweet to Sour," *Syracuse Herald-American*, April 29, 1984. *Columbus Dispatch* articles by Paige Lewis (June 30, 1980) and Eddie Fisher (April 14, 1981) provided background on Sgt. Dick Hoover's life and the Clipper card program. Details on Bobby Brown's time in Columbus were provided by Brown, Mark Warren, Dennis Werth, and Stan Williams. Other sources included Jack Torry, "Bobby Brown Balks at Going to Clippers," *Columbus Citizen-Journal*, March 24, 1981; Jim Massie, "Ex-Yank Brown Disenchanted after Demotion to Columbus," *Columbus Dispatch*, March 27, 1981, and "Brown Snubs Yank Orders," *Columbus Dispatch*, May 7, 1981; also John McNeely, "Bobby Brown May Be Wrong Patient for Dr. George," *Columbus Dispatch*, March 29, 1981; Tim May, "Yankee Yo-Yo Yanks Brown Up from AAA," *Columbus Dispatch*, April 5, 1981; Bob Hunter, "Trip to Columbus Helped Restore That Old Bobby Brown Confidence," *Columbus Dispatch*, June 1, 1981; and Madden and Klein, *Damned Yankees*. Robertson's early career and crucial play in the 1979 Governors' Cup finals were re-created via interviews with Robertson, also Chuck Bellinger, "Leal, Grilli Check Mud Hens as Chiefs Roll, 5–3," *Syracuse Post-Standard*, August 30, 1979, and "Tables Turned on Chiefs, Mistakes Were Costly," *Syracuse Post-Standard*, September 17, 1979; also John McNeely, "Clippers Clinch Cup on Holt's RBI Single," *Columbus Dispatch*, September 16, 1979.

"A pitch is never thrown," "Are we poor," "You're going to love playing," "How could you throw a pitch like that?" and "Alright. Let's load up the car": Marshall Brant interview, 2015.

"I've gotta tell you" and "I guess we'll see": Diana Brant interview, 2015.

"Don't you lie to me" and "It's from Pawtucket": Dave Anderson, "Pawtucket's 32-Inning Game," *New York Times*, April 21, 1981.

"Alright, alright, I see": Paul Boris interview, 2013.

"Seaman Verdi!" and "I don't want any money": Frank P. Verdi interview, 2017.

"hollering, hustling, fighting kind of ballplayer": Jack Slattery, *Syracuse Herald-Journal*, May 15, 1953.

"Look out, Aunt Millie": Ford with Pepe, *Slick*, 43.

"Verdi! You go to shortstop!": Randy Turner, "Baseball Lifers Had Brush with Fame," *Winnipeg Free Press*, August 23, 1995.

"Time out!": Richard E. Goldstein, "A Day in the Lives of Big-Leaguers Was a Career," *New York Times*, June 14, 1982.

"I have to go back and do what's best": Jim Massie, "Brown Snubs Yank Orders," *Columbus Dispatch*, May 7, 1981.

"You can be the same player you were": Bobby Brown interview, 2015.

"It won't be the last one": Robertson interview, 2016.

5. Signs of Life

The night of Len Barker's perfect game was detailed in AP, "Jays Can't Touch Barker's Breaker," May 16, 1981; and Jim Massie, "Clippers Gun Down Chiefs with Assist from Callahan," *Columbus Dispatch*, May 16, 1981. Frank Ray, Joe Santry, Wayne Harer, and Ken Schnacke provided details on baseball's return to Columbus and the city's prior baseball history in multiple interviews. Other sources include Joe Santry, *Grazing through Columbus*; Tootle, *Baseball in Columbus*; Daniel Flavin, "Columbus Becomes Clipper Country," *Columbus Dispatch Sunday Magazine*, April 17, 1977; John McNeely, "They Were Just Singin' in the Rain," *Columbus Dispatch*, April 23, 1977; Jay Hoster, "The Columbus Clippers: A Minor League Club in a Great New Ballpark," *Cleveland Plain Dealer*, 1978; and Rob Phillips, "Leadership of Frank Ray '73 Shines Again," *Ohio State University Law School Magazine*, Spring 2009. Details on the life of Harold Cooper came from a tribute in the *Columbus Dispatch*, October 6, 2010, as well as interviews with Joe Santry and Ken Schnacke. Verdi shared stories from his Columbus Jet days with Kaye Kessler in "Clippers' Verdi a Baseball Original," *Columbus Citizen-Journal*, February 4, 1982. Dave Wehrmeister's career is described from interviews with Sam Ellis and two articles by Phil Collier in the *Sporting News*: "Padre Prayers Point to Wehrmeister," February 21, 1976, and "Padres Grubb Too Tense, Bat Cools," September 8, 1973; see also "Pacific Coast League Notes" in *Sporting News* from 1975, 1978, and 1979; Don Pfannenstiel, "Showing Puts Rookie Back in Running for Bullpen Spot," *Independence Examiner*, March 28, 1981; Jim Massie, "Ellis: Pitching Better Than '80," *Columbus Dispatch*, April 13, 1981; and Jack Torry, "Wehrmeister, Clipper Pals Set for '81 Home Opener," *Columbus Citizen-Journal*, April 14, 1981. The Yankees' proposed trade of Dave Righetti to the Dodgers was reported in Stan Isle, "L.A. Could Have Had Righetti, Too," *Sporting News*, November 14, 1981. Other nixed Righetti trades and Steinbrenner's trading philosophy were detailed by Righetti and Stan Williams in interviews, also in "Two Yankees Dodged Bullet," *Sporting News*, October 31, 1981. Dave Stegman detailed his trade to the Yankees and time with Columbus. Other sources include Jim Massie, "Clippers Squander Righetti Effort, Fall 2–1," *Columbus Dispatch*, May 1, 1981. Background on Dennis Werth came from interviews with Werth and Bruce Robinson; also Tim May, "Werth Feels Cut Out for Big Leagues," *Columbus Dispatch*, April 5, 1981; audio of **WABC** and **WBNS** broadcasts, 1981; Kent Baker, "Werth Has Bloodlines, Mom's Tennis Balls, Too," *Baltimore Sun*, July 13, 1998; Dusty Rhodes, "A World Series Champ and His Phenomenal Family," *Illinois Times*, November 5, 2008; and Frank Lidz, "Get Out of My Hair!" *Sports Illustrated*, August 23, 2010. Details of Steve Balboni's early-season struggles and turnaround came from interviews with Balboni, Santry, and Glenn Stout. His five-hundred-foot home run against Richmond was described in Jim Massie, "Balboni Long Bomb Gives Clippers Two Over Braves," *Columbus Dispatch*, May 30, 1981; and Jack Torry, "Boris and Wehrmeister Pitch Clippers to Sweep," *Columbus Citizen-Journal*, May 30, 1981. Santry provided information on Josh Gibson's 1933 home run in Columbus. The Spokane Indians' win in the Northwest League title series was re-created with an audio tape of **KAQQ**'s post-game show from September 5, 1988. Other details came from three articles by Howie Stalwick in the *Spokane Spokesman-Review*: "Tribe Wins Division, Faces S. Oregon Next," September 2, 1988; "Indians Steal Championship," September 6, 1988; and "A Crazy End to a Crazy Season," September 7, 1988.

"Len Barker has done it!": Author's recollection of **WBNS** radio broadcast, Syracuse Chiefs at Columbus Clippers, May 15, 1981.

"We just bought old Jets Stadium" and "We're going to bring professional baseball": Frank Ray interview, 2014.

"I think we would have all changed": Frank Ray interview, 2017.

"Naw, scrambled eggs, that's it!": Kaye Kessler, "Clippers' Verdi a Baseball Original," *Columbus Citizen-Journal*, February 4, 1982.

"That's a stupid question": Jack Torry, "Wehrmeister, Clipper Pals Set for '81 Home Opener," *Columbus Citizen-Journal*, April 14, 1981.

"take the starch out of you": Jim Massie, "Clippers Squander Righetti Effort, Fall 2–1," *Columbus Dispatch*, May 1, 1981.

"You got any shoe polish?" and "You were throwing me nothing but fastballs": Dave Stegman interview, 2016.

"On a scale of one to ten": Murray Chass, "Judge, Legal Batteries Decide Baseball Fate," *Sporting News*, June 13, 1981.

"It was definitely an outward appearance": Steve Balboni interview, 2014.

"From the windup": **KAQQ** radio broadcast, Spokane Indians postgame show, September 5, 1988.

"We have been meeting most of the day": Katz, *Split Season*, 106.

6. Hello, Baseball

Rick Rizzs provided details on his own journey to the Majors in multiple interviews. Additional details came from an interview with Phil Neuman, in Jon Mark Beilue, "The Gold Sox Win the Pennant," Amarillo.com (website), September 13, 2011; Sandy Schwartz, "Rizzs Hopes Clippers Will Be His Ticket to Success," *Columbus Citizen-Journal*, April 10, 1981; David Laurila, "Prospectus Q&A: Dave Niehaus and Rick Rizzs," *Baseball Prospectus*, September 10, 2010; Damon Agnos, "A Chat with Rick Rizzs, the Other Voice of the Mariners," *Seattle Weekly*, August 3, 2009; and Mac with Kenyon, *My Oh My*. Information on Ken Schnacke's life came from interviews with Schnacke, Phil Neuman, and former Clipper players and executives, also from Katy Smith, "People to Know: Ken Schnacke," *Columbus Business First*, March 18, 2016. The scene at Franklin County Stadium on June 12 was re-created via the author's own memories, supplemented by interviews with Schnacke, Jim Massie, and Glenn Stout. Steve Taylor shared details of the evening and his baseball career in an interview, with additional information coming from "History of DSC Stadium," delawarestadiumcorp.com (website), 2007; and Meghan Montemurro, "Ex-UD Star, Respected Baseball Scout Dies at 58," *Wilmington (DE) News Journal*, November 18, 2014. Jack Aker's questioning of the June 14 postponement was included in George McClelland, "Still-Dazed Tides Washed Out," *Virginian-Pilot*, June 14, 1981. Stories from the Cardington tornado came from Evelyn Long, Jim Ullom, and Vickie Ullom, along with "3 Die as Tornado Rips Cardington," *Columbus Dispatch*, June 14, 1981; and Kathy Gray Foster, "Cardington Death Toll Rises to 4," *Columbus Dispatch*, June 15, 1981. The note on Lynn McGlothen referenced AP, "Lynn McGlothen Dies in a Fire," August 15, 1984. Rick Anderson's story is described from Hugo Kugiya, "After the Ball Is Over," *Seattle Times*, July 8, 1989; and Anderson's obituary in the *Sporting News*, August 14, 1989. Information on Bob Kammeyer came from interviews with Francine Kammeyer-Krug, Mickey Kammeyer, Jim Massie, and Bill Emslie, along with Jim Massie, "Clipper Stripes Not Appealing to Kammeyer," *Columbus Dispatch*, March 16, 1981; Jack Torry, "Former Clipper Players Find Minor League No Longer Pays," *Columbus Citizen-Journal*, April 2, 1981; William Juliano, "Melancon Has Nightmarish Outing, but Yanks' Kammeyer Still Owns Inning of Greatest Infamy," the *Captain's Blog*, April 18, 2012; Dan McGrath, "Old Friend Had Big-League Heart," *Chicago Tribune*, February 7, 2003; and Dan McGrath, "Those Who Can Inspire Youth in Short Supply These Days," Leo High School of Chicago (website), August 16, 2014. Joe Santry shared his life story and information on Huntington Park during multiple interviews. Additional details are from "Q&A: Joe Santry, Columbus Clippers Historian," Columbus Alive (website), April 2, 2014; and "Columbus' Baseball Museum of Huntington Park," This Week (website), July 25, 2009. The Tucker Ashford–ESPN story was described from an interview with Ashford, and also Thomas Rogers, "Baseball Strike Forces TV to Improvise," *New York Times*, June 27, 1981.

"Popped up, right side": Jon Mark Beilue, "The Gold Sox Win the Pennant," Amarillo.com, September 13, 2011.

"Ken, this is what you got into the game for": Ken Schnacke interview, 2013.

"It was like watching the game": Phil Neuman interview, 2014.

"Can you forgive me, ma'am?" and "the adult in the group": Jim Massie interview, 2013.

"There's something going on in Cardington," "like they were matchsticks," and "People just jumped in": Evelyn Long interview, 2015.

"The whole town is down": "3 Die as Tornado Rips Cardington," *Columbus Dispatch*, June 14, 1981.

"A tornado just hit Cardington," "half the fire station on top of the trucks," "I heard her on the other end," and "I cried": Interview with Jim and Vickie Ullom, 2015.

"per capita, the worst we've had": Kathy Gray Foster, "Cardington Death Toll Rises to 4," *Columbus Dispatch*, June 15, 1981.

"What are you, stupid?": Tucker Ashford interview, 2013.

7. "This Is Phil Rizzuto from Norfolk, Virginia"

Scenes from Phil Rizzuto's life and WABC's Clipper broadcasts were re-created via audio recordings of 1981 games, also from DeVito, *Scooter*; George McClelland, "New York Is Tuned into Norfolk VA," *Virginian-Pilot*, June 21, 1981; Loren Feldman, "Yankee Broadcasters Play It Loose in Minor League Assignment," *Columbus Dispatch*, July 3, 1981; and Kaye Kessler, "Rizzuto Is Having a Ball in the Minors," *Columbus Citizen-Journal*, July 9, 1981. The Clippers' June 19 game is described in Jim Massie, "Fans, Chicken Turn Out for Clipper Party," *Columbus Dispatch*, June 20, 1981; Bob Whitman, "Clippers Get Last Laugh from Victory," *Columbus Citizen-Journal*, June 20, 1981; and audio recordings of the WBNS broadcast. Additional information on Win Remmerswaal comes from an interview with Joe Morgan, and from Remmerswaal's Society for American Baseball Research biography written by Rory Costello, Chris Kalhout, and David Laurila in 2001. Marshall Brant shared details of his 1980 call-up, '81 slumps, and internal struggles during multiple interviews. Additional details came from Dick Schapp, "The Man Who Would Not Quit," *Parade Magazine*, August 7, 1983; and from an interview with Bill Livesey. Garry Smith shared his story in an interview. Additional sources were an audio recording of the WABC broadcast of Columbus at Pawtucket, June 29, 1981; Jack Torry, "Smith's Season May Be the Key to Career Future," *Columbus Citizen-Journal*, April 4, 1981; Jim Massie, "Smith Makes Most of Time, Circumstance," *Columbus Dispatch*, March 17, 1981; and Jim Massie, "'Awesome' Clippers Win on Power," *Columbus Dispatch*, June 30, 1981. Andre Robertson gave details on his family, upbringing, and early athletic career in multiple interviews. Other sources include interviews with Harold Fuqua, Kathy Fuqua, Roderick Robertson, and Ryan Robertson; also Wayne Coffey, "Yankee Shortstop Andre Robertson and Ballet Dancer Reclaimed Their Lives after Horrific Car Crash," *New York Daily News*, December 20, 2008; John Curylo, "WO vs BC—

Another Big Game," the *Port Arthur (TX) News*, September 26, 1974; John Curylo, "SP biggest test for BC," the *Port Arthur (TX) News*, October 3, 1974; "Tigers to Be in West Orange Friday," the *Silsbee (TX) Bee*, October 10, 1974; and AP, "Five All-Stars Drafted," June 13, 1976. Information on the Henry Hudson Parkway and West Side Highway came from Nowlin v. City of New York and Andre Robertson (court documents), 81 N.Y.2d 81, 612 N.E.2d 285, 595 N.Y.S.2d 927 (1993). Fake baseball tournaments, activities for players and coaches, and other aspects of life during the strike were described via multiple interviews with former players and coaches. Also from Joe Goddard, "Welcome to Working Class," *Sporting News*, July 25, 1981; Mel Durslag, "All Mexico Is Toasting Valenzuela," *Sporting News*, July 25, 1981; John McNeely, "Welsh, Righetti Eye Strike's Discomfort," *Columbus Dispatch*, June 19, 1981; Ralph Ray, "Issues Multiply as Strike Drags On," *Sporting News*, July 4, 1981; and Katz, *Split Season*; *Columbus Dispatch* 1981 "Best of Baseball" tournament articles by Bob Hunter, Tim May, Loren Feldman, Eddie Fisher, Herb Stutz, Kirk Arnott, and Candy Walters; and Skip Nipper, "Yogi in Nashville," 262 Downright (website), September 23, 2015.

"You look like George Burns": DeVito, *Scooter*, 204.

"This is Phil Rizzuto from Norfolk, Virginia": George McClelland, "New York Is Tuned into Norfolk VA," *Virginian-Pilot*, June 21, 1981.

"Poor Herb Score is drooling over there," Didja ever hear of deer flies," "They've got something going on out there," "I thought that thunder cloud had come over," and "The 3-0 pitch": Audio recordings of Columbus Clippers baseball games, Adler Communications, 1981.

"My listeners were not all of a sudden": Loren Feldman, "Yankee Broadcasters Play It Loose on Minor League Assignment," *Columbus Dispatch*, July 3, 1981.

"This was the great Washington's teeth" and "It's better to have half the teeth": Irvin Molotsky, "A Crime Half Solved: Part of Washington's Teeth Reappear," *New York Times*, August 30, 1982.

"You gotta be kidding me," "How do you do, Mr. King," "Hello Mr. Steinbrenner," "Gimme the program," "What are you doing?" "How long you been doing this?" and "Got a big league hit yet?": Marshall Brant interviews, 2013–18.

"I think Marshall Brant did about everything": Bill Livesey interview, 2015.

"Ground ball right side": Audio tape of WABC/Adler Communications broadcast, Columbus at Pawtucket, June 29, 1981.

"There are a lot of me's out there": Garry Smith interview, 2015.

"Are you sure you want to do that?" "I'm going to give you everything you need," "Don't start anything you can't finish," "But we didn't have many," "Look out the window," and "I keep telling Lanier": Andre Robertson interview, 2015

"Whenever Boe Robertson spoke" and "Why do we *lead off* with Andre?": Harold Fuqua interview, 2015

"You win some, you lose some": Loren Feldman, "Fox, Goose Spark Tigers' 15-Inning Win Over Nats," *Columbus Dispatch*, June 27, 1981.

"Gimme somethin' to do": Carl "Stump" Merrill interview, 2014.

8. The Grind

Details on Jim Massie, Jack Torry, and their coverage of the '81 Clippers came from interviews with both, along with recollections of former players and others around the team. The 1980 storyline from *General Hospital* was re-created via the General Hospital Wikia website and "Luke and Laura: The True History," www.angelfire.com (website). Marshall Brant recalled Roy Staiger's late-season complaint. Massie shared the story of Staiger and "Leather Lungs." Steinbrenner's visits to Columbus were recalled in Massie's "Steinbrenner Kept Ties to Columbus," *Columbus Dispatch*, July 14, 2010; and by numerous former players. George Frazier detailed his Columbus debut in an interview. Steve Balboni's midseason home run tear is described from interviews with Balboni, Massie, John Pacella, Stan Williams, Tucker Ashford, and Rick Stenholm. Also from Larry Harnly, "Glaum Hurls Riverside to NCAA Crown," *Sporting News*, June 18, 1977; "Bye-Bye Balboni," *Sporting News*, May 19, 1979; Steve Hummer, "Balboni's Titanic Home-Run Shots Stirring Wonder," *Sporting News*, June 9, 1979; Steve Wulf, "Hello Balboni, Bye-Bye Ball," *Sports Illustrated*, June 9, 1980; Sandy Schwartz, "'Bye-Bye' Balboni' Should Be a Big Hit," *Columbus Citizen-Journal*, March 4, 1981; Tim May, "Rookie Balboni Now Concentrating on Role as Clippers' First Baseman," *Columbus Dispatch*, March 31, 1981; Jack Torry, "Balboni, Showalter Victims of Surprise," *Columbus Citizen-Journal*, April 30, 1981; Jack Torry, "There's No Plate Like Home for Balboni," *Columbus Citizen-Journal*, July 28, 1981; Santry, *Grazing Through Columbus Baseball*; and Prato, *Just Out of Reach*. Balboni, Pacella, Massie, Paul Boris, and Mark Warren shared memories of Balboni's drinking exploits. Mike Bruhert's story was retold via interviews with Bruhert and Frank P. Verdi. Also from numerous articles in the *Columbus Dispatch* and *Columbus Citizen-Journal*, including Jim Massie, "Bruhert Complete Game Not Irrelevant," July 9, 1981. Frank Verdi's interactions with umpires were recalled in interviews with Bill Emslie, Frank P. Verdi, and Jack Torry, along with numerous newspaper articles. Emslie shared his own stories in two interviews. Additional background on Emslie came from Bob Broeg, "A Bonehead Merkle Was Not," *Sporting News*, January 25, 1975; Frank Slocum, "Who Loves Baseball More Than Umpires?" *Sporting News*, May 26, 1979; Thomas Rogers, "He'd Rather Be behind the Plate," *New York Times*, April 23, 1983; Dave Nightingale, "Trouble among the Umpires," *Sporting News*, May 23, 1983; Bob Hunter, "Umpire Emslie Back at 'Practice,'" *Sporting News*, June 6, 1983; and *Sporting News* American League and team notes from February 22, 1988, and November 26, 1990. Sam Ellis, Bill Livesey, and Larry Schmittou shared their memories of the Clippers' 1981 pitching shortage, with further details from Jim Massie's "Clippers Bombed by Resurgent Sox," *Columbus Dispatch*, July 20, 1981; and Jack Torry's "Red Sox

Rip Clips," *Columbus Citizen-Journal*, July 20, 1981. Jim Lewis and Marshall Brant provided background on Lewis's life, along with Jim Massie, "Clippers' Lewis Had 'Junk' Ball in Winter Loop," *Columbus Dispatch*, March 28, 1981; and Tim Tucker, "Bedrosian's Injuries Believed Minor," *Sporting News*, February 13, 1982. Background on Paul Boris came from multiple interviews with Boris, along with Jack Torry's "Pitcher Boris Has Improbable Success Story to Tell," *Columbus Citizen-Journal*, March 27, 1981; and numerous other articles in the *Citizen-Journal* and *Dispatch*. Andy McGaffigan shared his story in two interviews. Ellis provided additional background, along with Jack Torry, "Clips' McGaffigan Is Tight Over His Sore Elbow," *Columbus Citizen-Journal*, April 1, 1981; Jack Torry, "Licking ERA Wounds," *Columbus Citizen-Journal*, July 15, 1981; and Jim Massie, "McGaffigan Patiently Awaits Return, Shot at Yanks," *Columbus Dispatch*, April 23, 1981. The story of the Kansas City walkway disaster was retold from Mike McKenzie, "God Listened When Gale Prayed," *Sporting News*, August 8, 1981; AP, "111 Killed at Hotel," July 18, 1981; Mike McKenzie, "Sportswriter Watches as Catwalks Collapse," AP, July 19, 1981; AP, "Hotel's Lobby a 'Nightmare,'" July 19, 1981; AP, "Cause of Collapse Unknown," July 19, 1981; and "Hyatt Skywalk Collapse: A Tragedy Remembered," *Kansas City Star*, 2001.

"They wanted to see you there," "you better get used to it" and "Now batting for Columbus": Jim Massie interview, 2013.

"Man, I can't wait to go home": Marshall Brant interview, 2015.

"All of you guys know the rules": Jim Massie, "Steinbrenner Kept Ties to Columbus," *Columbus Dispatch*, July 14, 2010.

"Who's this new guy pitching?": George Frazier interview, 2014.

"Who's the sumbitch": Stan Williams interview, 2015.

"Where we goin'?" and "If he wanted to, he could break me in half": John Pacella interview, 2013.

"C'mon, pussy boy": Mark Warren interview, 2013.

"I don't remember that one": Steve Balboni interview, 2015.

"Mike, what's wrong with you?" and "You cock-knocker!": Mike Bruhert interview, 2015.

"They said he had a sore wing": Author's recollection.

"No YOU'RE out of the game": Jack Torry interview, 2013.

"Umpires say they can't": Jim Massie, "Verdi Blames Umps (Again) in 6–4 Defeat," *Columbus Dispatch*, June 29, 1981.

"Aw, you little cocksucker," "Look at that sumbitch," "the worst fucking diarrhea of my life," and "Let's go see George": Bill Emslie interviews, 2013 and 2016.

"Dobber, my God, we need pitching" and "if we screw this up": Sam Ellis interview, 2015.

"George loved Columbus": Larry Schmittou interview, 2015.

"We tried to win everywhere": Bill Livesey interview, 2015.

"Well, I guess you stuck that up my ass," "Too many Presidentes," "Women talk about being in bars," and "It was just an accident": Jim Lewis interview, 2015.

"You looked like shit tonight," "I have to have a decision from you," and "What the fuck are you doing to my car?": Paul Boris interview, 2013.

"Hi, I'm Andy McGaffigan," "I was scared to throw," and "Lunchmeat time": Andy McGaffigan interview, 2015.

"There has been a tragedy": Author's recollection.

"There's no way you can help them!": Mike McKenzie, "God Listened When Gale Prayed," *Sporting News*, August 18, 1981.

9. Flashing the *H*

Frank P. Verdi shared stories of his own upbringing and his family's life in Syracuse. Bob Snyder added other details. Additional information came from LeRoy Natanson and Peter B. Volmes, "Fire Rages at MacArthur Stadium," *Syracuse Post-Standard*, May 15, 1969; U P I, "Syracuse Chiefs Gypsies Until New Ball Park Is Built," May 20, 1969: Ed Reddy, "Chiefs Win Tense Finale," *Syracuse Post-Standard*, September 8, 1969; "Thank You, Chiefs!" editorial in the *Syracuse Post-Standard*, September 3, 1970; Ed Reddy, "Chiefs Wait 73 Years to Celebrate," *Sporting News*, September 19, 1970; and Jonathan Croyle, "Throwback Thursday: Syracuse Chiefs Left Homeless after Big Mac Burns," Syracuse.com, May 12, 2016. The Chiefs' game against Winnipeg was re-created via Frank P. Verdi and "Whips Void Clyde's Boo-Boo," *Sporting News*, August 29, 1970. Details on Frank Verdi's time in and out of baseball during the '70s were recalled by Frank P. Verdi and Bob Snyder, also in Mick Garry, "Verdi Back to Continue the Battle," *Sioux Falls Argus Leader*, June 2, 1995; Bob Snyder, "Sweet to Sour," *Syracuse Herald-American*, April 29, 1984; Bob Snyder, "Wall of Fame Welcomes Legendary Manager," *Syracuse Post-Standard*, June 30, 1999; and Matt Michael, "Verdi Proud to Be Included in 1999 Wall of Fame Class," *Syracuse Herald-American*, May 16, 1999. Jack Torry, Bruce Robinson, Wayne Harer, Andy McGaffigan, and Mark Letendre were among many who shared memories of practical jokes. Dave Coleman's struggles were described in Jim Massie, "Clipper Coleman Asserts Self," *Columbus Dispatch*, June 4, 1981; and Jack Torry, "A healthy Coleman Returns to Clippers," *Columbus Citizen-Journal*, April 20, 1981. Coleman's time with the Boston Red Sox was described via interviews with Coleman and Wayne Harer, also multiple articles by Bob Ryan in the *Boston Globe*, including "Sox Find Coleman Does It All," March 21, 1977; "White Sox Gopher Jenkins Twice . . . and Red Sox are 0 and 4," April 14, 1977; "Lynn's Ankle Almost Ready," May 3, 1977; and "Doyle Bails Out Red Sox in 11th Inning, 8–7," May 17, 1977. Articles describing Brad Gulden's exploits include Jim Massie, "Gulden Silences Red Wings," *Columbus Dispatch*, August 4, 1981. Harer, Sam

Ellis, and Jim Lewis provided additional information, including recollections of Gulden's scuffle with Howard "Hop" Cassady. Details from the royal wedding came from Natalie Finn, "The Epic Story of Princess Diana's Wedding Dress," E! News (website), July 9, 2017. Frazier described his call-up to the Yankees in an interview. Other sources include Malcolm Moran, "Yankees Lose to Rookies," *New York Times*, August 8, 1981; and Prato, *Just Out of Reach*. The Yankees' visits to Columbus in 1979 and 1980 were detailed in interviews with Ken Schnacke and newspaper clippings on file at Huntington Park in Columbus. Stories from the air traffic controller strike and the Clippers' bus ride home came from interviews with Jim Massie, Andre Robertson, and Marshall Brant; also Jim Massie's "Torrid Gulden Snubs Slump," *Columbus Dispatch*, August 6, 1981; also "Gulden Buries Wings" *Columbus Citizen-Journal*, August 6, 1981; and Joseph A. McCartin, "The Strike That Busted Unions," *New York Times*, August 2, 2011.

"Frankie, you work the scoreboard tonight?": Frank P. Verdi interview, 2015.

"C'mon, Ivy": Bob Snyder interview, 2017.

"Resident Genius of the Northside Ball Orchard": "Thank You, Chiefs!" *Syracuse Post-Standard*, September 3, 1970.

"Shut up" and "He needed baseball": Frank P. Verdi interview, 2017.

"To the Yankees, Verdi was": Bob Snyder, "Sweet to Sour," *Syracuse Herald-American*, April 29, 1984.

"I was trying to talk": Jack Torry interview, 2014.

"You might want to tell your friend": Wayne Harer interview, 2013.

"Zim wants to see you": Dave Coleman interview, 2017.

"It never should have happened": Sam Ellis interview, 2015.

"You're not going back to Columbus": George Frazier interview, 2015.

"Is this guy ever going to pass out?" and "Rise and shine!": Jim Massie interview, 2015.

10. Time to Get Up

Monica's story is described from a 2016 interview and also Karlen's *Slouching Toward Fargo*. Marshall Brant's mild-mannered, off-field behavior is described from interviews with Brant, his wife, Diana, and Tucker Ashford. Additional details on the "greenie game" came from a video tape of the USA Network broadcast of Rochester at Columbus, July 23, 1981; Jim Massie, "Brant Hits 18th Homer to Master Wings in 11," *Columbus Dispatch*, July 24, 1981; and Jack Torry, "Wings Clipped by Homer," *Columbus Citizen-Journal*, July 24, 1981. Additional background on greenies came from Jack Curry, "With Greenies Banned, Up for a Cup of Coffee?" *New York Times*, April 1, 2006. Wayne Harer discussed his baseball career in multiple interviews. Additional details are from interviews with Jack Torry, Rick Stenholm, Mark Letendre, and Dave Coleman. See also Jim Massie articles including "Harer's Hit Expands Clippers' IL Margin," *Columbus Dispatch*, August 13, 1981, and "Clippers Set for Shot at Playoff Title," *Columbus Dispatch*, September 3, 1982; and Jack Torry articles including "Harer's Hit in 9th Inning Nips Braves," *Columbus Citizen-Journal*, August 13, 1981. The author's own memories of Franklin County Stadium were supplemented by interviews with Ken Schnacke, Glenn Stout, Joe Santry, Paul Boris, and Jim Lewis, along with John Kolomic, "Bells Clang for Clippers," *Rochester Democrat and Chronicle*, September 12, 1981; and a description of the ballpark from the *Ohio State Lantern*, July 14, 1981. Henrietta Webster was profiled by Sandy Schwartz in the *Columbus Citizen-Journal* on April 17, 1981. Gene Nelson's return to Columbus was detailed in Jim Massie, "Nelson Gives Clippers Much-Needed Relief," *Columbus Dispatch*, August 12, 1981; and Jack Torry, "Nelson Saves Castro's 7th Victory," *Columbus Citizen-Journal*, August 12, 1981. Rick Stenholm's story came from interviews with Stenholm, Garry Smith, and Bill Livesey; and numerous *Columbus Dispatch* articles including Jim Massie, "Stenholm Battles Rare Bat Slump," August 8, 1981. Also "Standout Maine Coach Killed in Auto Crash," *Lewiston Journal*, November 17, 1979; and Adam Adkins, "Beefy Wright, First USF Baseball Coach, Passes Away," *Tampa Bay Times*, August 30, 2011.

"Watching the sun set in those ballparks": Interview with Monica K., 2016.

"Wow, what got into you?" "Okay, I know what happened," and "Let's play for these,": Marshall Brant interview, 2016.

"Ah say, ah say, ah say," "Take the hanger out of your shirt," "Why these things stick," and "They took my spirit": Wayne Harer interview, 2015.

"This wasn't 'Slapshot,'" "Ya right, Davis," "He jerked the 'slacker' right out of us," "If you clean up your act," "See you at spring training," and "If I were thirty years younger": Rick Stenholm interview, 2015.

"Col-um-bus Clippers, our team is number one": "Ring Your Bell" (Columbus Clippers fight song).

"If it bothers the opposition": John Kolomic, "Bells Clang for Clippers," *Rochester Democrat and Chronicle*, September 12, 1981.

"Just climb in the window": Glenn Stout interview, 2016.

"I hope your hands": Garry Smith interview, 2015.

"He was the epitome": "Standout Maine Coach Killed in Auto Crash" *Lewiston Journal*, November 17, 1979.

11. "I Guess I'm in Charge"

Leo Righetti's story was described from an interview with Dave Righetti, Jill Lieber, "The Relief Is Not So Sweet," *Sports Illustrated*, April 16, 1990; obituary of Leo Righetti by Mack Lundstrom, *San Jose Mercury News*, February 20, 1998; "Righetti to Play with Newark or Kansas City," *San Jose News*, May 23, 1944; Jim Kaplan, "He Went from Rags to Riches," *Sports Illustrated*, July 25, 1983; and Roger

Birtwell, "Balked at Third, Klaus Battles for Shortstop Berth on Braves," *Sporting News*, April 2, 1952. John Pacella's resurgence was described in interviews with John Pacella and Sam Ellis. Also from Jim Massie, "Pacella Is 'Awesome' in 10-Inning Defeat," *Columbus Dispatch*, August 5, 1981; and "Clippers, Pacella Drop Two-Hitter," *Columbus Citizen-Journal*, August 5, 1981. Details on the Clippers' coaching staff were shared by Sam Ellis, Jerry McNertney, Joe Altobelli, and numerous former players. Marshall Brant retold Mickey Vernon's story about Lou Gehrig. Additional background on Vernon came from Westcott, *Mickey Vernon*. Details on the life of Lou Gehrig came from the Society of American Baseball Research biography of Lou Gehrig by James Lincoln Ray. Jim Massie and *Citizen-Journal* writer Jack Torry documented the pennant race, season-ending awards, and the Clippers' celebration in numerous articles and interviews, including Massie's "Ashford Is Deserving MVP," *Columbus Dispatch*, August 23, 1981. Brett Butler's arrival in Atlanta was recalled from AP, "Butler Serves Braves Well," August 24, 1981. Tucker Ashford provided details on his late career. Andre Robertson detailed his journey from high school to college to the Majors in numerous interviews. Bill Bethea and Harold Fuqua provided other details, along with UPI, "Left-handed Pitchers Popular in Baseball Draft," June 9, 1976; "UT Inks Black Shortstop," *Abilene Reporter News*, June 29, 1976; Emil Tagliabue, "UT Magic Show Is Here," *Corpus Christi Times*, March 25, 1977; Jim Massie, "Yankees' Secret Shortstop Has Finally Been Discovered," *Columbus Dispatch*, March 30, 1981; Jim Massie, "Yankees Take Robertson as Clippers Lose," *Columbus Dispatch*, September 2, 1981; and Jack Torry, "Clippers Lose Game, Robertson," *Columbus Citizen-Journal*, September 2, 1981. For the story of Brian Holman's almost perfect game, the author's memories were supplemented by "Brian Holman—Seattle Mariners Pitcher One Out Away from Perfect Game," YouTube video, posted by "Paul Hoover," September 29, 2010; and "Brian Holman Remembers Almost Perfect Game," YouTube video, posted by "Mike Curkov," July 28, 2010.

"I feel like he should have made it" and "He talked about it filling an emptiness": Dave Righetti interview, 2015.

"all tensed up," "Go down to the bullpen," "Who's in charge?" and "To this day, Altobelli": Sam Ellis interview, 2015.

"I'm struggling and this guy's": John Pacella interview, 2015.

"No walks!" "What the fuck was that?" and "Changeup. What the hell": John Pacella interview, 2017.

"was a Major League pitcher tonight": Jim Massie, "Pacella Is 'Awesome' in 10-Inning Defeat," *Columbus Dispatch*, August 5, 1981.

"Why can't I bring my stopper in": Jerry McNertney interview, 2014.

"only man I know of in baseball": Westcott, *Mickey Vernon*, 25.

"God dammit, get those throws up!" and "I've never seen a guy get so drunk, so fast": Marshall Brant interview, 2015.

"He's done his job": Jim Massie, "Harer Hit in 9th Rescues Clippers," *Columbus Dispatch*, September 3, 1981.

"That's a nice jacket," "either in class or with my guys," "N——, *you ain't worth a shit*," "Look at lil' ol' me," and "Oh, some n—— parked there": Andre Robertson interview, 2018.

"Get your feet quick" and "He was the kind of kid": Bill Bethea interview, 2015.

"I haven't shut up since": Andre Robertson interview, 2015.

12. Postseason

Dave Coleman, Wayne Harer, Glenn Stout, and Dave Stegman shared their memories of the Clippers' postseason series with Rochester. Other details came from Stout's "A Tale of Two Prospects," *Verb Plow* (blog), June 29, 2013. Also from articles including Jim Massie, "Coleman Hero for Clippers," *Columbus Dispatch*, September 13, 1981; Jack Torry, "Clippers Breathe Life into Series" *Columbus Citizen-Journal*, September 11, 1981; Greg Boeck, "Finally, Something to Celebrate," *Rochester Democrat and Chronicle*, September 1, 1981; and John Kolomic, "Clippers Finish Wings, 2–1," *Rochester Democrat and Chronicle*, September 13, 1981. Coleman, Harer, and Dan Schmitz recalled George Steinbrenner's offer at the end of the series. Details for the Governors' Cup title series are from interviews with Rick Rizzs, Steve Balboni, Jim Massie, Jack Torry, and Mark Letendre. Also from Tom Haudricourt, "Clippers, Braves Vie in Finals," *Richmond Times-Dispatch*, September 13, 1981; Jim Massie, "Tired Clippers Grab Cup Lead," *Columbus Dispatch*, September 14, 1981; Jack Torry, "Clips Top Braves, 6–5, in 12 Innings," *Columbus Citizen-Journal*, September 14, 1981; Jim Massie, "Clippers, Wehrmeister Belted by Braves, 6–3," *Columbus Dispatch*, September 16, 1981; Jim Massie, "IL Playoff Teams Caught with Tarps Down," *Columbus Dispatch*, September 18, 1981; Jack Torry, "Wherever Clippers Are, Rain Is a Companion," *Columbus Citizen-Journal*, September 18, 1981; and Tom Haudricourt, "Old Story: Rain Delays Playoffs," *Richmond Times-Dispatch*, September 18, 1981. Roger Slagle's story is described via interviews with Slagle, Dan Schmitz, Sam Ellis, Rick Stenholm, and Marshall Brant. Also from Kurt Caywood, "Kansan Recalls His Moment in Pinstripes," *Topeka Capital Journal*, June 1, 2007; Jim Massie, "Ball's Scar Is a Reminder of Slagle's Fate," *Columbus Dispatch*, July 15, 1980; and Jack Torry, "A Pall Is Cast Over the Ballpark," *Columbus Citizen-Journal*, July 15, 1980. The Clippers' victory in the final series and ensuing celebration were recalled by Rizzs, Massie, and Letendre, among others. Articles from September 19, 1981, include Jim Massie's "Clippers Cherish Crown Despite Those Asterisks"; Jack Torry's "Three in a Row! Cooper's Canceling of Cup Series Doesn't Dampen Clippers' Parade"; and Haudricourt's "Finals Canceled; Clippers Get Cup." The 1981 World Series was recreated via interviews with Bobby Brown, George Frazier, Andre Robertson, and Dave Righetti; and tapes of numerous audio and video broadcasts including "1981 World Series Gm 3 (Scully-Anderson)," YouTube video, 2:37:08, posted by

"Don Zminda" on February 5, 2017; "1981 World Series Game 6," YouTube video, 2:53:46, posted by "MLB Classics" on October 4, 2010; and "ABC 1981 World Series introduct [*sic*] Los Angeles Dodgers New York Yankees Joe DiMaggio. mpg," YouTube video, 14:59, posted by "gibomber" on December 24, 2011. Also from Jim Kaplan, "All the Yankees Were Dandies," *Sports Illustrated*, October 26, 1981; Ron Fimrite, "The Series Was Up for Grabs," *Sports Illustrated*, November 2, 1981; Ron Fimrite, "A Last Hurrah for Los Angeles," *Sports Illustrated*, November 9, 1981; Phil Pepe, "Steinbrenner at It Again; Dresses Down His Players," *Sporting News*, October 24, 1981; "Dodgers 'Sky High' after Mad Scramble," *Sporting News*, November 7, 1981; Peter Gammons, "George, Billy, and Reggie: On Stage," *Sporting News*, October 31, 1981; Murray Chass, "Tales of '81: A Yankee Choke, A Boss Brawl," *New York Times*, June 17, 2014; Will Grimsley, "Yankee Pitching Goat Can Joke about Series Losses," AP, March 2, 1982; Thomas Rogers, "Sports World Specials: A Yankee in First," *New York Times*, September 21, 1981; Prato, *Just Out of Reach*; Schapp, *Steinbrenner!*; Golenbock, *George*; Madden and Klein, *Damned Yankees*; and Linn, *Steinbrenner's Yankees*.

"The pressure's on them": John Kolomic, "Clippers Whip Wings, 10–2," *Rochester Democrat and Chronicle*, September 11, 1981.

"And you know they'll beat the Clippers": Greg Boeck, "Finally, Something to Celebrate," *Rochester Democrat and Chronicle*, September 11, 1981.

"Gitcher head up, Bones," "Have you heard," "Why is Verdi letting a veteran sit," and "Just like big leaguers": Dave Coleman interview, 2017.

"He exuded confidence": Glenn Stout interview, 2018.

"the biggest clutch hit": Jack Torry, "Clips' Coleman Is 'Out of Gas' but Hit in Clutch," *Columbus Citizen-Journal*, September 15, 1981.

"like somebody dying" and "You're gonna be alright": Rick Stenholm interview, 2015.

"Oh God": Roger Slagle interview, 2013.

"As much guts as anyone breathing": Jim Massie, "Clippers, Wehrmeister Belted by Braves 6–3," *Columbus Dispatch*, September 16, 1981.

"hit a triple off his forehead": Author's recollection.

"It's over:" Rick Rizzs interview, 2013.

"cold feet": Jim Massie, "Clippers Cherish Crown Despite Those Asterisks," *Columbus Dispatch*, September 19, 1981.

"It's unfair to everybody": Tom Haudricourt, "Finals Canceled; Clippers Get Cup," *Richmond Times-Dispatch*, September 19, 1981.

"I want to go home": Jack Torry, "Three in a Row!" *Columbus Citizen-Journal*, September 19, 1981.

"Fuck you, you fat son of a bitch": Golenbock, *George*, 207.

"haven't won anything yet": Phil Pepe, "Bullpen Twins, George Give Yankees Impetus," *Sporting News*, October 24, 1981.

"I'm too old to be a sex symbol": Thomas Rogers, "Sports World Specials: A Yankee in First," *New York Times*, September 21, 1981.

"If I don't get as much applause" and "Remember how it feels, Andre": Andre Robertson interview, 2015.

"Goose Gossage": "1981 World Series Gm 3 (Scully-Anderson)," YouTube video, 2:37:08, posted by "Don Zminda" on February 5, 2017.

"This is the biggest game of your life": Prato, *Just Out of Reach*, 46.

"Why did my second bad start of the season" and "You never get over it": Dave Righetti interview, 2015.

"Why isn't Jerry Mumphrey in center field?": "1981 World Series Game 4," YouTube video, (no longer available).

"How about getting me ready": Madden and Klein, *Damned Yankees*, 104.

"You're going back to the animals": Schapp, *Steinbrenner!*, 292.

"I clocked them": Schapp, *Steinbrenner!*, 293.

"This is Young!": Madden and Klein, *Damned Yankees*, 248.

"Briefing, hell": Bill Madden, "Thirty Years with the Boss: There've Been Fights, Firings, Suspensions, and Championships," *New York Daily News*, June 21, 2005.

"It seems like most of the bad things": "1981 World Series Game 6," YouTube video, 2:53:46, posted by "MLB Classics" on October 4, 2010.

"My God, I can't believe he lost again": Will Grimsley, "Yankee Pitching Goat Can Joke about Series Losses," AP, March 2, 1982.

"It will be either George or Lemon": Linn, *Steinbrenner's Yankees*.

"It wasn't your fault, kid": George Frazier interview, 2014.

13. There's "Something I've Got to Tell You"

Frank Verdi's firing is described from interviews with Frank P. Verdi, Bob Snyder, Sam Ellis, and Stan Williams. Also from Jack Torry, "Verdi Won't Miss the Yankee Shenanigans," *Columbus Citizen-Journal*, October 18, 1982; "Yankees Give Verdi the Ax," *Columbus Dispatch*, October 18, 1982; and King with Rocks, *King's Legacy*. Andre Robertson's early years with the Yankees, the car accident, and its aftermath are re-created via interviews with Robertson, Rhonda Rawlings, Jim Massie, and Ken Schnacke; along with Wayne Coffey, "Yankee Shortstop Andre Robertson and Ballet Dancer Reclaimed Their Lives after Horrific Car Crash," *New York Daily News*, December 20, 2008; Nettles with Golenbock, *Balls*; Prato, *Just Out of Reach*; Moss Klein, "American League East Notes," *Sporting News*, March 27, 1982; William Glaberson, "Dancer in a Wheelchair: Jury Assesses the Blame," *New York Times*, December 19, 1990; "Jury Faults City Negligence in Case of Paralyzed Dancer," *New York Times*, December 21, 1990; "Jury Upholds Ex-Ballerina's Case," *Los Angeles Times*, December 21, 1990; A P, "Paralyzed Ex-Dancer Awarded $14 Million," December 22, 1990; Ira Berkow, "A Shortstop and a Dancer No More," *New York Times*, April 4, 1993; Peter Gammons, "Recovery of Vets May Be Key to Races," *Sporting News*, February 27, 1984; Moss Klein, "100-R B I Trio for Yankees?" *Sporting News*, August 5, 1985; court documents including Nowlin v. City of New York and Andre Robertson, 81 N.Y.2d 81, 612 N.E.2d 285, 595 N.Y.S.2d 927 (1993), and Matter of Robertson v. City of New York, 146 A.D.2d 456 (1989). John Pacella's memories of his post–1981 career were supplemented by interviews with Sam Ellis, Ken Schnacke, and Stan Williams; also "Revering Suffers Knee Strain," *New York Times*, April 4, 1982; and Jane Gross, "Rangers Defeat Yankees and Pacella, 4–1," *New York Times*, April 15, 1982. Wayne Harer shared the story of his final at bat in an interview, with additional details coming from Jim Massie, "Clippers Set for Shot at Playoff Title," *Columbus Dispatch*, September 4, 1982. Frank Verdi's time in Sioux Falls is described from interviews with Harry Stavrenos, Frank P. Verdi, and Brian Burkett; also from articles by Mick Garry in the *Sioux Falls Argus Leader*, including "Verdi Back to Continue the Battle," June 2, 1995, "Dietz Is New Birds Boss," June 14, 1995, and "Verdi Trying to Adjust to New Role," June 16, 1995. The final stops in Verdi's baseball career were detailed by Tony Zefiretto and Frank P. Verdi, with additional information from "Cerone Glowing with Pride after Bears Win First Title," *Newark Star-Ledger*, September 23, 2002; "Hurst Leads Bears into Playoffs Tonight," *Newark Star-Ledger*, September 18, 2002; and Brad Parks, "Bears Advance on Joffiran's H R," *Newark Star-Ledger*, September 20, 2002. The final years of Marshall Brant's career and his life after baseball are shared via interviews with Brant, Diana Brant, and Ken Schnacke. See also Bruce Weber, "Making the Case for Don Mattingly on His Last Chance for Cooperstown," *New York Times*, January 3, 2015; Dick Schapp, "The Man Who Would Not Quit," *Parade Magazine*, August 7, 1983; Randolph, *Yankee Way*; and Prato, *Just Out of Reach*. The Yankees' struggles in the '80s and early '90s are described from Bill Madden's joint effort with Moss Klein, *Damned Yankees*; Golenbock's *George*; and Prato's *Just Out of Reach*. Details on baseball's labor history since 1981 are from Helyar, *Lords of the Realm*; and Katz, *Split Season*.

"cut back on some things," "There's something I've got to tell you," and "What? F I R E H I M !": Frank P. Verdi interview, 2013.

"Bible-toting hypocrite": Sam Ellis interview, 2015.

"worst backstabber in baseball": Stan Williams interview, 2015.

"You mother fucker," "If it happens, it happens," "I should get my camera," "It was like the old movies," and "Boe's boy": Andre Robertson interview, 2015.

"He's so cute" and "my biggest fan": Rhonda Rawlings interview, 2014.

"the bridge to Jeter": Jim Massie interview, 2013.

"Sensational": Moss Klein, "100-R B I Trio for Yankees?" *Sporting News*, August 5, 1985.

"I was a dancing girl": William Glaberson, "Dancer in a Wheelchair: Jury Assesses the Blame," *New York Times*, December 19, 1990.

"I've got about a gallon of cortisone": John Pacella interview, 2015.

"It's two knuckleheads": John Pacella interview, 2013.

"Why the fuck is he telling me this?" "Matt, I'm gonna bunt," and "DROP IT!: Wayne Harer interview, 2013.

"some SOB": Frank P. Verdi interview, 2015.

"If I die in the night" and "who's the smart guy?": Harry Stavrenos interview, 2015.

"If something were to happen to him" and "Hey Canaries, we've come to see you win": Mick Garry, "Verdi Back to Continue the Battle," *Sioux Falls Argus Leader*, June 2, 1995.

"are you flying me there" and "Frank Verdi?": Tony Zefiretto interview, 2015.

"It's Cerone": Frank P. Verdi interview, 2013.

"Here are the orders I have," "He struck out tonight," "How old are you, anyway," "The next time he was up," and "Do I want to hit?": Marshall Brant interview, 2013.

"Holy cow, he did it!": Bruce Weber, "Making the Case for Don Mattingly on His Last Chance for Cooperstown," *New York Times*, January 3, 2015.

"Emotionally, he was very strong": Lanier Robertson interview, 2015.

"It was gone": Frank P. Verdi interview, 2015.

14. Heroes

Dave Coleman shared details on his life after baseball in a 2017 interview. Marshall Brant provided additional information in multiple interviews.

BIBLIOGRAPHY

Barry, Dan. *Bottom of the 33rd: Hope, Redemption, and Baseball's Longest Game.* New York: HarperCollins, 2011.

DeVito, Carlo. *Scooter: The Biography of Phil Rizzuto.* Chicago: Triumph, 2010.

Fathow, Dan. *Steinbrenner: Quotes, Hits, and Legacy.* Metairie LA: Megalodon Entertainment, 2010.

Ford, Whitey, with Phil Pepe. *Slick: My Life in and Around Baseball.* New York: William Morrow, 1987.

Golenbock, Peter. *George: The Poor Little Rich Boy Who Built the Yankee Empire.* Hoboken NJ: Wiley and Sons, 2009.

Helyar, John. *The Lords of the Realm: The Real History of Baseball.* New York: Villard, 1994.

Kahn, Roger. *October Men: Reggie Jackson, George Steinbrenner, Billy Martin, and the Yankees' Miraculous Finish in 1978.* New York: Harcourt, 2003.

Karlen, Neal. *Slouching Toward Fargo: A Two-Year Saga of Sinners and St. Paul Saints at the Bottom of the Bush Leagues with Bill Murray, Daryl Strawberry, Dakota Sadie, and Me.* New York: Avon, 1999.

Katz, Jeff. *Split Season 1981: Fernandomania, the Bronx Zoo, and the Strike That Saved Baseball.* New York: Thomas Dunne, 2015.

King, Clyde with Burton Rocks. *A King's Legacy: The Clyde King Story.* Chicago: Masters Press, 1999.

Linn, Ed. *Steinbrenner's Yankees: An Inside Account.* New York: Holt, Rinehart and Winston, 1982.

Lyle, Sparky, with Peter Golenbock. *The Bronx Zoo: The Astonishing Inside Story of the 1978 World Champion New York Yankees.* Chicago: Triumph, 2005.

Mac, Billy, with J. Michael Kenyon. *My Oh My: The Dave Niehaus Story.* Redmond WA: Sheepdog Press, 2017.

Madden, Bill. *Steinbrenner: The Last Lion of Baseball.* New York: HarperCollins, 2010.

Madden, Bill, and Moss Klein. *Damned Yankees: Chaos, Confusion, and Craziness in the Steinbrenner Era.* Chicago: Triumph, 1990.

Nettles, Graig, with Peter Golenbock. *Balls.* New York: Pocket Books, 1985.

Prato, Greg. *Just Out of Reach: The 1980s New York Yankees.* Self-published, 2014.

Randolph, Willie. *The Yankee Way: Playing, Coaching, and My Life in Baseball.* New York: HarperCollins, 2014.

Santry, Joe. "Grazing through Columbus Baseball." Unpublished manuscript.

Schapp, Dick. *Steinbrenner!* New York: G.P. Putnam's Sons, 1982.
Shalin, Mike. *Donnie Baseball: The Definitive Biography of Don Mattingly.* Chicago: Triumph, 2011.
Tootle, James, R. *Baseball in Columbus.* Mount Pleasant SC: Arcadia, 2003.
Westcott, Rich. *Mickey Vernon: The Gentleman First Baseman.* Philadelphia: Camino, 2005.

INDEX

Mount Gilead OH, 104
Moyer, Jamie, 240
MTV, 176
Mumphrey, Jerry, 2, 22, 234
Munson, Thurman, xix, 48, 117, 194
Murcer, Bobby, 155, 233–34, 237, 238
Murray, Bill, 180, 226
Murray, Jim, 7

Napp, Larry, 69
Nashville Sounds, 5, 32, 35, 36, 45, 121, 150,
    157, 216; Balboni with, 4–5, 18, 140–41;
    Berra sent to coach, 129; pitching staff
    of, 151; Rizzs as announcer for, 97; Show-
    alter with, 14–15, 85; Slagle with, 221, 222;
    Taylor with, 99–100
National Labor Relations Board, 87
Nelson, Gene, 4, 190; in International
    League postseason, 217–18, 225; in Major
    Leagues, 36, 190
Nettles, Graig, 26, 229, 230, 238
Neuman, Phil, 99, 159
Newark Bears, 257–58
New York NY, 126–27, 247
New York Giants (baseball), 148
New York Mets, 1, 40, 60, 61, 144, 207;
    Steinbrenner loathing of, xvi, 25, 36
New York Post, 29
New York Yankees: in American League
    divisional and conference playoffs, 227–
    29; approach to Minor League prospects
    by, xvi, 32, 34, 193, 264; Balboni as player
    for, 55, 87–88; Brant as player for, 54–55,
    117–19; Brown as player for, 22–23, 227,
    234; Clippers' exhibition games against,
    175–76; coaches for, 27, 31, 202, 205, 252;
    Frazier called up by, 174–75; free agent
    signings by, xii, xvi, 21, 234–35; hiring
    and firing of managers by, xviii, 27, 31;
    Kammeyer as player for, 106–7; Nelson
    as player for, 36, 190; Pacella as player
    for, 251–52; pitching rotation of, 34–36;
    Righetti called up by, 48, 53, 81; Robert-
    son as player for, 126, 207–8, 216, 227, 230,
    244–46, 249; season of 1981 of, xii–xiii,
    174–75, 227; Steinbrenner purchasing of,
    29; Verdi as player for, 67–68; in World

Series of 1981, 229–38; in years after 1981,
    264–65. *See also* Steinbrenner, George
nicknames, xix–xx, 15–16, 18, 46, 153, 184–
    85, 191
Niehaus, Dave, 93–94, 240
Nimitz, Chester, 65
Nixon, Otis, 216, 220
Nowlin, Shenikwa, 246–49, 250–51

Oakland A's, 53–54, 79, 211, 260–62; in
    playoffs, 227, 229
Oates, Johnny, 203, 258
Oester, Ron, 129
Oglivie, Ben, 227
Ohio State football, xiv, 28, 217
Ojeda, Bob, 207
Orosco, Jesse, xviii

Pacella, John: background and youth of, 39;
    and Balboni, 142; career of, 40, 252–53; and
    Clippers' pitching rotation, 4, 35, 81, 190;
    and control struggles, 39–40; and Ellis,
    198–200, 202; in Major Leagues, 198; mar-
    riage to Caryn by, 52, 53; mustache of, 1, 2,
    139; one-hit shutout by, 201–2; photos, 2,
    199; pitching delivery and mechanics of,
    198–200; postseason appearances of, 217,
    225; in regular-season games, xix–xx, 39,
    52–53, 200–202; and Righetti, 51–52; season
    turning around for, 200–202; strikeout of
    Aaron by, 40–41; struggles of, 1, 52–53, 81,
    198–99, 200; traded to Yankees organiza-
    tion, 1–3; as Yankees player, 251–52
Pagel, Karl, 38
Paige, Satchel, 66, 267
Palmer, Jim, 237
Parks, Danny, 62
Patkin, Max, 96, 139
Patterson, Mike, 114, 170, 177, 178, 184, 206;
    background and career of, 53–54
Pawtucket Red Sox, xvi, 7, 185–86, 216;
    games against, 46, 47, 53, 73, 114–15, 119,
    121–22, 145–46, 152, 200; longest game
    played by, 62–63
Peña, Alejandro, 231
perfect games, 74
Pettitte, Andy, 265
Phelps, Ken, 213–14